BEYOND PROGRESS AND MARGINALIZATION

AC Adolescent Cultures,
SS School & Society

Joseph L. DeVitis & Linda Irwin-DeVitis
GENERAL EDITORS

Vol. 48

PETER LANG
New York • Washington, D.C./Baltimore • Bern
Frankfurt am Main • Berlin • Brussels • Vienna • Oxford

Beyond Progress and Marginalization

LGBTQ Youth in Educational Contexts

Corrine C. Bertram,
M. Sue Crowley,
Sean G. Massey
EDITORS

PETER LANG
New York • Washington, D.C./Baltimore • Bern
Frankfurt am Main • Berlin • Brussels • Vienna • Oxford

Library of Congress Cataloging-in-Publication Data

Beyond progress and marginalization: LGBTQ youth in
educational contexts / edited by Corrine C. Bertram, M. Sue Crowley,
Sean G. Massey.
p. cm. — (Adolescent cultures, school and society; v. 48)
Includes bibliographical references.
1. Gay high school students—Social conditions. 2. Lesbian
high school students—Social conditions. 3. Bisexual high school
students—Social conditions. 4. Transgender youth—Education
(Secondary) 5. Marginality, Social. 6. Homophobia in high schools.
7. Sexual minorities—Education (Secondary) I. Crowley, M. Sue.
II. Massey, Sean G. III. Title.
LC2575.M37   373.1826'64—dc22   2009011340
ISBN 978-1-4331-0672-9 (hardcover)
ISBN 978-1-4331-0671-2 (paperback)
ISSN 1091-1464

Bibliographic information published by **Die Deutsche Nationalbibliothek**.
Die Deutsche Nationalbibliothek lists this publication in the "Deutsche
Nationalbibliografie"; detailed bibliographic data is available
on the Internet at http://dnb.d-nb.de/.

Cover and interior photos by Jes T. Kaminski

The paper in this book meets the guidelines for permanence and durability
of the Committee on Production Guidelines for Book Longevity
of the Council of Library Resources.

© 2010 Peter Lang Publishing, Inc., New York
29 Broadway, 18th floor, New York, NY 10006
www.peterlang.com

All rights reserved.
Reprint or reproduction, even partially, in all forms such as microfilm,
xerography, microfiche, microcard, and offset strictly prohibited.

Printed in the United States of America

Table of Contents

Foreword
David Kilmnick   vii

Acknowledgments   xv

Introduction
M. Sue Crowley, Corrine C. Bertram, and Sean G. Massey   1

Chapter One "My Voice Is Being Heard": Exploring the Experiences of Gay, Lesbian, and Bisexual Youth in Schools
Marjorie Cooper-Nicols and Lisa Bowleg   15

Chapter Two The Roles of Gay-Straight Alliance (GSA) Advisors in Public High Schools
Maria Valenti   52

Chapter Three Becoming an Ally: Straight Friends of LGBTQ High School Students
Darla Linville and David Lee Carlson   89

Chapter Four Attitudinal Ambivalence in the Developmental Contexts of LGB Adolescents
Sean G. Massey   111

Chapter Five Aspirations, Inspirations, and Obstacles: LGBTQ Youth and Processes of Career Development
Jeneka Ann Joyce, Maya Elin O'Neil, and Ellen Hawley McWhirter   126

Chapter Six Working with LGBTQ Youth with Disabilities:
How Special Educators Can Reconceptualize CEC Standards
Thomas Scott Duke   149

Chapter Seven School for the Self: Examining the Role of
Educational Settings in Identity Development among Gay,
Bisexual, and Questioning Male Youth of Color
Omar B. Jamil and Gary W. Harper   175

Chapter Eight Strategies for Building a Learning
Environment of Inclusion and Acceptance for LGBTIQ
Students
Kim A. Case, Heather Kanenberg, and Stephen "Arch" Erich   203

Chapter Nine Telling Stories Out of Class: Excavating
LGBTQ Youth Knowledge from Liminal Spaces
Corrine C. Bertram   227

Chapter Ten Defining Themselves: LGBQS Youth Online
M. Sue Crowley   250

Chapter Eleven Runners-Up: How Lesbian and Gay
Sidekicks in Mainstream U.S. Cinema Can Influence Lesbian
and Gay Youth and Those Who Work with Them
Diane R. Wiener and Christine M. Smith   280

Bibliography   291

Contributors   313

Foreword

WHEN MICHAEL, a 15-year-old student at a Long Island high school, was spat on daily at his school and bumped and hit in the hallways, the school administrators decided to remove him from the day schedule to an after-school program. When Anthony, a 14-year-old male, decided that he wanted a sewing machine, one county social services department decided they could not help him and instead moved him to another county for assistance. And Ryan, a 13-year-old transgender male teenager, was told that he could not be called by his preferred gender, and he should not dress like a boy — for if he did, then the school could not help him if kids teased and bullied him.

The responses to Michael, Anthony and Ryan all ignored their daily life experiences and their right to have a safe learning environment. In all of these situations, the response was to remove the person instead of removing the violence, bullying and harassment that a significant number of lesbian, gay, bisexual and transgender (LGBT) youth face on a daily basis.

Jennifer, Eric, and Debbie have had different experiences. Jennifer, 14, who identifies as bisexual, started a Gay-Straight Alliance at her school. Eric, 16, who is gay, is a leader on the safe schools team at Long Island Gay and Lesbian Youth (LIGALY) as is Debbie, 13, who is a straight ally. These young people represent a growing number of today's generation who are making sure their voices are heard to demand safe schools and fair treatment for LGBT youth.

Beyond Progress and Marginalization: LGBTQ Youth in Educational Contexts in many ways, represents the stories and the lives of Michael, Anthony, Ryan, Jennifer, Eric and Debbie. It provides a modern and contemporary look at the life of LGBT youth, in and out of school, as it exists today. Most books that portray the lives of these youth are outdated and represent the culture of the 1970s and 1980s and have not moved to seeing the assets and strengths of our LGBT young people and the progress made over the years. And while progress has been made, we are reminded that there is a lot more work to do, both in and out of the classroom. It is my hope that after reading this book, everyone, regardless of their sexual orientation, will accept the charge and responsibility to change the world and make it a better place for all, especially our LGBT youth.

Many individuals and institutions define the problems that LGBT youth face as a result of homophobia. Here is where we need the biggest shift in our mind-set. Homophobia, as a term and construct, merely reinforces the LGBT community's "lesser than" status and inferiority. Many people continue to have an irrational fear of homosexuality. This fear, homophobia, results in dislike or even hatred of homosexuals, resulting in prejudice and hostility toward the LGBT community. We need to challenge ourselves and start taking a look at people's lives and experiences through the lens of heterosexism instead.

Heterosexism or the assumption that heterosexuality is normal and right and that other forms of sexuality are abnormal and wrong is a persistent social problem for LGBT persons. Heterosexist attitudes, consciously held or not, prevent LGBT persons from obtaining good health care, from safety as they pursue their education, from full property rights, and from living daily life without fear of harassment and violence. Though attitudes toward LGBT persons have changed for the better in recent decades, discrimination remains, and the cost of this discrimination — economically, socially and personally — is high.

Curricula about sexual orientation that acknowledge the psychological, social, physical and spiritual aspects of sexuality should include discussions of socio-political issues that have implications for LGBT people. Some of these issues reflect a society that lacks information and understanding of the diversity of human sexuality and tends to discriminate or isolate that which lacks familiarity. It also tends to ignore and not listen to or refuse to hear LGBTQ youth voices. Moreover, familiarity and understanding of the range of LGBT life experiences provide for more comfort and sup-

Foreword

port not only of the issues but also of the individual. It is important in all of these efforts that we start to see tolerance and tance as heterosexist terms and instead move toward support, nurturance and admiration for our fellow human beings. To rate or accept someone for who they intrinsically are is to continue to degrade them. LGBT youth and persons do not need to be tolerated or accepted — they need safe classrooms, equal rights and opportunities to work and love and the safety to live their lives and succeed and be happy.

LGBT civil rights is a topic many feel uncomfortable discussing in school and out of school. People chalk this up to "politics." However, civil rights issues are important to the LGBT community because in many circumstances LGBT people do not have the same basic rights other citizens in our country enjoy. In many states and cities an LGBT person can legally be denied housing, employment and public accommodation simply because of his or her sexual orientation and or gender identity and expression. Organizations opposed to gay rights claim that LGBT people have some hidden plan to tear apart the moral fabric of American society and often refer to LGBT communities' efforts to obtain equal rights as the "gay agenda." To the contrary, most LGBT people are simply seeking equal rights and equal protection of their rights to housing, employment, public accommodation and the ability to offer financial and legal security to their families. The invention of the "gay agenda" is nothing more than a scare tactic employed by anti-gay organizations in an effort to place fear in the minds of the American public. That fear, or "homophobia," is then used to justify discrimination.

One may wonder why I am getting "political" in this foreword. Throughout my 16 years of serving as the executive director and CEO of LIGALY and my years of teaching in several universities, I have witnessed the ease with which folks talk freely in the classroom about how they think LGBT people are evil or how they shouldn't be able to get married or serve in the military or even live next door. As an instructor, I address this directly in my own classroom. However, every single week in the academic year we at LIGALY hear stories of how this is unaddressed in hundreds of classrooms. Or if it is addressed, it is chalked up to a difference of opinion. Herein lies another problem — speaking up and saying that LGBT people do not deserve equality, that they are evil folks committing sin, is more than a difference of opinion — it's downright mean, discriminatory and sets up an unsafe environment for LGBT young people and their families. To put this in context, other forms of prejudice such as racism and sexism are less likely to be expressed overtly, and if they are, they're identified as a form of hate and are dealt with in the classroom as such. Heterosexism, however, is addressed differently. Heterosexism for many remains a socially acceptable form of prejudice (Massey, 2009). When individuals express their anti-LGBT feelings, many rationalize and justify their feelings under the guise of a difference of opinion or "religious belief." Leaving it at that is unacceptable. Heterosexist language and comments must be confronted in the same manner as one would confront racist or sexist remarks.

It is essential that school communities provide a safe environment for learning while simultaneously supporting and nurturing the growth of LGBT youth. Every school has LGBT students or students whose families have someone who is an LGBT person. Harassment, verbal abuse, discrimination and violence in schools create a hostile environment and must not be tolerated.

School communities need to create and enforce policies that move toward this goal. It is a rather simple thing to do once we look at the issues and the lives of LGBT people through the lens of heterosexism. Institutions can add sexual orientation to their existing non-discrimination policies. This will provide legal protection from discrimination against LGBT students, teachers and school staff and help to create a safe and supportive learning environment. Just as important, enforcement of policies must treat all students equally. All students, regardless of sexual orientation, should be held to the same standards of conduct, behavior and appearance.

Michael's experience of being spat on and bullied in the lunchroom and hallways speaks to the need to confront violence and harassment. Making schools a safer place requires school staff to immediately confront harassment, discrimination and violence each and every time they occur. And we must talk about LGBT issues in the classroom. There are so many ways to do this in an effective and productive way. Issues about LGBT people should be included in discussions of families, relationships, communities, diversity, health, bias and discrimination.

One of the most frustrating things for LGBT folks in the classroom is their nonexistence and invisibility. Throughout all the different colleges and disciplines I have taught in and at, I have had to rewrite the curriculum to include knowledge about LGBT people and issues. Many instructors who I know do this see the rewrite as a one-shot deal — a "Gay Day" of sorts in the semester. However, it is critical that we incorporate LGBT people and issues throughout the entire semester's curriculum where appropriate. Imagine being an LGBT student in a Family Course in Sociology, Social Work or Psychology and not hearing anything about your family or your life or only hearing about it from a pathological perspective. Is it any wonder that they feel left out and silenced and that their lives and experiences don't matter? By not including LGBT issues throughout the curriculum we continue to be part of the problem and not the solution.

While there's much work to be done in creating safer schools, we have seen a lot of progress through the growth of Gay-Straight Alliances (GSA). A GSA club can be formed for LGBT and heterosexual students to address anti-LGBT harassment, discrimination and violence by increasing awareness through school activities and programs. The last few years have seen an explosion of these clubs throughout the United States, and they are making a big difference in many people's lives and also in their schools and communities.

Jennifer started a GSA at her high school so that people would be more aware of LGBT issues and in particular anti-LGBT language. The phrases "it's so gay" or "you're so gay" have become so commonplace that when they are said, they are often overlooked by students, staff and families, and they are unrecognized as being anti-LGBT. The use of the word "gay" in derogatory ways, as a person-directed or object-directed comment, is not meant to describe an individual's orientation but is perceived as a "put down" by LGBT adolescents overhearing it. Anti-gay language affects most students. It is offensive to the LGBT students and those students who have a friend or family member who is LGBT. It is also offensive to anyone who respects and supports diversity. Not intervening when this language is used sends an approval message and suggests the language is acceptable.

Jennifer heard "it's so gay" and "you're so gay" so many times, even from LGBT people, that she said a club that could promote awareness and education was necessary to eliminate this insidious problem. Through LIGALY's National Coming Out Day Campaign, she was able to organize more than 1,000 students to participate in wearing stickers and buttons that exclaimed that they were "Coming Out for Safer Schools." Thousands of young people, like Jennifer, are also starting GSAs and are becoming not only the leaders of tomorrow but also the leaders of today in helping to change school and community climates. We must support these efforts and give students all the assistance that is needed — it is our duty and responsibility to do so.

The authors of this book skillfully and effectively help us look at what can be the sometimes puzzling state of LGBT affairs — that is, the argument of "things are much better today for LGBT young people" versus "things haven't changed...LGBT youth continue to be victimized, marginalized and oppressed." While we have seen some progress in safer schools work, policy initiatives, and the media, including major television networks and shows that have LGBT characters, one area that is lagging far behind in this "progress" is research.

Recently, we were preparing a grant in response to a Request for Proposals for Pregnancy Prevention. Many people would say this goes against all logic — gay youth needing pregnancy prevention? However, recent studies have shown that gay and bisexual adolescents have higher rates of pregnancy than their heterosexual peers. This was the easy part — making the case and developing the needs statement. However, one of the requirements was to choose an existing evidence-based model to develop our program without adapting the model in any way, whether it be for a different population or a particular intervention. Not one of the evidence-based models provided mentioned or included the lives of LGBT youths. This is unfortunately a common occurrence as the needs of LGBT youth are generally not a priority when it comes to research, which is a reflection of the heterosexism that exists within our society and that which has infected academia. The lives and voices of LGBT youth are silenced and we must change that — this book provides us with the direction that we can follow.

Previous research that has been conducted about LGBT youth has mostly looked at negative behaviors and from an "at risk" perspective. Future research needs to change its focus to looking at youth assets and positive behavior.

Effective research today about LGBT youth needs to take a positive youth development approach. Positive youth development theory posits that youth are far better served by developing their assets rather than preventing negative behaviors. In fact, approaches incorporating positive youth development theory are showing greater success in preventing negative behaviors and health outcomes than programs based on out-of-date approaches that look at deficits.

Youth in this model are used to change the environment, even though they are not the problem — heterosexism is in this instance. Jennifer, Eric and Debbie's work in their GSAs and LIGALY's Safe Schools Team provides illustrations of positive youth development being employed in an effective way that is creating change. Research on their work and others is needed to develop evidence-based models that promote how youth can be more engaged in their schools and communities. It is this kind of research in which LGBT youth voices are heard and matter. It is this kind of research that can provide these models for replication and ones that will include the lives of LGBT youth the next time a Request for Proposals for Pregnancy Prevention is released.

The longtime exclusion of LGBT youth from conversations about health, safety and education means there is much catching up to do. LGBT youth must be a priority in increased resources for support and nonprofit organizations, for research and for LGBT studies and history curricula. Universities must include local nonprofits in their work. Local nonprofit organizations must include universities as well. Nonprofit groups have access to the population and universities have expertise in conducting research. By working together, evidence-based models to promote health and safety for LGBT youth will be developed and become a priority for increased resource support.

In 1978 the late Harvey Milk said, "I cannot prevent anyone from getting angry, or mad, or frustrated. I can only hope that they'll turn that anger and frustration and madness into something positive, so that two, three, four, five hundred will step forward, so the gay doctors will come out, the gay lawyers, the gay judges, gay bankers, gay architects. ... I hope that every professional gay will say 'enough,' come forward and tell everybody, wear a sign, let the world know. Maybe that will help" (Shilts, 1982, p. 374). Harvey knew what he was talking about. Research, including my own (Kilmnick, 1996), has shown that knowing someone who is LGBT significantly changes minds and attitudes and in doing so changes the world we live in. It is our charge and our responsibility to come out as educators, researchers, social workers, psychologists, parents and citizens in support of safer schools and environments. We need to do this so that Michael, Anthony and Ryan's voices are heard and matter. And we need to do this so they and all young people have an environment and world in which they can achieve their fullest potential.

David Kilmnick, PhD, MSW
Chief Executive Officer, Long Island Gay and Lesbian Youth
www.ligaly.org

Acknowledgments

WE HAVE many people to thank for the opportunity to bring this book to fruition. Primary among them are the young people who agreed to participate in the research presented herein. Too little is known about the experiences of lesbian, gay, bisexual, transgendered, queer, and questioning youth at the outset of this new millennium and we hope the chapters in this volume address the need for further understanding and scholarship. Next, we wish to thank all the contributors to the volume who have worked patiently and diligently with us over the past two years to complete this project. They represent many different fields of study and areas of expertise. The richness of the information and insight we hope readers will experience is due to them and their dedication to the task.

We would also extend our appreciation to the *Adolescent Cultures, School & Society* series editor, Dr. Joseph DeVitis, whose encouragement and guidance have been irreplaceable. One of the editors for this volume, Sue Crowley, has known Dr. DeVitis for many years and considers him to be an exemplary colleague whose efforts have furthered the multidisciplinary endeavors of many young scholars over the years. His patience, intelligence, and willingness to share his experience have served us well. Thanks, Joe.

Individually, we each have many family members, partners, friends, and colleagues to thank for their support. Sue Crowley would like to thank her "bff" for many many years, Dr. Brenda L. Seery, and the supportive members of her weekly writing group at Emma's Writing Circles in Ithaca, NY. Dr. Bertram would like to thank Dr. Lubna Chaudhry for her thoughtful counsel during this project and Miller Hoffman for being patient with the character (and characters) of academic life along with her. Dr. Massey would like to thank his partner, Loren, and son, Alfie, for their patience through the many projects that have taken time away from them.

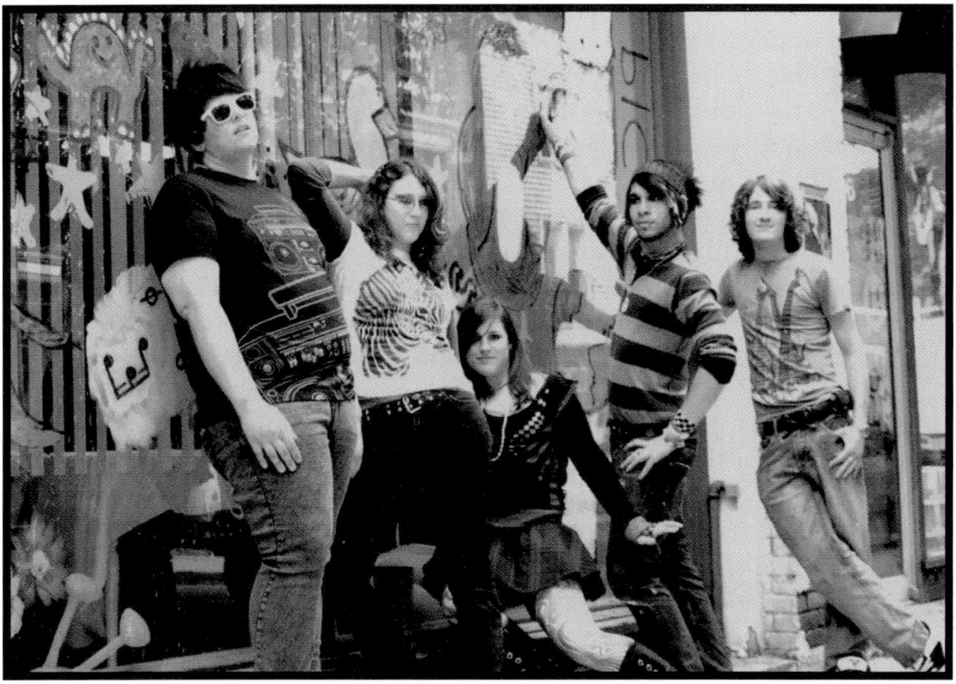

Introduction

M. Sue Crowley, Corrine C. Bertram, and Sean G. Massey

AS INFORMATION about the lives of lesbian, gay, bisexual, transgendered, and queer or questioning (LGBTQ) youth has increased over the past couple of decades, two competing narratives have emerged. Some recent research narratives reflect much improvement in the lives of LGBTQ people in general, while other anecdotal and research evidence shows continuing victimization, marginalization, and oppression.

One example of the narrative of progress can be found in the work of Savin-Williams (2005) and others (Talburt, 2004). From their perspective, the lives of LGBTQ youth have improved dramatically when compared to those of people who came of age a generation ago, "the rapidity of the cultural makeover since the birth of the modern gay era has been nothing short of astonishing . . . the younger generation is reasonably optimistic because a sea change has occurred" (Savin-Williams, 2005, p. 14). Legal initiatives and victories against anti-sodomy laws (*Lawrence v. Texas*, 2003) have given hope to many young people. Both public and private role models abound, and their straight peers are seen as much more open and accepting of LGBTQ people. In many workplaces, they will find equal benefits and protections, as well as a number of well-established organizations that represent their needs. Among youth in school settings, the most prominent example of such organizations can be seen in the emergence of Gay-Straight Alliances (GSAs). Developmental psychologists have linked the narrative of progress with the ability of youth to manage their impulses and desires in ways that do not openly challenge heterosexist norms (Savin-Williams, 2005). This stance is potentially damaging stance in so far as it places responsibility for such problems within the LGBTQ youth, isolating the issue itself from the varied social contexts within which LGBTQ youth are coming of age.

The counter narrative is represented by anecdotal and research reports of LGBTQ youth who encounter discrimination, harassment, bullying, and ostracism, problems reflected in higher rates of suicide attempts, drug and alcohol use, and homelessness relative to their straight peers (GLSEN, 2005). From this perspective, young LGBTQ people remain at greater risk than their heterosexual peers for a host of challenges that complicate their development during an already complicated period in the life-span (NMHA, 2002; Ryan & Futterman, 2001). These challenges are especially evident within high schools where "hatred in the hallways" (Bochenek & Brown, 2001) remains all too evident. The narrative of victimization and oppression, however, risks perpetuating negative stereotypes about the lives of LGBTQ people. Insofar as this is the case, youth may feel discouraged, even afraid, to explore their own needs and interests.

We have designed this volume to examine the conflicting narratives of progress and victimization as they play out in educational settings, both formal and informal, for LGBTQ youth today. By contextualizing their experiences in schools, communities, and wider social circles, we sought to present a more nuanced approach to the study of LGBTQ youth in the twenty-first century. Their experiences reveal the extent to which both oppression and opportunity commingle and interact to create paradoxical reflections of their still emergent identities.

Because we hope this volume will add to people's understanding of the lives of LGBTQ youth, particular emphasis has been placed on their own depictions, expressions, and representations. The following overviews of each chapter begin this process by focusing on excerpts that include the voices of LGBTQ youth, because the messages they send to those of us who are older and/or straighter, as well as to one another, are their efforts to make sense of the conflicting narratives and expectations for what life is or ought to be for them. Narratives of progress and oppression are interwoven in their words, giving expression to the challenges they confront, and presenting challenges to us as well. It is our responsibility to listen and to learn.

Section One
High Schools: Conflicted Contexts

I don't want to be out yet 'cause our school is horrible.

A lot of people are [out] but I just don't feel comfortable being out.

I would be devastated if the whole school knew.

In Section One of this volume, we present research conducted primarily within high school settings. High school remains perhaps the most ubiquitous and central social context in which young people begin to practice adult roles by experiencing firsthand the meanings of various social locations and non/dominant social positioning by class, ethnicity, disability, sexuality, gender, and race. Life in high school is a learning experience almost all adolescents must negotiate. These experiences provide important lessons about where one belongs, is appreciated, and encouraged, as well as where one does not belong, may be humiliated, and discouraged. For LGBTQ youth, negotiating high school can involve a minefield of conflicting emotions and expectations. These chapters provide important insights into how administrators, teachers, and peers can either help or hurt the process of developing self-respectful, hopeful identities among LGBTQ youth.

In Chapter One, Marjorie Cooper-Nicols and Lisa Bowleg point out that research on LGB youth in school has increased over the past decade (D'Augelli, 2002; Jackson & Hendrix, 2003; Szalacha, 2004; Smith, 2005), but only one study (Lasser & Tharinger, 2003) involved a qualitative approach that allowed youth to describe their experiences in detail. Cooper-Nicols and Bowleg bring those experiences to the forefront in the words of 13 teenagers who were participants in a community program, Project 10 East, that collaborated with local high schools in support of LGBTQ students. This study took place in the relatively tolerant political atmosphere of Boston, Massachusetts, where statewide educational guidelines recommend action to support and protect LGBTQ students in schools. The authors discover that policy guidelines do not necessarily translate into practice. In the words of a 15-year-old student:

> Early in the year someone wrote "Kill gays" on our bulletin board, but nothing ever happened. They never tried to find out who did it.
>
> It's just a mission, just a saying, but nobody ever acts on it.

The authors also discovered, however, that individual teachers can make a great deal of difference in the lives of LGBTQ youth for both good and ill: "I know my English teacher . . . If she's talking about something, she won't say 'your boyfriend.' She tries to incorporate a discussion of stereotypes."

Another young man, however, was berated by a male teacher in front of the class to "walk like a man!" In response to this humiliation he noted, "I thought about reporting it [the incident] and then I thought they [administration] wouldn't do anything. So, I just told the GSA."

Maria Valenti's research for Chapter Two is drawn from the experiences of faculty advisors for GSAs. It follows up on findings in the previous chapter about the potential of individual teachers to improve the lives of LGBTQ students. GSA advisors are involved in a set of complex, multifaceted roles within the school. They may need to interact with all constituencies across hierarchical levels of the system. This can include negotiations with administrators and school boards, organizing staff training sessions, and defending GSA programs at parent-teacher organization (PTO) meetings. Although these activities may read like an all-purpose list of responsibilities, they don't include the primary and most significant role: being student advisor. In that role, they serve as a caring adult and a touchstone for safety, advice, and understanding. As such, they are positioned to provide the most essential form of support LGBTQ youth need to negotiate the challenges of high school. In the words of one participant:

Introduction 5

> I'm still just so glad that the group has been here . . . and frustrated.
>
> I guess that on the other side just to know that people that I think should be aware of protecting and helping all kids are not doing so, and they are caving in to some kind of perceived political pressure.
>
> And I think if you're gonna be a leader in a school district you have to lead the way and that comes down to this issue.

In Chapter Three, Darla Linville and David Lee Carlson examine the significance of friendships between LGBTQ students and their straight allies. Peers, as well as adults, can make a tremendous difference in the lives of LGBTQ youth, again, both for good and ill. This study explores the experiences of 12 students involved in an after-school group focused on social justice issues. Although they are a small, self-selected group, these students were drawn from diverse ethnic backgrounds and neighborhoods, representing different social class positions. What they shared in common was an urban environment and an interest in social justice.

Drawing on Foucault's understanding of the ways in which we "fashion ourselves as ethical persons" (p. 105), Linville and Carlson explore how straight friends "have to refashion themselves within their friendships . . . make new choices about what they think and who they want to be in the friendship" (p. 108). The authors present a nuanced discussion of the challenges straight-identified friends encounter, both within themselves and in interaction with others. These narratives reveal young people of immense integrity and courage, such as "Omar" (a pseudonym):

> Omar is creating new spaces of freedom for straight boys in his school by standing up for his friend, speaking out unabashedly about non-heterosexual sexualities, . . . and also playing on the football team. He crosses the borders that students often cannot transgress—those that keep normative masculinity and heterosexuality on one side and homosexuality on the other.

The authors frame these young activists' endeavors as encounters between old power structures and new knowledge, generating various forms of negotiation and resistance. "It is the personal self-fashioning or continual re-fashioning of oneself that can alter both the political and ethical landscape. It is, in short, where both change and freedom occur" (p. 111).

In Chapter Four, Sean Massey discusses the ambivalent attitudinal contexts that gay youth navigate both in schools and the towns in which they live. This context is illustrated through the voices of high school students reacting to a local production of the play *The Laramie Project*, which described the reactions of residents of Laramie, Wyoming, to the murder of gay college student Matthew Shepard, as well as the reactions of members of an LGBT youth support group in Austin, Texas. One of the participants, Lea (17-year-old white female), describes the ambivalence found in her high school:

> You can't really compare Austin to any other city – especially in Texas because it's such a melting pot. The community is an accepting nurturing free-spirited type of place. So it's really not like any other town. . . but you couldn't really be openly gay at [my high school]. I mean a lot of people would be comfortable with it, but there are teenagers who would be so turned off by things that cause them to question their own image and the person they are trying to be.

Massey argues that the progress that has been made over the past half-century is remarkable, but not all aspects of the life space of LBGT youth have been equally influenced by this progress. He emphasizes the need for new ways of measuring attitudes toward gay men and lesbians that allows for the assessment of both progress and continued marginalization. To accomplish this, Massey presents a multidimensional measure of heterosexuals' attitudes toward gay men and lesbians that he developed as a possible tool for future research with youth.

Continuing the focus on high schools as a central context for youth experiences and development, the final two chapters in Section One present specific issues in education, career development, and disabilities studies, respectively, offering detailed recommendations to educators. First, in Chapter Five, Jeneka Joyce, Maya O'Neil, and Ellen McWhirter note that "vocational decisions and choices represent an implementation of self-concept" (p. 160), thereby linking career and identity development among LGBTQ youth. Using composite, fictional scenarios in which youth express

Introduction

the challenges of multiple identity issues, the authors offer insights into the ways in which teachers, counselors, and other caring adults may assist LGBTQ teenagers who are "coping with simultaneous developmental processes" (p. 165).

The authors conclude by presenting specific, comprehensive recommendations for practitioners, noting:

> Interventions should seek to support, educate, and provide resources for LGBTQ adolescents, as well as the families and schools within which they reside. . . . They have innumerable strengths and contributions to offer our communities if we can increase their well being . . . , promote their integration and self-exploration, and facilitate their goal achievement . . . , all of us will benefit. (p. 176)

In the final chapter of Section One, Thomas Duke re-visions the traditional standards set in place by the Council for Exceptional Children (CEC) for students with disabilities. Complicating the usual rhetoric in this field, Duke generates language inclusive of the particular needs of LGBTQ students. In doing so, he challenges educators to imagine youth with disabilities in all their complexity and diversity. It is a challenge that requires them to think beyond homogenized, singular labels to consider what is truly in the best interests of youth. Duke situates LGBTQ students with disabilities among many other young people who have been/are marginalized within schools that function as traditional agents of socialization and, therefore, sites of oppression.

Within the overarching 10 CEC Standards are 126 specifically defined core competencies. Duke begins by noting that only one of those includes a reference to respect for the diversity of sexual orientation. In this chapter, the author engages in a critical examination of *CEC Knowledge and Skills Standards*, concluding:

> The exclusion of knowledge forms related to the lives and experiences of LGBTQ individuals with disabilities . . . might lead one to assume that special educators do not need to know (or care) very much about sexual orientation or gender identity/expression to engage in safe and effective practice with LGBTQ youth with disabilities. (p. 194)

In response, he offers specific strategies to challenge school-based homophobia and heterosexism, while integrating LGBTQ-inclusive language in several core knowledge areas of the CEC standards.

Section Two
Beyond School Walls

> Just yesterday ... one of the guys in the car sticks his head out and yells "You're a fuckin' faggot!" I kept walking and ignored the comment.

Section Two of this volume consists of five chapters that extend beyond high school and most formal educational contexts. They discuss activism in universities, identity development in school and community settings, "liminal spaces" that exist outside formal interactions and adult supervision, youth-generated communities in cyberspace, and implicit messages in mainstream films.

In Chapter Seven, "School for the Self," Omar Jamil and Gary Harper lament the extent to which standard psychological theories of identity development "apply singularly to either sexual or ethnic identity development, and none have specifically detailed the process of identity development as it occurs for young men who are members of both sexual and ethnic minority communities" (p. 220). Their research argues that multiple identities develop concurrently and across diverse educational/community contexts.

These contexts include traditional school settings, community-based organizations (CBOs) focused on ethnicity and culture, and GBQ organizations and activities. Families, peers, and supportive adults across contexts facilitate identity development either singularly (e.g., ethnic minority or sexual minority) or multiply (e.g., learning what it means to combine multiple, minority identities). Although ethnic and sexual minority identities developed concurrently for participants in the study, it appeared that they were largely unrelated to one another.

Ethnic identity involved a public process of becoming affiliated with and being welcomed by one's community, while sexual identity was characterized as a private, individualized process, "often invisible to their parents" (p. 227). Schools also reflected these different processes of ethnic and sexual identity development. Again, ethnicity was negotiated more openly through interactions with peer groups across ethnic/racial similarities and differences. Emergent sexual identities could not be explored with the same openness. In the authors' words, "Despite years of movement toward the attainment of rights for LGBT individuals, discussing LGBT topics was viewed as still being taboo in schools by our participants" (p. 232). CBOs provided GBQ male youth of color with both opportunities and challenges in that they appeared to reflect and support separate rather than integrated aspects of their identity development. The authors describe a 17-year-old boy who felt more comfortable in a Latino CBO than an LGBTQ CBO due to the presence of gay-supportive staff.

> ...it's nothing but African American and White people over there [LGBT CBO]. So, I fit in, but it's kind of awkward around them. And if I find Hispanic LGBT men around in [Latino CBO], well, the people who I talk to there, they're really accepting and so I feel like I can openly talk to them about practically anything.

GB male youth of color appear to engage with an array of support systems and learning environments to explore their emergent identities as individuals who literally embody the status of multiple minorities. From family, friends, and CBOs they learn that it is possible to value one's ethnic heritage, even if their home communities are not always open to sexual minorities. From LGBT organizations and activities they can learn the value of living openly, of simply being free to be one's self.

> Just the fact that I could come there and be myself. Which I found out later wasn't really different from the person that I thought was so fake and phony. I was just accepting of myself when I was there, and then not accepting as soon as I left. But when I was there I felt comfortable just to think, yeah, oh my gosh, hey, I can look at guys and not be afraid. Yeah!

Chapter Eight illustrates how one courageous, dedicated individual can put in motion a broad-based activist movement to change institutional climate and culture. Those efforts took place in a mid-sized university near one of the largest urban areas in the United States: Houston, Texas. Like many educational institutions, particularly in higher education, the university had in place various mission statements that encouraged inclusion and diversity. As authors Kim Case, Heather Kanenberg, and Stephen Erich, point out, however, mission statements may not reflect the actual climate of an institution.

> LGBTIQ campus members experience various levels of exclusion ranging from prejudiced comments by faculty, staff, and classmates to name calling, threats to those working for transgender inclusions, damage to LGBTIQ displays and student property, and active resistance to equal rights for members of the LGBTIQ communities.

This chapter goes on to offer an example of complex resistance to entrenched, oppressive institutional norms. It is/was a daunting task. Changing institutional culture and climate requires concerted, consistent, and broad-based efforts across all levels of a university. It also requires a degree of personal courage from people who represent the full spectrum of constituencies in the institution. In this case, staff, professionals, students, junior faculty, and a few well-placed administrators exemplify how a relative few can confront injustice to effect positive change.

In Chapter Nine, Corrine Bertram discovers some of what we may learn from young people by becoming attuned to the "liminal spaces, locations and moments betwixt and between, on the edges of interviews" (p. 281), meetings, and other adult-organized and adult-created spaces for the edification, education, and service of LGBTIQ youth. Through openings that even the most well-meaning adult might miss, Bertram looks back on what she has learned from her involvement as a mentor in a weekly after-school group for LGBTQ youth.

The author reminds us that adolescence is a time when young people need to explore their desires, define their needs, and experiment with new roles in interaction with one another "outside of adult control and supervision" (p. 283). This may be especially true for LGBTQ youth, whose curiosity about and experimentation with their sexuality is so deeply feared by the adults around them, including LGBTQ adults. Much of what adults emphasize when discussing sexuality with youth involves harm, pregnancy, sexually transmitted diseases (STDs), and violence. As an illustration, the author describes a conversation in a van returning from a program sponsored by an acquired immune deficiency syndrome/human immunodeficiency virus (AIDS/HIV) non-profit agency. Awkwardly, the young people in the van questioned the adult mentor about the possibility of discussing sadomasochism (SM) in future programming. Their hesitance appeared to reflect an understanding

Introduction 11

of adult discomfort with the topic, a grown-up need to deflect discussions of sexual pleasure and desire into a discourse on psychopathology vis-à-vis safety and health.

Bertram's story is one of discovery framed by a critical analysis of both her own adult concerns and the ways in which LGBTQ youth are engaged in a process of knowledge production outside the formal, presumably safe spaces provided by adults. Framing her explorations in a series of scenes, she takes the reader to intersections of class, gender, and sexuality where working-class family backgrounds and low-wage, part-time work leave little room for coming to terms with the need for intimacy and sexuality. Her critical explorations also pass through sites of sexual fluidity where youth reject the boundaries of the alphabet adults have generated for them: L, G, B, T, Q. Here we encounter challenges *within* LGBTQ communities that cross generational lines and reveal the limitations of applying past coming-of-age experiences to LGBTQ youth today.

Because adolescents often learn important lessons about the ways in which they are socially positioned by observing representations of themselves and others, this issue speaks to the ways in which LGBTQ youth come to frame identities as part of the larger social worlds they inhabit or hope to inhabit. Therefore, the final two chapters in this volume consider how LGBTQ youth represent themselves to one another in cyberspace and how others represent them in films.

In Chapter Ten, Sue Crowley examines how LGBQS (straight) youth employ two online social networking sites, MySpace and Facebook, to form new avenues of connection. Within these sites, youths create ongoing conversations about their emergent sexual-social identities and new forms of representation. Rejecting the boundaries imposed by an alphabet soup of categories, L, G, B, T, Q, I, etc., they play with the language of identity and representation in ways that reflect their ongoing explorations—"I feel like a homo for being the only bi so far"—and the fluidity of their emotional and physical desires—"I don't like the word, because 'bi' means "two," and I certainly don't want to restrict myself to only the two "official" genders..." For many, rejecting past labels meant creating new ones. The most popular neologism was *mehsexual*, as in "meh, gender doesn't matter to me." This process also involved distancing themselves from the prejudice and hatred associated with LGBTQ labels. Many, both "Str8" and "meh," expressed the belief that, "HEY GANG what the fuck with the labels? . . . and it really doesn't matter it is 2007. labels r why gays have it so bad in the past...!"

The author contrasts their desire to reject old labels with the use of derogatory terms employed by those who continue to actively oppose human rights for LGBTQ people, even after 2007. Questioning the extent to which eschewing labels will result in escaping prejudice, the author expresses doubts about youthful reliance on the affective individualism that is evident in statements such as, "as long as ur happy," and "does not make one damn bit of difference to me." Although identity formation cannot be captured within the artificial boundaries created by identity politics, it also cannot occur in a psychological and personal vacuum dominated by individual desires. Ultimately, these young people are coming of age within sociopolitical frames of reference that contain broad social dimensions and meanings of identity.

Perhaps one of the most pervasive forms of public representation is found in mainstream media, specifically the movies. Unfortunately, it is rare to find films geared toward LGBTQ youth and their concerns. Seeking representations of gay life, LGBTQ youth may gravitate toward films that are outside the usual Hollywood teen movie genre. In Chapter Eleven, Diane Wiener and Christine Smith analyze the images and representations in one such film, *Under the Tuscan Sun* (2004). The authors explore ways in which teachers, social workers, and others who work with LGBTQ youth may examine and counteract representations of LGBTQ people that minimize the significance of their experiences by relegating them to the position of "sidekicks." This form of social positioning has been a Hollywood tradition for underrepresented minorities. Wiener and Smith argue that the same is true for sexual minorities.

Although youth have many more opportunities to observe LGBTQ images in the mainstream media than prior generations, those images tend to represent individuals who are "middle-class, intelligent, sophisticated, witty, thin, and usually white" (p. 353).

Introduction

Given the young people who populate other chapters in this volume, it is clear that such representations fail to capture the complexity of their multiple identities (Chapter Seven), abilities (Chapter Six), and social class positions (Chapter Nine). By relegating LGBTQ youth to the sidelines of both the teen movie genre and adult films with LGBTQ characters, youth receive clear, if often subtle, messages about who they are and can be.

The authors provide preliminary guidelines for engaging youth in critical conversations about the ways complex identities are framed in the mainstream media through illustrations from the film. Such conversations serve to expand representations of LGBTQ people's lives in ways that can be empowering to youth.

Coming of age at the tail end of the "culture wars," young people are situated within layers of influence across family, peers, schools, communities, and media. They are saturated in varied and conflicting images and political discourses. When adult researchers, teachers, and others impose their own assumptions, either of progress or victimization, they/we risk missing the point altogether. The extent to which LGBTQ youth are negotiating simultaneous, fluid contexts of opportunity and oppression are highlighted in many of the quotes that appear in the chapters that follow. It is not unusual for them to combine the positive and negative realities of their young lives in a single comment. They often display a level of epistemological complexity that their elders would be wise to consider.

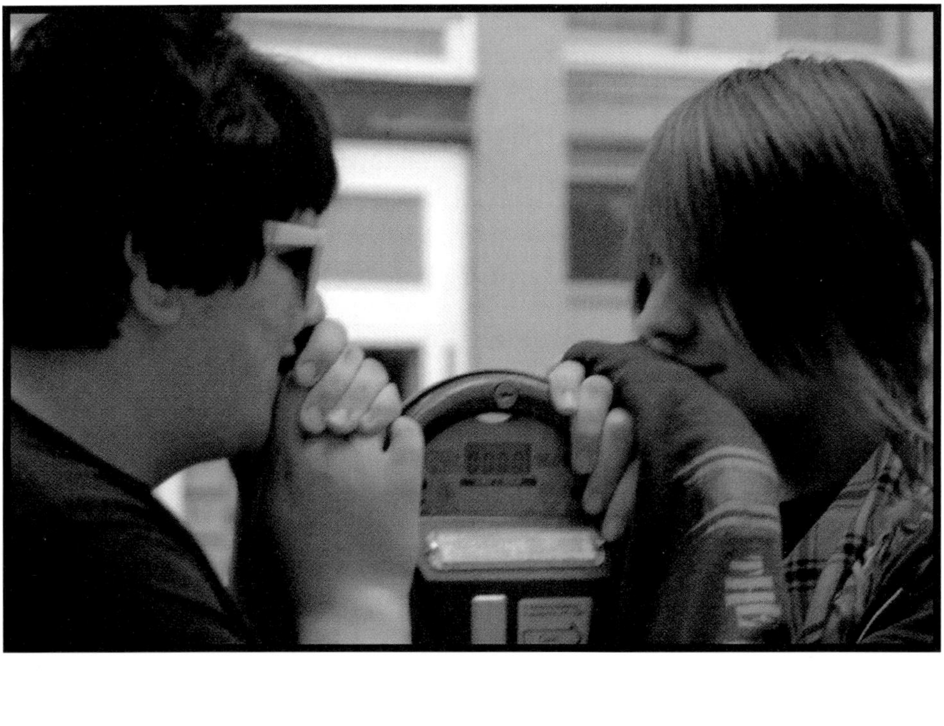

Chapter One

"My Voice Is Being Heard": Exploring the Experiences of Gay, Lesbian, and Bisexual Youth in Schools

Marjorie Cooper-Nicols and Lisa Bowleg

"THAT'S SO GAY! That's so queer!" Comments like these echo through many U.S. school hallways with the regularity of the change of the class bell. As such, far from being safe and welcoming environments, traditional U.S. schools contribute heavily to the feelings of isolation and stigmatization that many gay, lesbian, and bisexual (GLB) youth experience (Unks, 1995). Although middle school and high school can be rough for many adolescents, especially if they are somehow different from the "norm," GLB students often encounter extreme isolation as they explore their sexual orientation. With little recognition, few resources and minimal support from peers, family, and community groups, they are an at-risk population that schools too often ignore.

GLB youth are vulnerable to specific stressors that may impede healthy identity development. Stressors include depression, substance abuse, and heterosexist violence. Numerous studies indicate that GLB adolescents are two to three times more likely to attempt suicide than heterosexual young people, and they account for up to 30% of youth suicides annually (Faulkner & Cranston, 1998; Gibson, 1989; Remafedi, French, Story, Resnick, & Blum, 1998). GLB youth also use alcohol and marijuana at higher rates than the national average for all youth (Remafedi, 1987; Rotheram-Borus & Langabeer, 2001). Finally, anti-GLB youth violence is prevalent. For example, Faulkner and Cranston (1998) found that GLB students were more than three times as likely as their heterosexual peers to report not going to school because they felt unsafe due to being threatened and/or injured while at school. A Gay, Lesbian and Straight Education Network (GLSEN) survey conducted in 2005 found that 90% of GLB teens, versus 62% of heterosexual teens, reported that they were harassed or assaulted at school.

Heterosexism is the ideological system that denies, denigrates, and stigmatizes any nonheterosexual form of behavior (Herek, 1995). It is the assumption that everyone is heterosexual, or if not, should be (Friend, 1992). Heterosexism is manifested at individual, cultural, and institutional levels, thereby pervading societal customs and contexts. These three levels of heterosexism operate in our nation's schools. For example, at the individual level, peers and educators often perpetrate a great many jokes and put-downs and distance themselves from suspected GLB individuals. Examples of institutional heterosexism in schools include the lack of services and recognition for GLB youth, such as counseling, safe spaces, schoolwide anti-GLB discrimination policies, basic information and education for GLB and heterosexual students, health information, staff development, and school rules prohibiting same-sex partners at school-sponsored events such as the prom. Finally, examples of cultural heterosexism operating in schools include negative attitudes and stereotypes such as those promoting the ideas that girls and women who play sports are lesbians and non-athletic boys and men are gay, and the unstated rule that it is permissible to bully suspected GLB individuals, especially males (Bohan, 1996). Institutionalized heterosexism serves to deny the very existence of GLB students in schools. In turn, this denial and lack of affirmation perpetuates the GLB student's need to remain invisible (Fontaine, 1998).

Although some schools have begun to recognize the needs and concerns of GLB youth, most educators have received little or no training in how best to work with GLB adolescents (Mallon, 1997). There is a lack of school policy for working with GLB students, and GLB alliances are typically organized by GLB students and friends, not by school administrators (Leland, 2000). Additionally, educational personnel often display biased feelings and attitudes toward GLB individuals. For example, Sears (1992) found that teachers, counselors, and administrators exhibit distressingly high levels of homophobic attitudes and feelings, with 80% of prospective teachers and 66% of school counselors exhibiting negative attitudes toward GLB people.

Schools, as reflections of larger society, weave messages about normative culture through the formal and informal curricula. Adolescents by nature are progressing through a tumultuous time in life in terms of trying to resolve their own identities. Thus, school and peers, as socializing agents, assume a larger role than in childhood in helping adolescents shape their identities and experiences (Nichols, 1999). Many schools are not nurturing environments for GLB youth, and most schools have been reticent to address the issues of GLB students. Because of GLB invisibility and the sanctioning of harassment against GLB students in school, GLB youth learn that society views them through a pejorative and stigmatizing lens (Mallon, 1997). Most GLB youth choose to remain closeted because they have determined that it is not safe to be open about their orientation. Those who reject the strategy of hiding often encounter both verbal harassment and physical violence, especially at school (Mallon, 1997). Whichever option is exercised, hiding or living openly, most GLB youth fear losing their families and friends (Mallon, 1997). Such stigmatizing experiences cause a great deal of stress for the GLB adolescent, which may lead to complications such as isolation, trying to pass as heterosexual, or possibly risking harassment by disclosing one's sexual identity (Mallon, 1997). As their mission, most schools promise to educate all youth. More educators must come to realize that "all youth" includes GLB youth.

The formation of gay-straight alliances (GSAs) is a strategy many schools have implemented to assist GLB youth in coping with exclusion. GSAs have been a major factor in helping teenagers create openly gay lives. GSAs are school-based youth groups for GLB students and their allies that focus on support, education, and socialization, and they are typically facilitated by teachers or school counselors. GLSEN (2005) estimates that there are about 700 GSAs nationwide, most of which were formed in the wake of

Matthew Shepard's murder in 1998 (Peyser & Lorch, 2000). Some urban schools in large metropolitan areas have implemented different types of programs to help GLB students feel included and respected and to educate other students about homosexuality and the achievements of GLB people throughout history. To date, Massachusetts is the only state to have developed a statewide Commission on Gay and Lesbian Youth. Located in the suburbs of Boston, Project 10 East Inc. is an example of a community program designed to assist GLB youth. It is an organization that collaborates with local schools and communities to increase acceptance and support for GLB youth where they live and attend school.

Goals of This Investigation

Several researchers within the field of psychology have conducted qualitative studies with GLB adults recollecting their adolescent and school experiences (Anderson, 1998; Sears, 1991). Other researchers have used quantitative methods with GLB youth participants (Faulkner & Cranston, 1998; GLSEN, 2005; National Mental Health Association [NMHA], 2002). Researchers have also conducted GLB youth studies with school personnel (Fontaine, 1998; Sears, 1992). Despite the literature on GLB youth, there is a paucity of empirical research on the *actual experiences* of GLB adolescents in schools. Indeed, we are aware of just one qualitative psychological study that focused on youths' experiences in schools (Lasser & Tharinger, 2003).

This study examined the experiences of GLB adolescents in school and the impact that the school environment (e.g., peers, teachers, and school policy) had on their lives. We conducted this study in an effort to make educators (more) aware of the needs of GLB youth and to expose heterosexism in our nation's schools, because heterosexist and intolerant educational environments can only exist with the implicit and/or explicit cooperation of school officials and personnel. We worked in collaboration with Project 10 East.

Through the use of qualitative research methods, specifically semistructured interviews conducted with GLB adolescents, this study sought to examine the following questions: (1) How have schools responded to GLB youth? (2) What are some of the factors or experiences that help or hinder development of a healthy sexual identity for GLB adolescents?

Method

Participants

GLB youth participants included 13 adolescents who self-identified as gay, lesbian, or bisexual from 4 communities reached by Project 10 East. Participants' ages ranged from 15 to 18 years. Altogether, 3 participants identified themselves as lesbian, 4 as gay male, and 6 as bisexual (4 females, 2 males). Ten of the GLB youth participants were white; two were Hispanic; and one of the participants was Asian American. We also interviewed three teachers and one self-identified adolescent heterosexual "friend" of Project 10 East.

Procedures

The director of Project 10 East recruited the adolescents and teachers who participated in this study. After the director obtained a list of all interested students and teachers, we randomly selected participants. Because few GLB youth of color were randomly selected to participate in the study, we added ethnic/racial diversity by selecting three ethnic minority adolescents from those who stated an interest in participation. Participation in this study was voluntary. The Institutional Review Board of the University of Rhode Island approved all study procedures. To protect confidentiality, we have changed the names and identifiers of all participants. Interviewee demographics are included in Table 1. Community demographics of the 4 high schools represented in this study are included in Table 2.

Measures

Each interview was tape-recorded and transcribed. Interviews ranged in length from 1 to 2 hours. The interview guide followed a semistructured format (Flick, 1998) in which carefully worded and arranged questions were asked of each participant. However, flexibility in asking probe (follow-up) questions was permitted to explore certain subjects in greater detail (Patton, 1987).

Table 1

Demographic Information by GLB Interviewee

Name*	Age	Sex	Sexual Orientation**	School Attended	Race/Ethnicity
Jamie	18	F	Lesbian	Washington	Caucasian
Anna	16	F	Bisexual	Washington	Caucasian
Jane	15	F	Bisexual	Lincoln	Caucasian
Rachel	15	F	Bisexual	Washington	Caucasian
Steve	18	M	Bisexual	Lincoln	Caucasian
Linda	16	F	Lesbian	JFK	Caucasian
Sandra	16	F	Bisexual	Washington	Asian American
Mae	16	F	Lesbian	JFK	Caucasian
Chad	16	M	Gay	Washington	Caucasian
Robert	16	M	Bisexual	Washington	Hispanic
Mark	16	M	Gay	Washington	Caucasian
Juan	18	M	Gay	Washington	Hispanic
Chris	18	M	Gay	Roosevelt	Caucasian

* All names used are pseudonyms to protect confidentiality.
** Participants' self-described sexual orientation.

Table 2

Demographic Characteristics of the Schools Participating in This Study*

	School**			
	Washington	Lincoln	JFK	Roosevelt
Type of Community	Urban	Suburban	Urban	Suburban
Number of Students	1586	1316	1827	2080
Grade Levels	9-12	9-12	9-12	9-12
Race/Ethnicity of Student Body				
White	48.8%	66.6%	33.1%	80.9%
Black	18.5%	17.8%	42.7%	5.5%
Asian	8.2%	7.2%	8.6%	9.4%
Hispanic	26.4%	8.0%	15.2%	4.2%
Low-Income Families	57.4%	15.0%	42.9%	15.6%
Student's First Language Not English	50.3%	21.9%	38.1%	16.2%
Special Education	16.1%	16.5%	19.4%	19.1%
Number of Teachers	128	88	174	196
Student/Teacher Ratio	12.4/1	14.9/1	10.5/1	10.6/1
Attendance Rate	92.8%	92.5%	90.7%	95.5%

* Student body demographics were drawn from the Massachusetts Department of Education's Profile of Schools (2004–2005).
** All school names are pseudonyms to protect confidentiality.

Analytical Strategy

We used a modified grounded theory (Glaser & Strauss, 1967) approach to analyze the data. Grounded theory's clear and systematic procedures (Chamberlain, 1999) made it an ideal choice for our analyses. The coding phase of the data analysis proceeded in two main phases: open coding (i.e., broad coding of general themes) and axial coding (i.e., more refined coding of themes, then focusing on more central themes) (Glaser & Strauss, 1967). During open coding, the first author read all the interviews thoroughly and multiple times and attached descriptive labels to relevant sections of the transcript that best reflected the concept (Ryan & Bernard, 2000). We coded by grouping similar categories together (Flick, 1998). For example, the codes "school policies," "safety," and "school practices" were grouped, as were the codes "family" and "coming-out." During the axial coding phase, we further refined the coding from the open coding phase to focus on codes most relevant to the study's main research questions (Flick, 1998). Consistent with the constant comparative method of grounded theory (Chamberlain, 1999), we used an interactive process of comparing themes against each other to assess similarities on the one hand and negative or disconfirming cases on the other (Flick, 1998). In many cases, we found that we needed to elaborate on and refine initial categories.

We assessed the quality of analyses in this research study via three criteria proposed by Lincoln and Guba (1985): credibility, transferability, and confirmability. *Credibility* is the likelihood that credible findings and interpretations were produced (Merrick, 1999). Lincoln and Guba (1985) proposed several techniques to increase the likelihood that credible findings will be produced in qualitative work, such as: (1) prolonged engagement, investing sufficient time with the participants and data; (2) triangulation, checking the accuracy of data items by using different sources; (3) peer debriefing, engaging with others about what one is finding; and (4) negative case analysis, examining exceptions to the interpretations and thus possibly revising hypotheses. Lincoln and Guba (1985) conceived of the concept of *transferability* as the researcher's responsibility to compare whether the conclusions drawn from a study can be compared to other samples or theories. "Thick description" (Lincoln & Guba, 1985, p. 316) is provided to assist others interested in assessing the transferability of the study's findings. Finally, *confirmability* refers to the extent to which the study's methods, procedures, process of data collection and analyses, and conclusions have been described thoroughly.

Results

Research Question 1: Responses of schools to GLB youth. For this research question, we designed open-ended and specific questions to elicit what each participant would focus on with regard to defining and describing the school environment. Sample interview questions included: (1) "What things do you like the most/least about being a student at your school?" (2) "What are some of your school's policies towards prejudice, discrimination, and tolerance?" (3) "Tell me about the types of support that are available for GLB teens in your school." (4) "Was any teacher, counselor, or any other school personnel particularly supportive of this [coming-out] decision and process?"

Three key themes emerged: (1) Many schools followed statewide guidelines established by the Massachusetts Safe Schools Commission, which included the development of zero-tolerance policies, safe spaces, sensitivity training, counseling services, and GSAs. (2) School administrators generally responded reactively to GLB issues. (3) Although some teachers reached out to support GLB students, others ignored and/or harassed GLB students.

Theme 1: Following the guidelines established by the Massachusetts Safe Schools Commission. Twelve of the 13 GLB youth student participants discussed their school's zero-tolerance policies, safe space zones, and the support provided by their GSAs. All 4 schools participating in this study had adapted and publicized zero-tolerance policies that banned anti-GLB language and harassment on the part of faculty and students. Although 12 of the 13 GLB students articulated that they were comforted by these zero-tolerance policies, all of the youth, without exception, said that these school policies were somewhat vague and not clearly enforced. They described anti-GLB harassment as commonplace, said that faculty often failed to recognize it as harassment, and said that students often did not report harassment out of fear of peer retribution. Student interviewees also reported incidents when the zero-tolerance policies were not enforced. For example, Anna, a 16-year-old bisexual female and student at Washington High School stated:

> We have a zero tolerance rule, but it's not really enough. It's supposed to protect us. It's supposed to be in effect, but everyone ignores it. Like they say, "that's so gay," and "faggot" and "dyke" in any context, and they're like "I didn't mean it like that." And no one stops them.

Jane, a 15-year-old bisexual female and student at Lincoln High School, described an incident when individuals defaced the GSA bulletin board, and school officials did little to find the perpetrators or prevent future similar incidents:

> Early in the year someone wrote "Kill gays" on our bulletin board. But nothing ever happened. No one ever said anything and everyone knew what happened. They never tried to find out who did it. They didn't do anything about it. It's just a mission to have up in our school, just a saying, but nobody ever acts on it.

All but one of the GLB youth interviewees said that they were troubled by how commonplace harassment was against them and their friends, and how the zero-tolerance policies failed to protect them adequately.

The school environments appeared to be safer physically but not verbally for suspected GLB youth. All the GLB youth interviewees noted that they and their friends were often the targets of verbal harassment. Nor was physical harassment uncommon; 2 GLB youth interviewees noted that they had witnessed physical harassment, while Linda, a 16-year-old lesbian youth, reported that she witnessed a violent attack against a male friend suspected to be gay. Chad, a 16-year-old gay male, said that he was often physically attacked and threatened. Unfortunately, it did not appear that the Department of Education's zero-tolerance policies had clearly informed administrators how to deal with anti-GLB harassment incidents. All the youth reported that administrators typically wanted eyewitnesses to harassment to punish perpetrators. If a fellow student was caught harassing someone because of sexual orientation, school officials in all 4 school districts typically issued an initial warning rather than suspensions. The GLB youth also reported that perpetrators were rarely suspended, and on only very few occasions were parents summoned. In addition to inadequate disciplinary measures in dealing with acts of discrimination, there did not appear to be any penalties for failure to report anti-GLB harassment.

All 13 GLB participants discussed the importance of the GSA in their lives. They viewed the GSA as a safe place that enabled them to make friends, get educational material, find supportive counselors (if need be), and even get connected to the larger GLB community if they chose. Nine of the 13 participants noted that their GSA had received full club status at their schools, which meant after-school meetings, an advisor, a mailbox, and being allowed to make announcements to the general student body, hand out flyers, maintain a bulletin board, and sponsor school events. Six of the GLB youth described the GLB-related programming at their schools and how they believed that their GSAs had positively influenced school policies for GLB youth. For example, Linda, a 16-year-old lesbian and student at JFK High School, noted, "Every year we have a Coming-Out Day assembly and a thousand students attend. And we speak to every single freshman health class about GLBT issues. It's open enough that it's talked about." Similarly, Chad, a 16-year-old gay male and student at Washington High School, recalled:

> Well, since I'm in the GSA, we've had a lot of say in a lot of stuff lately. So I guess that's good 'cause we're standing out and getting to talk to people. My voice is being heard. So I guess that's one of the ups of being a student there; that I'm helping changing around the way people are thinking.

As part of the Massachusetts Safe Schools Commission, all public high schools are required to hold sensitivity training workshops to learn about GLB tolerance, diversity, services, and how and where to make referrals for GLB students in need. All 3 teachers discussed these workshops and noted that they perceived them as interesting and useful. That said, Mr. Lander, a teacher at JFK High School, said that no workshops had been conducted since the guidelines came out nearly 10 years ago. Ms. Smith, a teacher at Lincoln High School, reported that those workshops took place in her school 5 years earlier, and she was concerned that there had been a high turnover of staff in her school in recent years. Thus, many new teachers were not trained adequately. Additionally, both teachers interviewed for this study from Lincoln High School reported that portions of the sensitivity training workshops were optional. Thus, these voluntary workshops were not reaching *all* faculty members, and mandatory training was not happening annually as dictated by the Department of Education's guidelines. Moreover, all the teachers noted that closed-minded faculty members typically opted not to go to these workshops.

Theme 2: Most school administrators responded reactively or not at all to GLB issues. Four of the 13 GLB youth and 2 teachers discussed the specific role school administrators played in GLB matters. Sandra, a 16-year-old bisexual student at Washington High School, complained that Building Masters (i.e., class deans) were strikingly inconsistent when it came to taking action against students who violated antidiscrimination policies based on race versus sexual orientation. She noted:

> [When] you talk to your Building Masters about a racial slur or call a girl a "bitch," you'll get a suspension. So I asked the Building Master, "What about prejudice against gay people? All you get is a warning?" And he goes, "Oh, we'll call the person in and ask him if he said it." But all the time it's happened, they've never done anything.

Sandra further articulated that the administrators simply wanted a list of certain people to punish. When she and her friends asked for more preventive services, such as increasing awareness for both faculty and students, their requests were ignored. Sandra's concern was echoed by the 3 teachers; namely, that school administrators tended to be reactionary, rather than proactive, when it came to GLB matters.

Of the 13 student participants, only 3 mentioned positive experiences with the administrators and indicated that the administrators were supportive of GLB students. Jamie, an 18-year-old lesbian student at Washington High School, recounted the close relationship she had with her school principal and how he allowed many GSA-sponsored activities at school. Similarly, Linda, a 16-year-old lesbian at JFK High School, noted, "One of our deans is helping us create a teacher training about GLBT issues. And she's been to every meeting about it. She's helped us all along the way, and she's totally straight." Chad, a 16-year-old gay male at Washington High School, reported that he and fellow GSA members were welcomed at a teacher's meeting and that they had received positive responses from the teachers and administrators.

Two teacher interviewees also spoke about their school administrations' mixed reactions when dealing with GLB matters. Ms. Connor, a teacher at Lincoln High School, noted that her school principal "stays for all the [GLB] events until the end to make sure everything is okay. And, he's been very supportive. Everything we've asked for—the Coming-Out Day—anything, he has been very, very cooperative." In contrast, Ms. Smith, a previous advisor to Lincoln's GSA, did not share Ms. Connor's positive evaluation. Instead, Ms. Smith recalled two incidents that she perceived to be unethical. In one incident, the former headmaster insisted that the GSA remove a poster in the hallway created for a student carnival. Although the poster was approved and placed alongside other clubs' posters, the headmaster insisted that the poster be removed because it was "too big." In Ms. Smith's opinion, the real reason the poster was removed was because the carnival coincided with parent-teacher conferences week, and the headmaster did not want parents to see the GSA poster. In another incident, the superintendent of the schools banned the former Project 10 East advisor from entering the school building after the advisor complained to a local newspaper that the school did not allow general announcements informing the student body about National Coming-Out Day. The former advisor felt that this sanction was discriminatory because the school made announcements for Black History Month. A local newspaper had highlighted the incident, and in retaliation, the superintendent prohibited the advisor from entering the school building thereafter.

Theme 3: Some teachers reached out to GLB students, while others ignored and/or perpetuated harassment. Although the participants all noted that the majority of the adults in the building ignored anti-GLB harassment and/or did not get involved in GLB issues, a select few supported and took interest in GLB students in need, supported events, and even curtailed harassment. Eleven of the 13 GLB students spoke about helpful and concerned teachers befriending and assisting GLB students at their schools. It appeared that these teachers were self-selected, in the sense that the assistance they offered GLB youth was voluntary, and they went beyond the call of duty in terms of the teaching requirements. GLB youth expressed their admiration and gratitude for their teachers. Rachel, a 15-year-old bisexual student at Washington High School, noted that her teacher worked hard to promote equality in the classroom:

> I know my English teacher, my favorite teacher I had in my entire life. If she's talking about something, she won't say "your boyfriend." She tries to incorporate a discussion of stereotypes into our discussion. She's really good about that kind of stuff. She's very accepting.

Similarly, Sandra mentioned that, although the majority of teachers did not stop harassment, "There are certain people, of course, who do stop it." After Chad, a 16-year-old gay male, came out to his parents, he experienced serious depression and anxiety in response to his father's verbal harassment and repeated threats to kick him out of the house. In response to his plummeting grades, Chad recalled the support that one of his teachers provided:

> The only one I told was my English teacher, Ms. B., 'cause she kind of understood, 'cause at that point when I was depressed I was failing my classes for the year, and she understood, and she helped me bring my grades back up after I told everybody. And, my grades started coming up. But I still didn't have enough good grades. So, she kind of urged my teachers. . . that's when she told my teachers, "He'd just come out. His parents were uncomfortable with it. He was all depressed about it. That's why his grades went down." So, they pushed me up and I passed for the year.

Eight of the 13 GLB students perceived honors classes to be more accepting environments for GLB students, in stark contrast to mainstream classes or school hallways. Because the majority of students in high schools are in mainstreamed classes, are required to take nonacademic classes such as physical education, and need to walk through the hallways, GLB students may spend the good part of their school day in discriminatory environments. The teenagers in this study noted that most honors teachers and students made a "nonissue" of sexual orientation, meaning that they did not react or give their opinion one way or another on GLB issues and typically treated GLB students with the same level of respect as any other student. Honors teachers also often invited discussion on topics such as equality and diversity, as Robert, a 16-year-old bisexual male and an honors student at Washington High School, stated:

> Most teachers are good, at least my teachers. If someone says, "That's gay" in class, most of them will stand up for it and tell them not to say that. I think it's better in the honors classes 'cause they [teachers] care more. . . I just think that most teachers are understanding, so I didn't have to hide it from them.

Although interviewees thought there were helpful teachers at all 4 schools, they also reported that, other than in health class, GLB matters were never fully incorporated into the school curricula. Neither the accomplishments of GLB people nor the U.S. GLB Rights Movement was ever mentioned. To start rectifying this situation, GLB students from both Washington and JFK High Schools were working on projects through their GSAs to get gay-friendly reading material and literature by GLB authors into their school libraries. The students' proactive work is laudable, but the onus for such activities should be on the educators, not the students.

Unfortunately, for every positive example these youth had of caring and accepting teachers, all the GLB youth had many more examples of teachers who either ignored harassment, treated GLB students as if they were "invisible," or even verbally harassed GLB students.

Male youth recounted more tales of ridicule at the hands of teachers than did female youth. Three young men from Washington High School reported problems with particular teachers. Chad reported what his health teacher "said in front of everybody, embarrassing me totally. We were talking about gender [and] he's like, 'Anybody who's confused with their sexuality can come see me after class to talk about it. Right, Chad?'" Robert, a 16-year-old bisexual male, recalled a teacher who harassed him. "I had this one teacher, this geometry teacher who was horrible. He tells me to walk like a man." Mark, a 16-year-old gay male, spoke about an episode in which his health teacher was condemning specific sexual acts. "And then he was like, 'Oh yeah, some perverted people like to engage in what we call analingis.'"

Research Question 2: Factors and experiences that help or hinder development of a healthy sexual identity for GLB adolescents. Examples of open-ended questions for this research question included (1) Why did you decide to come out to your peers at school? (2) What are some things that you think might happen if your teachers in school knew that you were GLB? (3) How does your family feel about your sexual orientation? (4) Do you have people or organizations in your life that you can turn to in times of trouble or stress?

According to participants, the development of a healthy sexual identity was facilitated or hindered by: (1) the overall school environment (i.e., the presence and enforcement of antidiscrimination policies, rates and nature of harassment, teacher support, the actions and support given from the GSA, and peer support and acceptance) and (2) relationships with friends, family, and community.

1. The overall school environment

School life plays a major role in every teenager's developing sense of self. Thus, it would make intuitive sense that levels of acceptance and nonacceptance, support given by adults and peers, and the presence or absence of organizations designed to improve the situation for GLB adolescents would all have an impact on a GLB teen's acceptance of his or her sexual minority status. In many ways, the issues discussed below echo and expand on the themes that emerged in response to Research Question 1 above.

All 13 GLB youth and the 3 teachers appeared to find some level of comfort in the zero-tolerance policies at their schools. For example, Jamie, an 18-year-old lesbian at Washington High School, stated, "They actually have it [anti-GLB discrimination policy] in the rule book. They kind of don't follow it as strictly as other rules, but at least they have it in the book." Chris, an 18-year-old gay male at Roosevelt High School, noted that:

> [No discrimination] is tolerated. Oh, students report it. [Administrators] actually speak with the kid and give him a suspension. At my school they officially have a policy of zero tolerance, but it varies with teachers with how they implement it.

Although the overwhelming majority of GLB youth interviewees regarded the existence of zero-tolerance policies positively, they also acknowledged that such policies were not consistently enforced. Six of the youth perceived that this lax enforcement would change as a result of their advocacy. For example, Mae, a confident and well-spoken 16-year-old lesbian at JFK High School, said that she often confronted her peers when they used hate speech:

> I hear in school the word "faggot" every day, every day. And it just goes through me right now. I kind of like it that way too. It shouldn't really bother me. But then again, people say it and teachers don't say anything. Other students don't say anything. And every day I give the same speech. . . basically I'd just say "[be] careful of . . . what you're saying." And a lot of times I've gotten rebuttals. "Oh, what about you? Are you gay?" And sometimes I'll be like, "Yeah." Sometimes it does matter. When you're like, "Well, actually yeah, I am gay." They're like, "Oh sorry." It does catch their attention when a person they've known for two years and sits next to them in class is gay, especially, 'cause, I guess I don't look like a lesbian might look. So, it shocks people.

Chad, a 16-year-old gay male at Washington High School, was upset when he and many of his GLB peers were repeatedly harassed in school. Realizing that the antidiscrimination policies were not protecting him adequately, he initiated a strategy:

> The school didn't want to talk to the kids about [the harassment]. . . . So, we had to end up going to the teachers at one of their meetings, on a Wednesday night, and talked with them face-to-face, and [told] them it needs to stop. They followed [some of our suggestions], and . . . now it's starting to get better again.

Chad's and Mae's statements appeared also to imply that their grassroots work in attempting to solve this verbal harassment problem enhanced their self-confidence. This opportunity notwithstanding, 6 of the youth responded to this inconsistent enforcement of zero tolerance with a combination of anger and fear. For example, Anna, a 16-year-old bisexual female at Washington High School, who is partially out at school, stated:

> We have a zero-tolerance rule, but it's not really enough. It's supposed to protect us. It's supposed to be in effect, but everyone ignores it. Like they say, "That's so gay," and "faggot" and "dyke" in any context, and they're like "I didn't mean that." And no one stops them . . . if a student said the word "nigger," they'd take out a detention slip or send them to an administrator and they might get suspended. To this they're like "Don't say that again." But most teachers don't even do that! They pretend they're deaf.

Anna also described an incident in which she was walking by the gym area and a male student spat on her. She told the administration of the incident, but because she did not know his name, the administrators were not able to assist her (the school's typical response when a perpetrator's identity is not known). By the time Anna did learn his identity, the story had gotten around the whole school. She was afraid to inform the administrators of the perpetrator's identity by then because she was frightened that the school would not protect her if the perpetrator and some of his friends sought revenge. When she saw him in the hallway, she tried to avoid him.

After Robert's teacher yelled at him for accidentally spilling coffee and berated him to "walk like a man" in front of his whole class, he felt embarrassed and angry. Yet, because there was little follow through when GLB students reported harassment incidents, Robert decided not to report this occurrence. He was also afraid of repercussions: "I thought about it [reporting the teacher] and then I thought that they [the administration] wouldn't do anything. So, I just told the GSA. I don't think—it wasn't that bad to report him or anything."

In reality, Robert's teacher had violated many of his profession's ethical standards, as well as his school policies on antidiscrimination. Yet, despite this flagrant violation and highly offensive comments, Robert did not believe that his teacher's actions warranted reporting or discipline. Perhaps it was just a matter of

Robert not believing that administrators would believe or support him. He may have also been embarrassed to explain the situation to his administrators, reveal his sexual orientation, and challenge a teacher. In short, the school's antidiscrimination policies failed to protect Robert.

As the GLB youth's narratives attest, GLB verbal harassment in schools is common. All study participants stated that verbal harassment was much more common than physical harassment. Some teens said that they spent years denying their same-sex feelings or chose not to come out because of the widespread harassment. Because of this harassment, Rachel, a 15-year-old bisexual female at Washington High School, recalled that she had gone to great lengths to hide her same-sex attractions from other students:

> I don't want to be out yet 'cause our school is horrible. A lot of people are [out] but I just don't feel comfortable being out. I would feel devastated if the whole school knew. I see what happens to people who are out. Maybe I'm being selfish, but I don't want that . . . I change "she" to "he" when I'm talking about my girlfriend in school. It gets very confusing.

The 3 teachers in this study affirmed that verbal harassment was fairly common in their two schools (Lincoln and JFK) and that many GLB youth remained closeted in school. For example, Mr. Lander, a teacher at JFK High School, reported that his school environment was:

> Not the worst, but it's not the best. I mean, kids report that people make remarks all the time. You know, "fag." I hear "fag" and "dyke" and whatever, and I don't doubt it. There are even some faculty who have said insulting things to kids.

Six of the youth shared incidents involving serious physical harassment of gay/bisexual males they knew at school. Two participants shared stories involving violence toward suspected lesbian or bisexual females. Mark, a 16-year-old gay male at Washington High School, reported that he had been the victim of verbal and physical harassment since elementary school because his peers perceived him to be effeminate. Chad recalled how he was shoved into a locker and threatened multiple times after he came out at school. Five of Chad's peers who participated in this study from

Washington High School also recounted Chad's story of physical harassment, a testament to the impact of this event in their own lives as GLB students.

It is also clear from these interviews that nongender-conforming individuals faced more threats to their safety than did individuals who did not threaten proscribed gender roles. Gay males who appeared effeminate seemed to evoke the most violence and hatred from their peers, but females who violated gender norms were not immune from harassment either. Although transgendered students were not a specific research category in this study, the experiences of Chad, Mark, and Linda (three self-described nongender-conforming individuals) suggest that transgendered students are routinely taunted in schools. The term *transgender* does not imply any specific sexual orientation. Rather, it can be defined as "nonidentification with one's gender assigned upon birth." Interestingly, most of the stereotypes about GLB individuals are related to gender-role nonconformity, not sexuality. Given that society values "masculinity" more than "femininity," feminine boys, who are seen as abandoning a position of power, are generally a greater source of concern than are masculine girls (Bohan, 1996; Gonsiorek, 1995; Herek, 1993). "Sissy boys," regardless of sexual orientation, are tortured and publicly humiliated in schools, because bullies perceive them as refusing to be real boys or as acting "girlish" (Rofes, 1995).

Although harassment was prevalent, some students appeared to feel empowered to respond to Chad's situation; they were angered to action. This in turn seemed to strengthen their resolve and acceptance of their sexual identity. For example, Jamie, an 18-year-old lesbian at Washington High School, explained that since she was going to be harassed with or without the antidiscrimination policies at her school, she wanted to have a positive impact on her peers:

> People will harass me and not support me as much if I wear a dress. I'm like it's not going to change who I am. . . . I want to be a role model. If you have a problem with that, then I'm gonna get more in your face . . . We had a Day of Silence, where everyone had to be quiet for a day. I walked right up to a group of kids who always made fun of us and gave each individual one a paper. They looked at me and threw it on the

My Voice is Being Heard   35

ground and said, "Oh, this is so gay." I started laughing. I didn't say anything. I'm like, think now, Day of Silence, gay harassment and violence. Yes, it is so gay, that's why we're doing it. People try to use gay like it's so stupid or disgusting. I try to turn it around and use it as something good: "This drink is extremely gay. Um, it's good."

The negative reactions of peers and teachers, however, were not the only story. Ten of the 13 GLB youth spoke about a teacher(s) or other adult(s) at their school who supported them, enabling them to feel a sense of acceptance. For example, in addition to the aforementioned help from his English teacher, Chad noted that both his guidance counselor and his history teacher were extremely supportive. He reported that his guidance counselor disclosed that his son was also gay, and Chad felt that he was able to talk to his guidance counselor about "anything; he's right there." The fact that 10 of the 13 teenagers readily discussed how teachers assisted them and accepted them implies that teacher support may have contributed to their own self-acceptance in their sexual minority status.

The GSAs seemed to give the youth an opportunity to gain an understanding of diversity and differences, inspired youth activism, taught skills for combating discrimination effectively, and instilled a sense of optimism that one individual could make a difference. All 13 of the youth described the programming that took place in their schools and how the GSA had positively influenced school and community policies for GLB students. More importantly, they reflected on how they had each contributed to the GSA programs and how this improved the climate for GLBs at their schools. This support and programming, in turn, increased their own self-esteem. For example, Linda, a 16-year-old lesbian, reported that her GSA "changes people's thoughts 'cause we put on stuff at our school every year. And thousands of students see it. Just having the door itself with gay posters, and people see that, and rainbows." Chad, a 16-year-old gay male, reported that since he was in the GSA, "my voice is being heard. So I guess that's one of the ups of being a student there; that I'm helping changing around the way people are thinking."

Steve, an 18-year-old bisexual male, discussed how the GSA at his school had influenced many different types of people:

We have people show up for all kinds of meetings. Some people show up, like "My sister is a lesbian" or "My dad is gay." People come in and say things like that. We had one person come in 'cause they saw the Matthew Shepard special on MTV and it moved them. We have people there for all sorts of reasons, and things like that.

2. Relationships with friends, family, and community

The social support of friends appeared to be an important factor in the process of sexual identity developmental for the 13 youth who all highlighted the salience of friendships. Within these relationships, the youth processed issues related to their sexual orientation and made decisions about identity management. Friends also protected the youth from victimization and often helped advocate for their rights.

For example, Mae, a 16-year-old lesbian at JFK High School, shared a story in which she came to accept her same-sex attractions and feel a sense of belongingness through her recently acquired friends:

> One day during lunch she [Linda, another study participant] brought me into Project 10 East and I was so scared the first time I was in there. I joined as sort of questioning. But before that I knew I wasn't into boys, but I wasn't sure if I was into girls yet. And like, she took me in the back door. And I just walked in and saw all these gay books and friendly people that came up to me and introduced themselves. And the next day, I went there for lunch and they remembered me and I thought, "This is cool."

Through these new friends, Mae eventually came to understand and accept her same-sex attractions and came out to others, including her family.

Anna, a 16-year-old bisexual, said that her friends continuously "backed her up," especially as she dealt with upsetting family news about her mother's serious illness: "I was having a lot of trouble with my family. Then I had my friends, most of them in the GSA. They're really a good support network for each other. Most of my friends are gay."

Robert noted that, although he initially struggled with disclosing his sexual identity to others, his secure relationships with his GLB friends led him to take the risk to come out:

> I kept to myself and was like, "Should I come out, should I not?" It's weird, it's like your life totally changes a lot and everything. And, I had a lot of support there. I got it mostly from my friends and from Ashlee [the director of Project 10 East].

To Mark, a 16-year-old gay male, heterosexual friends were especially important to coming out because:

> When you carry that secret, it's like you know something that no one else does. It's sort of this thing you have inside of you. And then you tell people, you get it out of the way. And, that kind of like, sucks. I think telling people overall though, makes you feel better about yourself. Before with my friends, I couldn't talk about certain things around them. It was just very restrictive, and then they'd ask me about girlfriends. But now, I can just like, talk about guys, and talk about guys to my girlfriends and all that stuff.

Five of the 13 GLB youth interviewees noted that peer support networks were more valuable than families, especially when teens were either not yet out to their parents or experienced negative reactions upon disclosing their sexual identities to them. Chad recounted:

> I've been out for like three years, but [my parents] still don't accept it. It's not good. But I don't really treat my family as family, if you know what I mean. My friends come before my family now, just 'cause they care more about me. My dad had been saying, "You're not my son, I disown you. You'll never amount to anything." So, I got wicked depressed. And then when I told the rest of the high school and I found out that most of the people that were in my classes were accepting to it, it took a lot of weight off my shoulders. And I was like, "If my parents don't care, then I got more than that behind me."

Mark, Anna, Juan, and Robert also relied on friends for social support almost exclusively. Within these relationships, these youth made calculated decisions about disclosure. Supportive alliances enabled some of them even to risk coming out to parents and heterosexual peers in an attempt to improve these relationships or feel authentic about their real and presented selves. In turn, they experienced unanticipated levels of support from parents and heterosexual friends that they might not otherwise have known was available.

Next, youth described their families as ranging from highly accepting and involved to nonaccepting and prejudiced. Three of the youth, Linda, Jamie, and Rachel, grew up with gay parents. Rachel's gay father did not live with her family. Linda and Jamie grew up with the support of mothers who were in long-term lesbian relationships. Parents and other significant family members seemed to lay the foundation for positive self-esteem. Indeed, all the GLB youth reported that they grew up in loving, caring households, despite their parent's attitudes about GLB individuals.

Of the 13 GLB participants, 5 of them (Juan, Robert, Sandra, Mark, and Jane) were not out to their families; 3 of these 5 individuals remained closeted due to fear of disclosure to their parents (Mark, Juan, and Robert); 2 of these 5 planned on disclosing their sexual identities when they felt the time was right, but were not overly fearful of their family's reaction (Jane and Sandra). Two people (Chad and Anna) experienced highly negative reactions from their parents upon coming out to them. Six of the 13 GLB youth (Jamie, Linda, Steve, Chris, Rachel, and Mae) were out to their families, and reported high levels of social support from them. Regardless of the type of family reaction and level of support, all the GLB youth noted that their parents' attitudes and actions had influenced them.

Linda, a 16-year-old lesbian, noted that her lesbian mother, herself a GLB rights activist, often accompanied Linda to various events:

> I have thousands of brothers and sisters now 'cause they all want my mom. She's involved with P10 obviously. We went to a speak-out training together, and she went to Pride with me. Yeah, I actually spoke at Pride this year and she came to watch. She was like, "Yeah!" How cool is that?! My mom's like watching me speak at Pride.

Besides both of her mothers' support, Jamie, a 16-year-old lesbian, also reported that her older sister supported her:

My sister is extremely supportive of me though. We share a room right now, and I've got my gay flag up and my little swirly gay flag up. And she's real helpful and helping me look up information to help other kids. And she goes to some Pride marches and dances.

Jane, a 15-year-old bisexual female, disclosed her sexual identity to her father who, to her surprise, reacted positively to the news:

> I told him that I was voted president of the GSA, and I know he doesn't feel too strongly about gay people. He's told me that he thinks that people who are gay need mental help. He was OK with it when I told him. So I was like, "What would you do if I had a girlfriend?" And he was like, "I'd still love you and I'd like to meet her." He's like, "You'd still be you."

Thus, despite her father's negative views of homosexuality, he was able to offer his daughter unconditional support. Jane reported that she planned on telling the rest of her family members (her parents were divorced and she lived with her mother and siblings) at some point.

Parents sometimes differed in their reactions to disclosure. For instance, Linda was out to her mother, but she could not disclose her sexual orientation to her father because she feared he would then despise her and refuse to pay for her college. Although Anna's father was highly accepting when she disclosed her sexual orientation to him, she lived with her mother and grandparents (recent immigrants) who were not as open-minded. Her situation was further complicated by the fact that her mother was battling cancer at the time of the interview. Their highly negative reaction when she came out to them only added to the burden her family was experiencing with respect to her mother's illness:

> I was walking home with my mom and grandma one day and they were talking about something like when I grow up and get married. And they were like talking about stuff like boyfriends and how I don't have any. I got really mad and I was like, "I don't think that I like boys!" I was just telling them how I felt. I wanted to just tell them how I felt [being bisexual] but I didn't think they'd accept it, like if I was like, "I'm bi." But if I was like, "I'm gay" they would have to acknowledge it. But it hasn't worked out that way. My mom was crying and upset for days. . . . Being at home was horrendous after I came out. I was just never home.

Anna experienced anxiety and depression over her mother's serious illness and reported that she often spoke to counselors for support.

Chad was physically and verbally threatened by his father when he came out. In addition, his father asked him to leave the house when he turned 18. Yet, he was still able to get love and support from his mother, which he seemed to treasure:

> [My mother] just looked at me [after I came out]. She went, "All right," and she went to doing the dishes and I left. And I came back, and I walked in. She came and gave me a hug. I was like, "Oh, you're talking to me?" She was like, "Why wouldn't I be?" I was like, "Because I'm gay." And she's like, "My love is unconditional. It doesn't matter." I was like, "Oh." That was nice. So then the next day we went shopping for clothes and she bought me makeup.

Thus, some GLB youth were able to use their parents' support as a resource to manage stress. In contrast, GLB youth who experienced negative reactions to disclosure from their parents or feared that they would, sought loving and supportive relationships from friends rather than family members.

Finally, involvement in GLB support groups and/or community resources also played a significant role in the development of healthy identity. All 13 GLB adolescents were connected to and participated in at least one GLB-related support group. A connection to a GLB social support group and/or the GLB Rights Movement appeared to be related to the development of healthy sexual identities, particularly with regard to coming out. For example, Jamie noted:

> When I'm mad about something, [P10 East staff] talk to me. They say don't go to any parties, don't drink, don't use drugs. They're around my age, so they know where I'm coming from. They're all open, and practically all young, my age, you know. It's easy to connect with.

Chad also spoke of many of the wonderful benefits he experienced for being involved in Project 10 East:

> I love [P10]. It's like, a sanctuary, you know? I'm really comfortable with all the people that are here. I know everybody by name and face. They planned and executed a forum at my high school on safe space in my

town. There were at least over 200 people at the forum. It was really good, really positive.

Jamie, an 18-year-old lesbian with a great deal of confidence, reported that with the assistance of Project 10 East:

> I'm helping as many people as I can. I go to all the conferences I possibly can. I'm on the board of Project 10 East, as one of the kids. I'm a member of my GSA. I go to as many rallies and parades as I can. I talk to as many people as I possibly can in school.

Some students remained quite optimistic about the future of GLB Rights because they were seeing positive changes as a consequence of their involvement in Project 10 East and the broader GLB Rights Movement. For example, Juan noted:

> I think that's gonna happen naturally, like with time, people are gonna start accepting homosexuals. They already are, like many people, they don't care. I don't think they like it better, but they just don't dislike you anymore. So I think it's gonna happen naturally. In like 30 years, there's probably gonna be no discrimination.

Discussion

This qualitative study examined the school environment through the eyes of 13 GLB adolescents. Additionally, this study explored the variables that affected the youths' sexual identity development. Three key themes emerged regarding how schools responded to GLB youth: (1) Many schools followed statewide guidelines established by the Massachusetts Safe Schools Commission. (2) School administrators seldom responded proactively to GLB issues. (3) Although some teachers reached out to support GLB students, others ignored and/or harassed GLB students. The youth's sexual identity development was greatly affected by the overall school environment and their friendships, family reactions, and involvement in GLB support groups and/or community resources.

Although the state guidelines helped to establish some general parameters in working with GLB students, the youth in this study noted that the guidelines were not broad enough, and often, administrators and teachers did not adhere to the established policies. Although most administrators and teachers did not actively support GLB students, the establishment of GSAs in the schools in this study had a positive impact. Consistent with the theoretical literature on GSAs (see Mallon, 1997; Peyser & Lorch, 2000; Robinson, 1994), membership in GSAs allowed these teens to feel safe, afforded them opportunities to socialize and befriend others, and helped to educate them about a variety of issues relevant to their sexual orientation. Many teens also benefited from supportive adults running or associated with the GSA and consequently became involved with the larger GLB Rights Movement. Findings from this research support the notion that GSAs should be established in all U.S. high schools.

GLB people and issues were largely absent from the school curriculum, as is the case in schools across the nation (see Leland, 2000). The exception for all 4 schools was health class, the one curriculum recommendation dictated by Massachusetts Department of Education's Safe Schools Program for Gay and Lesbian Students (MDESSPGLS). As required, the 4 public high schools in this study had to allow their GSAs to make public announcements, maintain a bulletin board, and sponsor dances and events. The schools also supported the annual Day of Silence and National Coming Out Day in support and recognition of GLB individuals. The young interviewees reported that these schoolwide events helped them feel accepted by the school populace. Thus, they should be encouraged in all high schools by administrators and schools officials who develop curriculum.

Although some participants said that school administrators were supportive of GLB students and issues, the majority criticized their school administrators. They described administrators as reactive when it came to GLB issues rather than proactive, and that occasionally, administrators ignored GLB students' requests for help. This finding reinforces the need for rewriting policies, implementing new training, and holding school administrators (and teachers) accountable for anti-GLB acts that occur in their schools.

Teachers were also an important source of social support, particularly with regard to making the youth feel accepted at school. In listening to both the youths and 3 teachers, it became clear that the adults who offer support to GLB students in school do so out of personal motivations rather than professional obligation. Indeed, all the youth reported that only a handful of teachers were compassionate and provided support, usually on their own time. This suggests that only a small proportion of school staff understand the stressors GLB adolescents face and/or that only a few individuals are willing to advocate for GLB youth. Education programs need to revamp their curriculum to provide training that includes ethical and professional responsibilities for working with GLB youth. School administrators should also increase incentives for motivated teachers to assist GSAs and GLB students (See *Applied Recommendations*).

The high level of harassment reported by GLB study participants was consistent with reports in the theoretical and empirical literature (Faulkner & Cranston, 1998; GLSEN, 2005; NMHA, 2002). Most of the youth discussed experiences with verbal harassment. Others recounted that GLB students had been violently assaulted, with no response from the school administration after these events. Some teens even discussed how teachers suspected of being GLB were harassed by students. Research such as the recent GLSEN (2005) survey of schools in the United States has demonstrated that schools that have antidiscrimination policies designed to protect GLB youth report less harassment than schools without these policies.

Yet interviewees perceived that harassment was quite prevalent in their schools, even schools that included GLB students in their antidiscrimination policies. Extrapolating from the GLSEN (2005) and current study findings, the level and frequency of harassment against GLB individuals in schools without policies must be staggering. GLB teens in schools without antidiscrimination policies may face more threats to the development of healthy sexual identities than those in schools with such policies.

The failure of schools to enforce antidiscrimination policies made a few of the youth angry, unhappy, and unwilling to come out. Consistent with the findings of Cohen and Savin-Williams (1996), some of the teens even denied their same-sex attractions to themselves to avoid the harassment that their out GLB peers were experiencing at school. In contrast, other participants expressed that they were motivated to find acceptance in their sexual minority status *because of* school discrimination and their resulting anger.

Consistent with the findings of previous research on GLB youth (see Anderson, 1998; Cohen and Savin-Williams, 1996; Diamond, 1998), all 13 youth interviewees discussed the importance of the social support of friends to their sexual identity development. Within these friendships, GLB youth were able to process issues related to their sexual orientation and explore their identities, and they were supported in making decisions about disclosure. Five of the youth had friends only to rely on because they could not depend on family support. All the youth discussed how their friends, both GLB and heterosexual, supported them unconditionally and often defended them if they were attacked. It is possible that the urban/rural towns represented in this study are more socially progressive than many other areas of this country (Herek, 2000). GLB teenagers in other regions might not have such positive experiences when coming out to heterosexual friends (Sears, 1991).

Consistent with other literature on GLB youth (Savin-Williams, 1998), all GLB interviewees discussed the importance of families to their sexual identity development. In this study, 8 of the 13 youth were out to their parents. Two of these youth encountered a great deal of negativity upon coming out to parents, while the parents of 6 GLB teens offered unconditional support. GLB youth interviewees unanimously recommended that adolescents make careful and planned decisions about disclosing sexual orientation to parents, because hostile and unaccepting parents could negatively affect the development of a positive sexual identity.

Community resources were also integral to these teens' ability to achieve a healthy sexual identity (Cohen & Savin-Williams, 1996). The adolescents related stories about the connections and friendships they were able to make by frequenting these organizations. Schools and media forums should make people aware of available community resources for GLB individuals.

Novel findings also emerged from this study, including: (1) zero-tolerance policies were not clearly written and enforced by high school faculty members; (2) honors, college-track students and teachers were perceived to be more accepting of GLB individuals and issues than general education classes and teachers; and (3) in addition to friends, some peers were accepting of GLB issues and people although many engaged in verbal harassment.

Zero-tolerance policies were enacted in all 4 schools represented in this study, as mandated by MDESSPGLS. Yet, according to the participants, these policies were not being written clearly or properly implemented. Almost all the interviewees described high rates of harassment and discriminatory practices against suspected GLB individuals in their schools. Even though there were policies in place, all participants noted that responses by school officials to anti-GLB victimization were inadequate. Penalties mandated by zero-tolerance policies were rarely imposed on suspected perpetrators (students or teachers). Several of the youth in our study advocated for stronger zero-tolerance policies for GLB discrimination.

Alas, stronger enforcement of zero-tolerance policies is no panacea. White middle-class youth who defy zero-tolerance policies tend to have families with resources that can liberate them from severe sanctions; not so youth of color, especially girls, who often bear the harshest brunt of zero-tolerance policies (Chesney-Lind & Irwin, 2004). In light of this disparity, school officials must consider the disproportionate impact of zero-tolerance policies on ethnic minority youth and devise policies to ensure that antidiscrimination measures are established and communicated clearly, and that the punishment of infractions is equitably distributed for perpetrators, regardless of race, ethnicity, gender, class, disability status, or sexual orientation. Additionally, school officials and teachers need to be held accountable to enforce these policies to provide a safe learning environment for all their students regardless of sexual orientation.

The GLB youth and teacher participants perceived that honors, college-track students and teachers were more accepting of GLB individuals and issues than general education students and teachers were. The interviewees noted that honors teachers and students in their schools made a "nonissue" of sexual orientation, respected their students/peers, and even invited discussion on topics such as equality and diversity. This stood in sharp contrast to the high level of derogatory remarks GLB interviewees said that they often heard in hallways and in regular education classes. It appeared that peers in general education classes displayed a much higher level of openly prejudicial behavior toward GLB individuals and that adults in these settings had a higher level of tolerance for these offensive actions. Furthermore, because heterosexist youth may have less direct exposure to GLB issues and people (because these issues are not being raised in general education classes), they may continue to view GLB people as nonexistent and sinful. This finding gives more impetus for educators to incorporate diversity issues, especially on topics relevant to sexual orientation, into *all* classes.

Psychological research has demonstrated that young people are more accepting of diversity than older people (Herek, 2000). The Center for Information and Research on Civic Learning and Engagement (Circle, 2005) highlighted multiple survey studies demonstrating that, compared with their older counterparts, youth supported laws that prohibit discrimination against GLB individuals and extend equal rights and protection to GLB people. Coinciding with this research, the interviewees perceived that many of their peers were accepting of GLB issues and people. The participants noted that, in their opinion, verbal harassment had more to do with ignorance, insensitivity, and societal practices than true hatred of GLB people (although it still causes psychological harm). Half of the participants reported that when they confronted their peers about verbal harassment, the perpetrators often apologized and stopped the harassment. This finding indicates that it is possible for GLB students to counter anti-GLB prejudice using direct confrontational strategies. Yet direct confrontation on the part of offended GLB youth should not be the sole strategy to combat discrimination. GLB youth need institutional support from their teachers and administrators and through school policies so that the burden does not fall on these youngsters alone.

Applied Implications

The results of this study point to specific recommendations for changing policies and procedures at the schoolwide level. Teachers, administrators, counselors, and school psychologists should be agents of change who help all marginalized populations in the school.

Recommendation 1: Create support groups and/or become the faculty advisor to the GSA. One way educators can begin helping GLB youth is to provide school-based support, in a safe environment that does not demand that members disclose their sexual orientation to the group. The GLB youth in this study all discussed the benefits they received from school-based support. Heterosexual young people also need opportunities to talk openly with their GLB peers to dispel heterosexist stereotypes and address issues such as the coming out of close friends/family members. Educators can facilitate this process by becoming faculty advisors of these groups. Once established, the faculty advisor should look for community support to give GLB youth opportunities to make friends in neighboring towns (Uribe, 1994).

Recommendation 2: Develop school policies that protect GLB students. Study participants indicated that written, formal school policies can help minimize discrimination and harassment against young people perceived to be GLB and are associated with many GLB youth feeling safer and advocating for themselves at the individual and community levels. Therefore, school districts should adopt and publicize antidiscrimination policies that ban antigay language and harassment by faculty and students and highlight clear consequences for these incidents.

This study also demonstrated, however, that too often educational personnel do not recognize anti-GLB epithets as harassment. Antiharassment rules must be written so carefully that they punish conduct that targets a person for assault and threat on the basis of the victim's actual or perceived race, ethnicity, religion, national origin, disability, sex, gender, and/or sexual orientation. Additionally, educational personnel must inform perpetrators that verbal harassment is not acceptable when they observe it and explain why—not because it is "against the rules," but because it (1) perpetuates stereotypes, (2) is psychologically harmful to GLB people, (3) offends many fellow classmates and family members who are GLB, and (4) interferes with the educational environment, resulting in legal decisions against school districts.

Recommendation 3: Educate school personnel on heterosexism. An essential component in creating safer environments for GLB students is in ensuring that all school staff members are equipped with accurate and relevant knowledge about GLB young people (Friend, 1992; Uribe, 1994). Educators should help in raising awareness about the need to develop appropriate and safe environments. They can coordinate staff development strategies, such as annual presentations about GLB students for all teachers (perhaps during staff development days) using expert speakers and panels and facilitating a discussion of heterosexism and its effects on all students.

Educational personnel should also provide their peers with material and information on recognizing and reducing prejudice against sexual minorities. They should also be familiar with community and counseling resources for GLB youth and their families and be able to make referrals to any interested parties (Nichols, 1999).

Recommendation 4: Make information for GLB students available in school libraries and include content about GLB people in the curriculum. Recognizing the contributions that GLB individuals have made to history, literature, arts, and sciences, discussion about GLB issues can be integrated into many subject areas in an age-appropriate fashion. Educational systems must commit resources to examining current curricula for combating bias and provide for faculty development to assist teachers in developing competence in fighting school heterosexism (McFarland, 2001).

Young people who are, or think they might be, GLB frequently do not have access to accurate information about sexual orientation. Young people with questions can benefit tremendously when resources and information about GLB issues are readily available in school libraries (Friend, 1992). Such information can include videos, books (especially those written by young people for young people), pamphlets, and other materials for use by students, teachers, and parents. Libraries that develop reading lists of books on GLB issues can build acceptance and awareness by periodically displaying these books in a highly visible area and/or creating exhibits similar to what many schools do for Black History Month (Rofes, 1995).

Limitations

This small exploratory study has a number of limitations. First, the small sample size and method of recruitment (i.e., participants were recruited by Project 10 and not randomly sampled) limit the extent to which these findings can be generalized to GLB youth from other social and educational contexts. All the students interviewed for the study belonged to a community support organization (Project 10 East) and to their school GSAs. Thus, they were members of a tight-knit social network that benefited them. Youth who are not connected to a community or school support organization may or may not experience similar protective and self-esteem boosting friendships.

Another limitation of this study is its restricted ability to examine gender, ethnic/racial, community, and socioeconomic (SES) differences in the school experiences of GLB youth. Interviewees were predominantly white, middle-class, liberal/urban adolescents who participated in P10. It is possible that these sociodemographic identities and the privileges associated with them may have influenced their perceptions of the school environment, their sexual identities, as well as the coping strategies they used in response to heterosexism encountered in their schools. Diversity is an important consideration in GLB research because the literature suggests that stress is often exacerbated among poor and/or ethnic minority GLB individuals (Alquijay, 1997; Chung & Katayama, 1998; Greene, 1997; Monteiro & Fugua, 1995). Thus, more research with diverse samples of GLB adolescents is needed to assess the effects of SES and race/ethnicity on perceptions of the school environment for GLB youth.

Accordingly, future research should include more diverse GLB youth (in terms of ethnicity/race and SES) as well as those who do not have contacts with GLB agencies or who are isolated from any kind of GLB community. Although such GLB youth may be difficult to find, it is likely that their experiences are quite different from those who have the social support of organizations such as P10. More diverse samples are needed to learn about schools' responses, factors that shape the development of a healthy sexual identity, and the impact of a community organization on GLB youths' self-acceptance and positive community affiliation. It is important to understand whether and how the experiences of diverse GLB youth are similar to or different from the predominantly white, middle-class GLB youth in this study.

Conclusions

Many compelling reasons exist for making schools safer places for GLB young people. Affecting changes in attitudes and beliefs can lead to more affirming environments and competent practices with GLB youth and their families. This requires education, training, and self-exploration on both individual and institutional levels. Educators should be in positions to *name* this oppression so that other educators cannot continue to pretend that it does not exist (Marinoble, 1998).

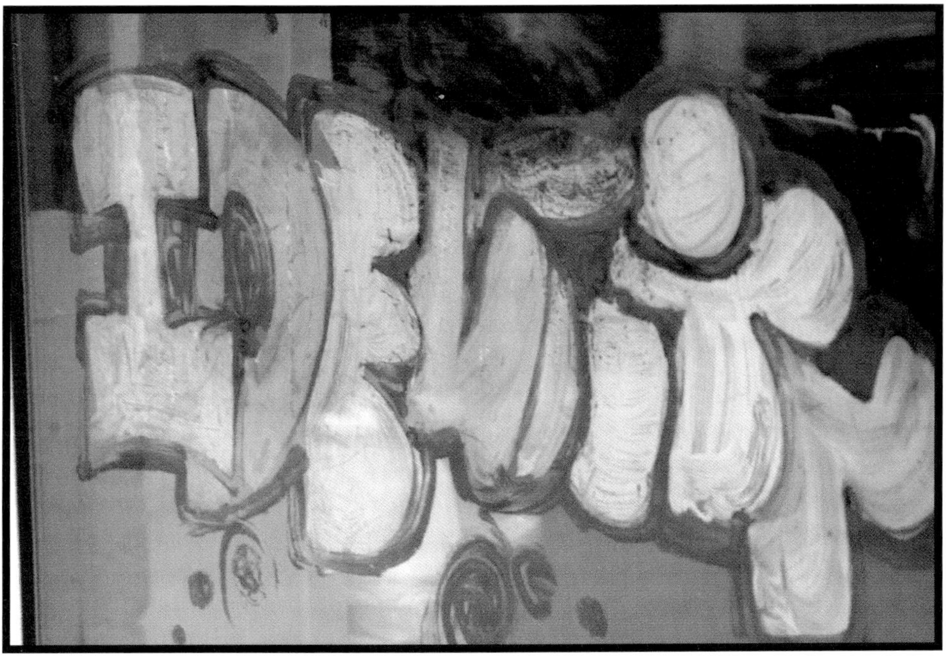

Chapter Two

The Roles of Gay-Straight Alliance (GSA) Advisors in Public High Schools

Maria Valenti[1]

YOUTH ARE EXAMINING their sexuality at earlier ages than in years past, leading to an increase of lesbian, gay, and bisexual (LGB) youth who disclose their sexual orientation at school (Bochenek & Brown, 2001). Unfortunately, self-identified LGB youth are not always welcomed in the school community, where they may experience overt or subtle acts of homophobia. However, one place in the school where they may be accepted is at Gay-Straight Alliance (GSA) club meetings. This chapter explores the role the GSA advisor plays in the GSA and in the broader public school community regarding the often-contentious topics of sexual orientation and gender identity. The chapter begins with a discussion of homophobia and a description of the literature on GSAs. The chapter will then describe a phenomenological study with GSA advisors in which the thematic results revealed the multifaceted roles GSA advisors play in dealing with students, colleagues, administration, and the community regarding sexuality and gender issues.

Homophobia

Various forms of homophobia affect high school students, staff, and administration. One form, institutional homophobia, involves dis-

---

[1] The author would like to thank Drs. Rebecca Campbell, Cris Sullivan, and Deb Bybee for their guidance and support in making this research project a success.

crimination against LGB people in social policies, and/or laws. In general, this includes ignoring the existence of lesbian and gay people in insurance policies and wills, in hospital visiting rules allowing "immediate family only," and by mass media portrayal of the world as entirely heterosexual (Herek, 1986). At the school level, it could include the school system not allowing a GSA to be formed, even though the Equal Access Act of 1984 (EAA) mandates that schools receiving federal funding cannot discriminate against student groups and noncurriculum clubs. Student clubs need to be allowed the same resources and opportunities as any other club (Berkley, 2004). In addition, institutionalized homophobia could include the lack of policies protecting staff and teachers from being fired for being a sexual minority.

Another form, overt homophobia, is the "verbal and physical abuse of sexual minority [people] or those who are perceived as being sexual minorities. This harassment is expressed in name-calling, queer jokes, AIDS jokes, snide remarks, gay bashings, and other hate crimes" (Malinsky, 1997, p. 38). Overt homophobia occurs on a regular basis during the school day (Buston & Hart, 2001; Smith, 1998). Approximately 75 to 90% of high school informants in various studies report hearing negative remarks, such as "fag," "dyke," or "queer" and the sayings, "that's so gay," "you're so gay," very often or frequently (Burn, 2000; Buston & Hart, 2001; Gustavsson & MacEachron, 1998; Kosciw & Cullen, 2001; Peters, 2003; Smith, 1998). Most of these homophobic slurs come from other students, but as many as 25% of the harassers are faculty, staff, and administrators (Kosciw & Cullen, 2001; Mason & Palmer, 1996; Peters, 2003; Savin-Williams, 1994).

A covert manifestation of homophobia is also prevalent in the school community. Researchers have used the term *heterosexism* in conjunction with homophobia to describe this subtle version (Buston & Hart, 2001; Little, 2001; Malinsky, 1997). In essence, the absence of gay and lesbian positive images creates a deafening silence about the homosexual reality (Herr, 1997; Lee, 2002). Fewer research studies examine this subtle version, but there is evidence of this type in the school context. Homophobic remarks often go unchallenged at school (Buston & Hart, 2001; Jordan et al., 1997; Kosciw & Cullen, 2001; Peters, 2003; Telljohann & Price,

1993). There has also been evidence that teachers actually encourage antigay talk (Buston & Hart, 2001; Malinsky, 1997; Smith, 1998).

The focus of research concerning the effect of school homophobia on LGB youth has been largely about negative outcomes (Anderson, 1998; Ryan & Futterman, 2001; Savin-Williams, 1994). Research has shown that homophobia in school puts LGB youth at risk for feeling unsafe and isolated, which can lead to absenteeism, substance abuse, and suicide. About 72% of LGB youth feel afraid at school, which consequently leads to being absent (Elliot & Kilpatrick, 1994; Rivers, 2000; Vare & Norton, 1998). This absenteeism limits their school interaction, leading to social isolation, which can hamper LGB youth in the accomplishment of certain developmental tasks such as the attainment of a sense of identity, the capacity for intimacy, and a sense of self that contributes to psychological and physical independence (Kivel & Kleiber, 2000; Vare & Norton, 1998). It is well documented that school-based homophobia can lead to abuse of alcohol and drugs (Rotheram-Borus, Rosario, VanRossem, Reid, & Gill, 1995; Russell, Driscoll, & Truong, 2002; Savin-Williams, 1994). Research also supports findings that the rates of suicide among LGB youth are much higher than that among their non-LGB peers (Elliot & Kilpatrick, 1994; Garofalo, Wolf, Wissow, Woods, & Goodman, 1999; van Heeringen & Vincke, 2000; Vare & Norton, 1998; Wichstrom & Hegna, 2003).

Gay-Straight Alliance (GSA)

Although evidence of homophobia in school is growing, efforts have been made to counteract it. One approach has been Gay-Straight Alliances (GSA), which are extracurricular clubs for students in school who are lesbian, gay, bisexual, or transgendered (LGBT), who are questioning their sexuality or gender identity and expression, who have family members who are LGBT, or who consider themselves allies to LGBT issues and people (GLSEN, 2000). These groups offer LGBT youth the opportunity to develop a sense of belonging and community, as well as the possibility of exploring different aspects of themselves in a safe environment that promotes self-understanding and acceptance (Anderson, 1998). GSAs are essentially for all youth, regardless of their sexual orientation or gender identity. They allow youth to build coalitions and community that can work toward making a safer school environment for all people (GLSEN, 2000). GSAs may also be a piece in the overall strategy to ensure schools provide the best education possible in a safe environment (Blumenfeld, 1994).

The first high school gay support group, Project 10, was founded in 1984 (Lipkin, 2004; Uribe, 1994). Virginia Uribe developed this program to address the underserved needs of gay and lesbian students by providing education, reducing verbal and physical abuse, preventing suicide, and disseminating accurate AIDS information. Uribe created workshops for teachers, counselors, and other support personnel and established support groups for students dealing with sexual orientation issues. The goals were to improve self-esteem and to provide affirmation for students suffering the effects of sexual orientation stigmatization and discrimination. This idea of having a school group took hold, and GSAs began forming throughout the country. Griffin, Lee, Waugh, and Beyer (2004) found that GSAs contribute to the school setting in four primary ways: (1) providing counseling and support; (2) providing a "safe space"; (3) raising awareness, increasing visibility, and providing education within the school; and (4) engaging in broader school efforts raising awareness, increasing visibility, and offering education about LGBT issues in the school and surrounding community.

Emerging research suggests that GSA involvement by LGBT youth greatly increases their positive interaction with the school. Lee (2002) interviewed GSA-involved students and asked questions based on how belonging to the alliance affected their academic performance, relationships with school stakeholders, their comfort with being out, and if they felt as if they belonged to the school community. She also asked them if the GSA provided strategies for handling heterosexism, if the students felt safer, and if the students thought that they could "make a difference" in society. She found that the students did experience some hopelessness and despair common to sexual minority youth, but that the GSA helped them "move beyond" and gain stronger identities. They learned that their perceived problems were society's problems.

They also reported increased positive relationships with school stakeholders, self-pride, feeling safe, and a sense of belonging (Lee, 2002).

Current Study

No research to date has examined the roles and tasks of GSA advisors and how they negotiate the challenges of their responsibilities. GSA advisors must establish links with students involved with the club and with administration, colleagues, and perhaps parents. Therefore, the research question examined in this study was: What is the GSA advisor role in the school environment? This project explored how GSA advisors are a resource to LGBT youth and their school communities. To answer these research questions, this study used a qualitative approach. Several characteristics made qualitative methods compatible with this research project.

First, qualitative methods have the potential to give voice to informants' lived experiences. Because GSA advisors may not have had the opportunity to discuss their roles and responsibilities, this research project provided them an opportunity to share their stories and to have their experiences documented. Second, qualitative methods also provide researchers with conceptual road maps into previously uncharted territory, helping to identify contextually salient variables while avoiding inappropriate norms and constructs based on other populations. Third, qualitative methods provide flexibility, which means that data collection times and methods can vary as the study proceeds. This was beneficial because little is known about GSA advisors' experiences; there was room to modify the protocol if needed to further investigate emergent topics. This allowed more complete and detailed information to be captured from the interview (Miles & Huberman, 1994).

Phenomenology explores the meaning, structure, and essence of lived experience. It is committed to the description of experiences with an emphasis on wholeness by elucidating the various perspectives encompassing the phenomenon (Moustakas, 1994). Phenomenology attempts to explore how people transform their experience into consciousness, both individually and as a shared meaning (Patton, 2002). This was synergistic with the goal of the study, which was to explore the experience of GSA advisors, whose subjective experience is their reality. Therefore, this project used a phenomenological qualitative method with individual interviews.

The sampling frame included 78 registered high school GSA advisors from one midwestern state. Informants were found through the National Gay, Lesbian and Straight Education Network (GLSEN) Web site where GSA information is available. The contact information from the GSA list was found online through school system Web sites and phone books. All schools listed on the Web site were called to see if the club still existed and to obtain the current advisor's name and contact information. If the advisor's contact information was not available from the person who answered the phone, the Internet was used to obtain the contact information (e.g., e-mail address) from the school Web site. From this initial round of phone calls, private schools and GSA clubs that were not currently functioning were removed from the list, which left 43 clubs. A letter or e-mail was sent to the advisors of all 43 clubs to inform them of the study and request their participation.

Because it typically requires more than one contact to secure participation in a research study, a protocol was developed for more targeted recruitment that would ensure programs across the state would be represented. The 43 clubs were clustered based on geographical location. Thirty-two clubs clustered around the 5 major cities in the state (i.e., they were located within the city or surrounding area). A sixth sampling cluster was formed, which consisted of the remaining 11 clubs that were not city-identified (i.e., they were geographically dispersed and not close to one of the 5 major cities). Each of these 6 sampling clusters had between 4 and 12 clubs. Within each cluster, a randomized list of programs was created that specified the order in which the advisors would be contacted for intensive follow-up. For example, the advisor from the first program within each cluster was contacted repeatedly by phone and e-mail to request participation. If she or he agreed, then an interview was scheduled. Once an interview had been scheduled, then the next program on the list was targeted for intensive recruitment. If after 3 attempts to recruit (spaced over 2 weeks), advisors did not respond, the next program on the randomized list was selected. During this process, it was discovered that 3 clubs were no longer in existence, so they were removed from the sampling frame.

These recruitment procedures were repeated for each geographic cluster until 14 participants were interviewed, with at least 2 from each geographical location. Specifically, 2 advisors were interviewed from each of the 5 city-based clusters ($n = 10$) and 4 from the noncity-based cluster. Four advisors did not respond to the e-mail, letter, and/or phone call. The targeted sample size was between 10 and 15, which is typical for phenomenological qualitative research (Creswell, 1998). Of the 14 participants, 6 were women, and 8 were men. Although no question specifically asked about sexual orientation, 5 self-identified during the interview as lesbian, gay, or bisexual. Twelve of the participants were teachers, and 2 were social workers. All the teachers mentioned having tenure, although they were not directly asked. Six described their school as being in an urban area, 6 a suburban area, and 2 a rural area. Six reported working in an upper-class or upper-middle-class neighborhood, 2 in a middle-class neighborhood, 4 in a lower-middle-class to lower-class neighborhood, and 2 described their neighborhood as being split between the two extremes of upper and lower class. Ten were advisors to the club when it first began. The ages of the club varied from 2 months to 8 years.

Measures

To begin, the interview questions pertaining to the research questions were asked. An example of an interview question is "What prompted you to decide to become a GSA advisor?" The interview questions were broad, open-ended questions that helped facilitate rich description. At the end of the interview, some demographic questions were asked to gain additional information about the informants and their affiliated schools (see the appendix for the full interview protocol).

Data Analytic Procedures

Phenomenological data analysis was both inductive and deductive. There was analysis of specific statements and themes and a search for all possible meanings (Creswell, 1998). To begin, using the ATLASti program, all text related to the research question was selected. Then open coding began, which is the process of developing categories of concepts and themes emerging from the data (Kerlin, 2002). To do this, words were chosen that summed up the collective meaning of the phrases. Quotes from the interviews discussing advisor motivation were extracted. From these quotes discussing motivation, open coding assigned meaning to the advisors' words. These open codes were then grouped together based on similar meaning, which led to the development of themes. Each theme was labeled based on the content of the open codes and quotations.

Both cross-case analysis (common themes across informants' transcripts) and within-case analysis (quotations from transcripts verbatim to elucidate the emerging themes) were performed. Saturation also occurred, meaning no new themes within the metatheme could have been created and any additional data would have had marginal influence (Glaser & Strauss, 1967). At least 3 participants needed to discuss the same essence of experience for saturation to occur.

Verification of the Results

Techniques were implemented to ensure that findings were transferable. One technique involved clarifying bias before the study started, which included writing out assumptions that could shape the interpretation and approach. Special attention was paid to probe around these areas during the interviewing process. Another technique included using "rich, thick description" when writing, which allowed readers to make their own decisions regarding conclusions.

This study also used member checks, which involved taking the conclusions back to the informants so they could give their opinions on the accuracy and credibility of the findings. Three informants who consented to future contact and seemed especially interested in the research topic were sent a section of the results and asked four questions: (1) Do the quotes I used to illustrate my point fit with what I wrote about? (2) How do my ideas fit into your experience as advisor? (3) Do you think I am missing anything major? If so, what's missing? (4) Overall, what do you think of the results?

Memoing helped to interpret the phenomenon. During data collection and the analysis process, the author jotted down general trends and possible meanings of what was said during interviews. This information helped to reveal essential features of the phenomenon. It also allowed for the linkage of different data into recognizable clusters moving from an empirical to a conceptual level (Miles & Huberman, 1994).

Results

The GSA advisor's role was multifaceted and somewhat complex. The various roles involved interactions with all the hierarchical levels of the school community from the students to the superintendent. The major roles informants discussed were (1) a role model or caring adult who is a "safe" person for students; (2) an inactive observer; (3) a monitor who ensures that GSA students comply with appropriate school behavior; (4) a liaison between the GSA, teachers, administration, and parents; (5) a resource for the school and broader community concerning LGBT issues; (6) a knowledge seeker; and (7) a teacher of leadership skills.

Role Model/Caring Adult

GSA advisors served as role models to the GSA students and the general student body. Advisors in the interviews may not have directly used the term *role model*, but they described themselves in a way that could be interpreted as such. They served as role models in the traditional sense meaning that they represented someone who the students could aspire to be like (imitate). Prior research suggests that there are few known adult LGBT role models for sexual minority youth in the school community. The advisors who are gay, lesbian, or bisexual could be the only visible sexual minority adults that these students know and represent people who have successfully navigated the "coming out" process, as well as continued to succeed professionally. Because two or more of the advisors were in same-sex partnerships (some with children), they also presented an image of a person in a successful same-sex relationship. In addition, both the sexual minority advisors and heterosexual advisors served as positive role models. The heterosexual advisors could be seen as allies for sexual minority people.

GSA advisors viewed themselves as "safe" people who were there for the students. Four advisors (3 heterosexual males and 1 bisexual female) discussed aspects of being a safe person. These advisors may in fact be safe people because students had felt comfortable enough with them to discuss their sexuality. Two advisors had students disclose their sexual orientation to them. As one heterosexual male informant stated:

> ...one girl who's like come out to me. And that's only to me . . . seems like she's dealing with it as well as about any kid, I guess. But, uh, she's also a kid who said she's known for a number of years that she was gay, so— she's only 14.

The second bisexual advisor stated:

> I have had eight students come out to me this year, which is more than I have ever known in the last three years that I have taught here. So I am like whoa like this is kids are feeling more comfortable with identifying who they are at a younger age.

The students trusted these advisors and felt free to disclose their sexual orientation. This seems to be an important role because sexual minority youth might not have support from friends or family or feel safe enough to talk with them about what they are going through. Thus, GSA advisors may be positive developmental assets for these youth.

As noted above, the GSA advisors served as role models in the traditional sense; they represented someone that the students could aspire to be like. Five advisors (4 were sexual minority) discussed traditional aspects of being a role model. The sexual minority advisors who disclosed their sexual orientation to the GSA students became a representation of what the future could bring. For some students, it may have been the first time they met a gay person, which may have been an opportunity for them to see gay people as "real" people.

> ... they'll [GSA students] say things like "when did you and your partner meet?" and . . . I'll explain how we met and stuff like that. So, I think that being gay, me being gay sort of normalizes the situation for them, it makes it easier for them to talk about it. I think also being the advisor what I done in the classroom is I started um using gender-neutral language ya know instead of saying to a young woman, "do you have a boyfriend?" I may ask, "are you dating somebody" or ya know leave the possibilities of what their life is like open.

This advisor not only openly discussed his same-sex relationship, but also made it an open environment for students when he used neutral language. He demonstrated an alternative to using gender-based language that the students could then replicate in their conversations with their friends creating a more inclusive environment.

The media and our culture seem to perceive and present sexual minority people as being extremely sexual. One gay advisor wanted to challenge this perception.

> Well, the kids will ask me personal questions, ya know, and so . . . and I feel comfortable talking about myself personally, as any straight teacher does. You know, the straight teachers talk about their wives or their husbands and their kids, and I try to show kids that our sexual orientation is not just what we do in a bedroom. You're, you exhibit your sexual orientation all the time. When you talk about yourself, and your plans for the weekend, or what you're doing for the holiday. So, I feel comfortable to talk to them about my own experiences, because I see myself as a role model for them.

This again reflected the idea that some advisors want to normalize the gay experience. If gay and lesbian people's lives were normalized, perhaps there would be less of a tendency to equate their lives only with sex. It could also dispel other misconceptions lessening the stigmatization. GSA advisors could also serve as leaders who can model protecting all kids. One gay advisor talked about how school districts needed to take a stand against people who disagreed with the GSA and that it was the school's job to intervene. A GSA advisor was being a "moral leader."

> I'm still just so glad that the group has been here, so I'm proud of that and pleased with that, and frustrated I guess on the other side just to know that people that I think should be aware of protecting and helping all kids are not doing so, and they're caving in to some kind of perceived political pressure. And I think if you're gonna be a leader in a school district you have to lead the way and that comes down to this issue. Yes, the community may or may not support it, but you have to lead and to teach them that it's right and that comes down to this issue.

The idea that administrators were not willing to take a stand to protect all students in their public school represented the institutionalized homophobia that may be underlying school culture.

Other advisors were role models in that they actively spoke out against homophobic actions. The students could see and hear adults openly stopping homophobic pejoratives. This may not happen with all teachers in all classrooms. They took a stand in creating an environment that was safe for sexual minority students and faculty. One gay teacher stated:

> I'm not for sure other teachers would do this, but we hear a lot of "that's so gay" in the hall and "fag" and "faggot this" and "faggot that," so I hear two young men yelling at each other, you know, "faggot" this, "faggot" that. And I pulled them aside and said "you know, there's really only two people that should be saying that, and that's one faggot to another, and unless you're sure about your friend, I would suggest that you not say it."

By confronting the youths, he let them know that gay slurs were not tolerated, thereby setting an example that encouraged others to intervene in similar ways.

A heterosexual advisor stood up for the GSA against the school assistant principal when the assistant principal tried to dissuade the students from creating a GSA. He thought that the students who wanted the GSA should just join the diversity club. After talking to the assistant principal, the advisor talked to the GSA students about this idea. The students really wanted to start a GSA and were not interested in the activities of the UNITE club, especially because some of the UNITE members brought up religious concerns about having sexual minority issues become part of their club. The advisor was willing to do whatever the students who wanted the GSA decided.

> I was behind whatever decision they wanted to do, if they wanted me to start going to the UNITE Club groups and being a presence there, I would, or I would start the group on its own as its advisor. We ended up saying, no; we want to go alone with it. I can tell you that on the side, not with the kids, when the assistant principal did first get the paperwork and hear what was going on, I don't think he realized that I was that strongly for it.

The advisor was willing to stand up for the kids despite his superior (the assistant principal) advising him not to start this club. This seems to have taken some bravery on the advisor's part because the assistant principal was his superior and controlled the future of the advisor's job.

Advisors also helped their students deal with life issues. Four informants (3 were sexual minority) discussed how, as GSA advisors, they gave life advice to the GSA students. Two advisors discussed religious issues surrounding sexuality with their students. Some dominant religions have strong antigay messages, and a few of the youth found conflict with the messages that they received from their religious practices and from their family. One male, heterosexual advisor stated:

> I knew that the two girls that had talked to me kind of like expressed like religious concerns with it so I just, since it was like an after school thing, I just told them, I said "I'm Catholic and the reason that I would want to do this is because I'm Catholic, that it complements how I feel a person should be treated and I don't find any qualms with it but you have to decide for yourself and what's going to work out best with your relationship with your parents" and that kind of thing.

Religious institutions that the students attend may send conflicting and rejecting messages about any sexuality besides heterosexuality. The sexual minority youth and allies in the club could feel dejected and alienated from the community that their family supports. The perspective this advisor gave may give solace to some students struggling with living in a religious community promoting antigay rhetoric.

Another gay advisor had a similar experience. The GSA invited the Bible Club to a meeting to discuss Christianity and sexual orientation. He knew that some GSA youth were struggling with religious issues. During the meeting, some GSA students were getting upset. At one point, the advisor felt the need to come to the defense of LGBT people.

> ...and I knew that it was not gonna be pleasant. And they were using, you know the line, "Oh we love you, but we hate the sin." And I came to their defense and said ya know I said, and ya know I'm speaking in a public school, "Listen, if sin is what separates us from God, I gotta tell ya, my homosexuality has never done that. It's only brought me closer." So I'm talking to the kids, because there were a lot of kids that were really upset. I said, "Truth is, it's probably hard to live a life that's so scorned by others, and not have faith in something." And I said, "And you know when we read these passages of the Bible that people are using, let me put them in context for you." So, that I think was real helpful to the kids, because a lot of them were struggling about how to be people of faith, and primarily Christian faith they were thinking of, and identify themselves as gay, and so I was telling them, you know, you can, you can be both. There isn't really any incongruence. So I think that was help for a lot of kids. And then the next—that was when one of the mothers who was attending brought a friend of hers in to speak to the kids on another Christian perspective. We call her "the rainbow cross lady," [laughs] because she brought all these little rainbow crosses in, she had them pin them on their backpacks and stuff. Actually, that year at graduation I wore mine at graduation, too.

This advisor offered an alternative perspective on Christianity of which the youth were unaware. He conceivably gave some of the youth dealing with religious conflict a new idea that the two identities could merge and were not necessarily at odds. He also served as a role model by wearing the rainbow cross to graduation. The students in the GSA, other students, and faculty perhaps saw that he was willing to present an image of himself as both a Christian and an openly gay man who could influence others with the same inclination to become more visible.

Another advisor gave advice to a gay student who was being beaten up in the school parking lot. She never saw the beatings happen but knew they were indeed happening on school grounds. Because she personally never saw it happen, she was not able to write up an incident report. However, she urged the student to file an incident report for himself.

> I told him that I was there as his advocate and that I would meet with people, I would do whatever I could but I wasn't a witness and so I could not, I didn't feel like I could go to the principal and write an incident report about it because I didn't see it happened, I only got that his report or from other kids and that kind of thing and so ya know I told him I don't want how many times, at least four times, at least four times that I told him this, you need to go file an incident report and I will make appointments, like for meetings with your mom, you, with the assistant principal whoever it takes, I would be there with you and I will do whatever I can support you . . . and he never followed through.

Although the student never did file the report, she kept reminding him to do it and to get help for himself. She was willing to stand up against the homophobic harassment this student was facing if the student was willing. Perhaps her presence in announcing the unacceptability of this type of harassment would encourage others to do the same. She could serve as a role model for her colleagues as well as for students in standing up against harassment.

Inactive Observer

The advisor's role as described by 7 informants was one of sitting back and letting the students take control of the GSA activities. The GSA advisor did not take charge of group activities or discussion content. As one advisor stated, "I really try to be just an advisor . . . it's their time to plan and think about what they want to do and what they want to accomplish, so I just kind of . . . sit back." The advisors said they were not there to play an active part in the meetings. "I'm usually more of just a fly on the wall here, you know." They seemed to have made a conscious separation between the club and themselves. Interestingly, 6 of the 7 advisors who endorsed this theme were male and heterosexual. Perhaps if a male advisor became involved with GSA activities, his colleagues would begin to question his heterosexuality. Although advisors may support students who are gay, lesbian, bisexual, and/or transgendered, straight male advisors may not be comfortable being seen as gay themselves. Some heterosexual advisors may have subconsciously internalized the heterosexism and homophobia that lurk in society and underlie the school context.

Monitor of Appropriate School Behavior

The role of a GSA advisor also entailed being a monitor who ensured that students were demonstrating appropriate school behavior. Three of the 4 advisors who discussed this theme were heterosexual, female, and from an urban high school environment. To begin, an important question was what exactly is appropriate school behavior? Once it became known that a GSA was going to be established, one advisor was brought into a meeting with the assistant superintendent and the curriculum director to discuss the issue.

> ...when we started talking about it seriously the, the uh assistant superintendent and the curriculum director asked me to go to a meeting and we sat down and basically what I heard they telling me was that I couldn't discuss sex or sex education sorts of topics at the meetings and if there were meetings going on, it was my responsibility to see that those things weren't discussed and if they were, it could be big problems for me and my job. I mean, and I didn't, I like both those men and I think that it could, uh, had we not already had a good rapport, a teacher might have found that like a threat like, but I really didn't and I don't think it was. They were just generally concerned about me and making sure I knew what was going on and so that I didn't get into a situation that I didn't expect because I didn't know. Um and so they told me to be really careful about that and I said that I would and I have been. And it really haven't been, it doesn't come up, it's not like. GSA's don't get together and talk about sex, it's just not.

The assistant superintendent and the curriculum director seemed to be truly concerned that the advisor was going to be put into a compromising situation. However, these administrators' concerns about discussions of sex reinforced the perception that sexual minority issues are entirely about sex. Although the advisor did not take the threat of losing her job seriously, it reinforced an image of intolerance and demonstrated that GSA advisors take risks on behalf of their sexual minority students. This quote also illustrates the underlying heterosexism and covert homophobia occurring in some schools, resulting in fear and hostile environments surrounding gay and lesbian issues in the school context.

Another advisor got a little frustrated with the administration because she had to reiterate quite a few times that the students demonstrated appropriate school behavior during the meetings.

> I guess they still, even though people knew or we stated that it was legal, that it was the legal right of students to have this group, they were still struggling with whether this was really appropriate ya know for a public high school to. And people were, even though I think I kept explaining a couple of the premises that you don't ask kids what their sexual orientation is and that we don't talk about sex, we don't talk about sex anymore than you'd talk about sex in Band under French Club or whatever but people seemed to have that idea that we must talk about sex. So they just seemed to misunderstand what goes on in the meetings and that got me a little frustrated.

Again, the perception that sexual minority issues revolve around sex led to a heterosexist assumption that GSA students violated appropriate school behavior simply by joining together. Covert homophobia by teachers and administrators is linked to the failure of public high schools to understand the legitimate needs of LGBT students and the purpose of GSAs.

Liaison

The GSA advisor also served as a liaison with the various levels of the school community. This theme was supported by all the advisors. There were variations, however, within this theme. Three basic ways the GSA advisors served as liaisons were between (1) the GSA students and teachers, (2) the GSA students and administration, and (3) the GSA students, parents, and administration.

The GSA advisor served as a connection between the GSA students and teachers. Many GSAs participate in the Day of Silence, which is a day when the students do not speak all day in protest of our society's oppression of LGBT people. One advisor and his co-advisors stood up during a faculty meeting to talk about the Day of Silence.

> Our main purpose is academics, so we'd have meetings, faculty meetings, and they'd refer to these things like the Day of Silence and say "well ya know we're not sanctioning this activity," but we [the advisors] just want you to know the kids will be participating in it. So, I had to stand up and explain to them, thankfully that was when it wasn't just me, I had the other two people [advisors] there with me, explaining what the purpose of the Day of Silence was and explain to them about this and that and that the kids should still be held academically accountable that um if they're missing points, then they're missing points. And I believe that personally. Because I think that's a form of the protest too. If you're going to protest something, ya know, if Gandhi, if Gandhi gonna fast he can't sneak food in the middle of the night, ya know. And, part of it is the suffering that you go through, so ya know the whole thing with the not getting points or oral quizzes or whatnot and they can't speak. I personally don't think there's a problem with that at all. Ya know, you take the hit if you feel strongly enough about something that, it's not let it go. But the teachers, nobody talked to me about it, not really. I didn't have good discussions with the teachers who didn't agree with me necessarily.

This quote demonstrates the opposition that GSA advisors may face with their colleagues. In addition, it shows the unfriendly reception GSAs may receive from teachers.

An advisor from another school was approached by teachers when the club was first initiated who suggested that the club be called a diversity club instead of a GSA. The advisor discussed this with the students and let them decide what they wanted to call their club.

> Um there was some teachers who came up to me for example and said, "do you have to use the word gay in the club name?, can't you call it . . ." and this wasn't even, it wasn't like the principal who was saying "call it a diversity club" um "and don't have it be focused on gays." It was the, a teacher who said, "fine have a club that's focused on these issues, but just don't call it gay because that . . ." And ya know, I put that to the kids and I said, "it's up to you ya know, but this is one of the things I'm getting in terms of feedback from teachers." And the kids said, "it's like we're being re-closeted, that's the whole point, there's nothing wrong with the word gay, so accept it."

Serving as a relay between the faculty and the students, this advisor exposed how the omission of the word *gay* would contribute to the invisibility and silencing of LGBT youth in the school.

Another advisor also started communication right from the start with administration. Counselors were trying to change the nature of the GSA, therefore, the advisor met with administrators to advocate for the club the students wanted. The administrators had various concerns about the GSA, including a negative reaction from parents and other students.

> Well, they started putting road blocks up, ya know not really anything that I couldn't deal with, but they kept trying to change the sort of what the GSA would be. First they wanted it to be something that the counselors did and it was completely anonymous and confidential and all that stuff and so I took that back to the kids and they said "no that's not what we want." So, I went back to the administrators and said "ya know that's not what they want, they want it to be like an after school club" and they [the administrators] had all kinds of concerns, my principal was concerned that parents would be taking out the kids out of my classroom if they found out, and our Athletic Director was worried that kids would be targeted, that would increase the amount of harassment and violence against gay kids or kids that were perceived to be.

As a liaison between students and the administration, the advisor revealed the administrators' automatic negative assumptions about the community response. GSAs represented problems for them rather than an opportunity to serve underrepresented students.

The role of liaison did not stop for the advisor once the GSA was formally or informally established in school. The need continued once the GSA was formed and organizing activities. For instance, one GSA was having problems in school with Day of Silence activities. There was a protest against the Day of Silence by a group of students. These students created T-shirts mimicking the students participating in the Day of Silence on the front of the shirt with perceived offensive writing on the back. The students were selling these T-shirts before the Day of Silence in school during school hours, which was breaking school rules. The advisors (there were 3) approached the principal and together they devised a plan to send the students wearing the offensive shirts to the principal's office where they would be forced to take off the perceived offensive shirts.

We went to the principal and talked about it and explained it to them and said, "look it, ya know the GSA, regardless whether or not its school sponsored, it promotes acceptance, tolerance, respect. . . . these objectionable shirts is fostering separation, divisive, humiliating kinds of things" and I said, "look it, if someone were to come in and wear a swastika or, or have a picture of a, of a Black person with a gag and say keep [name of school] white on it, you couldn't have it" . . . I said, "what's the difference? We've got these students with these shirts. You can't, you can't have people coming in with Nazi shirts on, it's just not." He agreed with us. He said, "those shirts will come off. They will not be allowed to wear those shirts on the Day of the Silence." I said, "Great. Thank you so much for doing this," ya know. And um, then the Day of Silence arrived about a week later. And since that time I was able to get one of the shirts . . . I showed that shirt to [name of principal] our principal at the time . . . it was just "keep [name of school] on the straight and narrow," but it had this demeaning depiction on the front. So, he said, "You know, great for showing me this and that ya, everything fine." He also gave us permission, [names of GSA's student co-presidents], to make out a sheet to put in all the teacher's mailboxes that said, "if you see these shirts send them to the office because that's not respectful." They need to bring those shirts in. And that letter also explained the Day of Silence and what's it supposed to symbolize. It's symbolizing silence and discrimination and that, really what it is, it's not broadcasting and advertising homosexuality, what it is, is it's just going against discrimination. So we put all these things in their mailboxes

The Day of Silence came, and there were students wearing the anti-Day of Silence T-shirts. When students wearing the shirts were sent to the principal's office, the principal did not make them take the shirts off. The advisor and the student presidents of the GSA met with the principal to discuss the ordeal.

Anyway, they didn't have to take their shirts off and so [names of student co-presidents] and I were "what is going on? Ya know, they were supposed to take them off. We just had this long discussion," but they couldn't talk. It was the Day of Silence. So, we had to go in there to talk to [name of principal] and they couldn't talk, so they are writing these things down and I'm reading the things. And he tried to explain it and he's just being kind of patronizing and just make us really upset. And he says, "well, I've thought it over and I've decided that we're going to do it this way and if the students aren't actually advocating violence, we're going to send them back to their classrooms so long as the teachers don't have any objections to them being in their class, so as long as it doesn't cause a learning disruption," he said, "we can let them have their shirts on."

The advisor was the connection that the GSA students used to communicate their concerns and frustration with the anti-Day of Silence T-shirts. He was right in the middle of the dispute, willing to advocate and confront the administration directly to protect the students.

Not only did the advisors serve as liaisons between staff at the school, but with parents as well. When one club was just beginning, the principal suggested that the advisor bring some of the GSA students to a PTA meeting where they could answer some questions and concerns raised by the parents.

> ...we had a new principal this year . . . had had a big GSA in his previous high school and he I think he was really overwhelmed with the change from an inner-city high school to suburban upper-middle-class high school. So I think the one issue he felt really comfortable with was the Gay-Straight Alliance because he had a lot of experience with that. So he was almost cavalier about it as opposed to the previous principal who had been so uptight about it . . . and a group of parents or some of the right-wing parents found out and so maybe five or six of them came to the meeting and sat in one corner of the room together and started asking kind of combative questions of the students and after a while the principal, we had the students leave because it was getting unpleasant and one of the sad things was and then he had us, the advisors leave, but the mother of the boy who had started the GSA was there and of course the other parents didn't know her so she was very, very upset by some of the comments that were made um . . . well they were very angry that parent permission wasn't required for kids to be well in the GSA. They ya know just stated their beliefs that it, we shouldn't have such a group and that kids were being recruited for the gay lifestyle um and even that there was some accusations and I have a little trouble remembering what was said in the meeting versus some of the phone calls and visits to me later where ya know that the gay lifestyle leads one to get AIDS and HIV and die and so I was facilitating the death of students you know by having this group or helping to have this group.

This quote demonstrates the risks faced by GSA advisors and students. They need to be prepared for direct confrontation and to defend their positions in difficult situations.

Resource

GSA advisors served as a resource in the school community. They assisted their peers, students, and community members on issues of sexuality and educated peers through in-services and presentations.

One advisor discussed her role as a point person for sexuality issues. If there was something going on in school concerning gender or sexual orientation, this advisor was told to provide her perspective.

> I mean there have been a few situations and um, I guess as the, being the advisor, one nice thing is that now I'm well known as the point person for these sorts of issues. Ya know, we had a student this year who doesn't want to wear a dress, she hasn't worn a dress since 4th grade and she's graduating and the requirement is that you have to wear a dress and this, ya know [laughs] and a couple teachers take me aside and say this is going on, okay, I guess I like knowing what's going on and being able to provide them with factual or legalistic information if I have it. Um, so I think there's among the staff an increased ability to do things properly because I could be a resource. . . . I feel like they, I feel like, you know um when an issue comes up surrounding GLBT issues, somebody lets me know what's going on, sometimes the students let me know something's going on, sometimes the faculty lets me know what's going on and I'm glad to do that because I probably do know more about these things then anybody else on the faculty. I would guess, so I'm glad that they let me know and let me give some input and do what I can to help.

In this instance, the school community looked to her as a resource for sexuality and gender expression matters. This advisor also seemed to take pride in her role, appreciating the ability to help students and perhaps her colleagues make informed decisions regarding LGBT issues.

Another advisor gave a colleague, who was teaching government, information about hate crimes that he could add to his curriculum.

> I found resources on Matt Shepard and other hate crimes, too and stuff like that. He took that up as part of the curriculum, so things like that. I like to think I'm making a difference.

This quote illustrates how GSA advisors can create greater visibility for LGBT issues, thus contributing to positive changes in the school culture.

During the Day of Silence, one advisor set out GLSEN lesson plans, ribbons, and door signs that other teachers could take to teach about sexual orientation issues during class.

> I have a Day of Silence and we have GLSEN lesson plans . . . so I set those out on the teacher's like counter by our mailboxes and just said ya know had our ribbons, and these are lesson plans and these are signs for doors if you want to have kids come in your safe room.

If other teachers wanted to include sexual orientation in their curricula or let students know that their classroom was a safe space by putting up a sign on their door, the resources were there. The advisor did not push the resources onto her colleagues, but left it open for them to be proactive in tackling gay and lesbian issues in their classroom if they were ready and willing. This approach may be necessary in a climate that is not fully open to acceptance.

GSA advisors have also given presentations and in-services to other faculty members about the GSA and youth sexual orientation issues. There was one advisor who gave a presentation to staff where a teacher asked how they should present the information to the class and how they should handle possible personal conflict during class discussion.

> ... I did an in-service about working with LGBT issues and this was an in-service for teachers. And I told one woman, she was saying about how she felt she needed to preface when she was going to be talking about LGBT issues and you know, if a parent, you know, "I know that all of you might not agree with this or blah blah blah," and I said, "Would you do that with anything else you taught in your social studies class?" And she said, "No," and I said, "Don't do with this either." I said, "Teach it, and, yeah, some of them are gonna disagree and some of them are gonna agree, but you need to stop sort of apologizing," 'cause that was kind of the reaction I was getting from teachers, I felt like they sort of like, "Ya know, I'm gonna teach this, but I know some of you aren't gonna like it." And ya know, trying to keep parents happy, and you know, it's like ya know don't, because what you're already saying there is that you're putting some judgment on it, and that may be unintentionally, but I feel like people pick up on that. Just, ya know, teach it. And let the students decide where they fall in this spectrum.

Teaching about LGBT issues without first apologizing can promote the normalization of gay and lesbian experiences. It also serves to create a more accepting school environment, leaving students to make their own decisions regarding these issues without being influenced by others with strong convictions.

Advisors also gave out resources to students during meetings or individually. One advisor gave a coming-out book to a student whose friend was dealing with coming out as a lesbian. This advisor discussed the book through a story that she told about talking to a parent over the phone.

> when I talked with this mom on the phone I said "you know your daughter came to me," actually her daughter didn't even come to me her daughter's friend came to me and said, "(respondent's name) I have a friend that thinks she might be a lesbian" and I said well here I have got this book that has like coming out stories. Give it to your friend, have her just read it, get some ideas about what other students have felt like and what they did when they came out and then if she wants to she can come and talk to me. So the next week she came and talked to me and we sat down and talked about some of the stories in the book and she said "I am just so scared if I tell my mom she is going to kick me out and it is going to be really bad" and I was like okay "well it might be kind of bad for a while" I was like but pointers are don't do it on the holiday, don't do it you know those are kind of cool things to know so she was going to go do it.

This quote also supports the idea that GSA advisors are considered safe people. This young woman came out to the advisor before her mother. GSA advisors may support a youth when support from home is not available, which could serve as a protective factor in their development.

Another advisor had a similar experience when a high school in a small town nearby wanted to start a GSA. He also had students from other schools visit because they were interested in GSA activities.

> Because this has been for years, the only GSA in this county, we've had students from other schools interested in what we're doing and how we're doing it and can they come to our social functions and so on. It's been open to them, like that Laramie Project night with Maya Angelou readings, we've had several kids from other schools came in. I actually recently had consulted with someone at [name of high school] which is a

real small town where the original GSA members used to joke, "yeah we'll never have one at [repeats name of high school]." They've got one going on or they're starting one out in [name of small town].

In another community, a parent came to one of the GSA meetings to talk to the GSA advisor about her son who was gay. She wanted to try to make the school environment safe for him.

> I had a parent came to me, and she outted her son to me at one of our initial meetings and um [laughs] she kind of figured I was gay as well. But, ya know she said, "what can you do to make this environment safe for my son?" and that was in '98 when I put up the display in '98 as a way to sort of, to see her son to see himself reflected both disciplinary program, to see himself reflected in culture, in science and ya know other areas.

These two quotes offer examples of the ways in which active, sustained GSAs serve as models that encourage others to become more proactive in their efforts to support LGBT youth. Consultation and networking are key resources the GSA advisor can provide.

Knowledge Seeker

In order for a GSA advisor to serve as a resource, the advisor must be knowledgeable enough to serve as one. The advisor role consisted of finding information and developing expertise so they were informed, especially of their legal rights. A few advisors needed to learn about their legal rights regarding the legitimacy in establishing a formal GSA.

> I did some research, or the kids maybe already knew about the federal Equal Access Act and I did some research on it. I included in the proposal something on the bottom that said, "under the federal Equal Access Act this is something that is by law, something that has to be permitted in any school that has any other clubs" and I might have even cited a case or two where recently the courts have ruled in favor of GSAs and I put out there that this federal law that you have to do this. Somewhere along the lines the lawyer got called in. I did not call him. I didn't even know who this attorney was for the district. He was very cooperative with me in sitting down and the principal and talking out here are the different options. There wasn't any opposition really from within the school administrative structure or the school board.

Another advisor was having a difficult time with administration in accepting the GSA as a school club. She gathered resources and invoked the American Civil Liberties Union (ACLU), which halted the opposition.

> And finally I guess it was—I think it must be in January or so, I finally gathered enough resources and I found a letter—an open letter to administrators and teachers about the rights of students to have a GSA and I made copies of that letter and gave it to all of them. And once I evoked the ACLU, they pretty much left me alone [laughs].

The teacher who had the anti-Day of Silence T-shirt incident previously mentioned also sought information through the ACLU. He contacted them to determine whether it was legal for the students to wear the anti-Day of Silence T-shirts because they were offensive.

> We contacted the ACLU about the shirts, by the way and the lawyer that we spoke with said that there was nothing we could do about getting them removed because they didn't have violent language on them. They didn't promote violence, necessarily. That's what the lawyer said. The symbolism, but that's interpretive. He said he needed something that wasn't gonna be in court and an interpretation issue . . . , so if it had hate terms on that shirt, they couldn't wear them. They are just toyin' with that that edge of acceptability and it's in a gray area.

Teacher of Leadership Skills

As previously discussed, students take on the role of leading the GSA meetings in content. It is important to remember that these students are still developing skills they can use in the future, and some may not be experienced in leading groups or activities. Therefore, one role of the advisor is to help students hone their leadership skills. The advisors tended to do this in two ways: by teaching logistical leadership skills, such as helping leaders develop meeting agendas and organizing activities, and teaching emotional leadership skills, such as guiding them to make mature decisions, strategize effectively, and act professionally.

A GSA advisor may help the group think about activities and plan them out. The advisor takes the knowledge that she or he has about the school environment and helps students execute various school activities. As one advisor stated:

> I help them with ways to think of something, like the different activities that we have done, and to help try to consider how to plan it, how to carry out, how to consider what kind of reaction it's gonna get. So, I think of myself as just a voice in their head that just kind of is the experience or knowledge of the district to let them know how to tackle or how to handle certain things . . . it has to be student initiated and it has to be student-run.

Again, this advisor reiterated that the GSA should be student run, and the students were in charge of their own activities. The advisor was there to help GSA students make their ideas a reality by helping them think through the steps of planning an activity. By helping the students with planning activities, the GSA helped students indirectly learn the needed steps and skills to create and execute activities independently in the future.

Another advisor felt as if the president of the club needed to take on more leadership responsibility in the group. The president had not been correctly planning agendas for meetings and, thus, the group was not being productive.

> I would with the leadership I'm working with, I gave her [GSA president] sort of an ultimatum, I said, "You know, you have to have a written agenda for me at least at the beginning of the day, otherwise won't be meeting." . . . but the truth was that I really—the group, if it's not gonna be active in a way that is a contribution, which really we're hoping for to just create a safe space if we can get it, but also to be an educational component, both within school and the community, and if we don't have any agenda to do that or we don't have any plans or ya know sort of strategies to do that. And then, you know [laughs] . . . [what he says to the president] communicate with me and I'll, you know, I can advise you as to how to gather materials, and what kind of fund-raising things are available and this and that. But, you know, if you just come in and you're wingin' it or you got no agenda at all, then I'm, sorry. Nine months—er, eight months they've had to figure this out.

This quote illustrates some of the difficulties advisors face when working with an inexperienced and ever-changing group of students. As with most student clubs, the faculty advisor needs to direct members toward better organizational and leadership skills.

Part of the job of a GSA advisor was keeping students on task and getting them to begin to think about what they wanted to accomplish. For example, one advisor asked the students the necessary questions about how to execute activities, such as helping resolve a problem of unsupportive staff.

> So, we are like a safe environment. They run when they come in, they end up sharing all sorts of information, hanging out. So, at times I have to be "okay, we need to get some stuff done, stop the social hour, ya know we have this plan now and how are we going to this done?? . . . I throw out ideas um but, I really want to be, where do they think the need is, what do they see is the problem in the building and what could we do to kind of change it? Earlier in the year we had one of my students um wanted to really, felt as though that we needed to do something for the staff again. After some discussion, they've come up about oh people hearing things, staff not being as supportive in the classroom as they should as I said, "Well okay if you think that is a need well then lets put together some sort of plan to present to the staff" so they came up with some ideas. And then my role is to say, "well if we are going to do this, these are the hoops that we have to jump through, these are the processes, these are the steps."

This advisor took what the students were saying about the staff problem and then helped them generate a plan. After a while, the students could learn from the steps that the advisor generated and apply them to different situations for solving other problems in the school community.

Not only did students learn the logistics of leading a group from the GSA advisor, the students also learned there was an emotional side of leadership. Being a leader takes more than knowing how to plan and execute activities. There are also personal and emotional aspects of leadership, such as being mature and professional. GSA advisors advised the students on how to approach possible conflict. For instance, one advisor discussed ideas with students on how to approach the administration about the sexual orientation harassment problem in the school. One of the students immediately wanted to confront administration with a lawsuit. The advisor suggested that he be delicate with his wording when addressing the administration or they were going to react negatively.

> ...I'm a teacher I have some insight as to what the administration might want more than the kids. So, I'd say "why don't you try it this way or why don't you say, when you write your letter ya know put this kind of thought into the letter, don't come at him like [bangs on the table] ya know so demanding and it's got to be like this rah rah rah, we're going to get lawyers." That would be a great way to start, ya know. . . . and I'm like, "no, that's not going to work." So ya know . . . "try it this way, it'll be more positive, you'll get farther." So, ya know that's kind of the things that I did. I didn't do a whole lot, but ya know that was, just trying to show them the right direction to do it without getting all super passionate about it and turning people off before they could get started . . . he wanted just to blast in there with guns firing. And ya know so I had to like, "okay slow down a little bit, you go in there like that, they are definitely going to say no because I know that I would ya know chill out a little bit." So I just had to like pull the reins on him and not let him go to fast, too strong or something like that to get, because if he just would have gone in there the principal would have just squashed him and said "bring on the lawsuit" ya know. So, teenagers can be passionate so ya know that sort of thing....

This advisor tried to guide the students to take a more low-key approach when dealing with administration. Threatening a lawsuit right away would not be an appropriate strategy and would perhaps close doors on any communication to resolve the harassment problem. In the future, students could transfer this approach to other instances where strategic confrontation is necessary.

One GSA planned an activity where all the students watched a video about sexual orientation issues that the group had created. The video was meant to generate awareness and sensitivity, but it backfired. Some members of the general student body reacted negatively and started name-calling and harassing GSA students. The advisor addressed the GSA students about how to deal with their anger and resentment.

> ...they, they [GSA students] were hurt, I mean, it was . . . Then they were angry, because, you know, kids were talking about it, and they were overhearing conversations and they were mad, so . . . It got them riled up, and then ya know . . . Sometimes, those types, my types, my students may get riled up and they can, they can do the things that I tell them not to do. They can be just as bad as the people that are harassing them or being mean. And that too, that's always my basic message to them that, ya know, think about the message you're trying to send. If you're gonna resort to their tactics, their low level of, ya know, name-calling, ya know,

all that sorta stuff, you know better than that . . . that's where I have to sit down and kind of, as my role is to say, "Listen, ya know, this is, ya know, this is[n't] the perfect world we think we should live in, this is reality. And you need to know how to deal with people in a real world. Sometimes you gotta bite your lip, ya know, but don't resort to those tactics, because that's not gonna get you anywhere in the long run." And ya know, I use the examples of, ya know, look at the civil rights movement and those sorts of things.

Advisors need to help prepare GSA students for the backlash that may greet their efforts to educate others. Safe space and inclusion are goals rather than realities. Negotiating the most useful and effective means to counter harassment requires GSA advisors to serve on the front lines of social change. Strong leadership skills may be required to provide a careful balance between reactive anger and proactive strategies.

Discussion

This chapter explored the roles GSA advisors play in the school environment. GSA advisors had almost parental feelings for the youth, wanting to create an environment that keeps them safe and free from discrimination. This is shown through some of the roles that advisors play in the GSA. They serve as role models, are seen as safe people, give life advice, and are resources for the youth. For example, by being seen as a role model and caring person who is there for the youth to talk to, the GSA advisor helps to create an environment where the youth can feel safe. In addition, by giving life advice and resources, the advisors may be seen as helping the youth develop skills for successful living, which reinforces that they care about them and want them to succeed. GSA advisors become another adult in their lives for advice and opportunities to foster positive youth development. Positive relationships with caring adults encourage positive development, especially for young people who must overcome prejudice and adversity (Rhodes, Ebert, & Fischer, 1992; Scales & Gibbons, 1996).

For some advisors, becoming involved with LGBT issues did bring about confrontations with administration, fellow teachers, and parents. For example, one advisor was involved with a lawsuit concerning a display that he put up in his classroom about LGBT history, another advisor was approached by other teachers about calling the club a diversity club instead of a GSA, and one advisor had a confrontation with a parent who accused the advisor of facilitating the death of students from HIV. Although these are negative experiences, none of the advisors interviewed had their jobs seriously threatened, and some had no serious confrontations at all. It is not known, however, if other GSA advisors who did not participate in this study lost their jobs or had them threatened as a result of being a GSA advisor. The advisors in this study who did face confrontations held to their convictions and beliefs. While discussing the problems that they faced or are currently facing, the advisors seemed to become more solid in their beliefs that they made the right decision to become an advisor. No advisors disclosed that they were considering abandoning the GSA or were becoming too worn down by conflict. In fact, the opposite seemed to be true. It is interesting to note, however, that 38 of the 78 GSAs registered in the state were not currently in operation at the time of the study. Therefore, the advisors sampled in this research could represent those that exist in more conducive environments for establishing a GSA. Also, these advisors could represent the GSAs that have been best able to withstand opposition.

Using Herr's (1997) definition of homophobia involves interrelated mechanisms of silencing: systematic exclusion that involves rendering LGB people invisible and systematic [negative] inclusion in which discussions place sexual minorities in a negative context. There was evidence of systematic exclusion, such as the administration trying to convince GSA supporters to join the diversity club, lack of repercussions for the students who wore the anti-Day of Silence T-shirts when it was previously decided they were not allowed to wear them at school, and the superintendent demanding that a bulletin board with LGB history be taken down. There were also elements of systematic [negative] inclusion, such as the perception that during GSA meetings the students talk about sex and that gay people have HIV. It is interesting to note that heterosexual advisors, as well as the sexual minority advisors, experienced the effects of homophobia. Previous research has focused on the experiences and effects of homophobia on gay, lesbian, and bisexual people, but the effects on heterosexual allies may be greater than expected. In addition, there is a tendency to focus on the gay part of the Gay-Straight Alliance while ignoring the straight element of the club. It is an alliance meaning that these two groups (gay and straight) meet together to discuss issues. It is important to consider what message that sends to straight students as well as gay students.

Being a GSA advisor can be a lonely task in a working environment where hostility around gay and lesbian issues is an undercurrent. The GSA advisor may be the only person advocating for the club against the opposition of his or her colleagues and superiors, which requires some degree of courage. GSA advisors, therefore, need more support in the school environment, especially because they may be key actors in creating an environment that is safe for gay and lesbian students and faculty. There are many ways that the school community could be more welcoming of GSAs and their advisors.

First, the administration should adhere to the Equal Access Act and keep personal viewpoints about gay and lesbian people and issues out of the public school system. Administrators need to be role models for teachers, staff, students, and parents. If the administration is seen as being fair and welcoming, this attitude could filter out into the broader school community. Administrative and principal support has been connected with effectively changing school practice and culture (Fullman, 1985; Reitzug & Burrello, 1995; Taylor-Greene et al., 1997). The school climate could be a reflection of the administration's reaction to the GSA.

Second, the advisors often used the tenure policy as a protection against being fired as a result of their GSA involvement. GSA advisors might also be more likely to take on the advisor position if there were protections in place to ensure that their jobs would not be jeopardized, such as a nondiscrimination policy that would protect against firing a teacher or staff member for being a sexual minority or ally. This layer of protection may sway a teacher to get involved.

Some GSA advisors in this study faced various challenges and difficult confrontations. One benefit of the study is that it documents for advisors that they are not alone in their challenges. Perhaps starting an online support group or chat room for GSA advisors might be beneficial for sharing stories and giving advice to one another. This might be especially helpful for those advisors who have never advised a club before. They could establish a connection with other advisors across the state or nation to discuss what has worked and what has not worked when dealing with sexual minority issues in high schools. Together they could support each other in creating school environments that are accepting and welcoming of students of various sexual orientations and genders.

APPENDIX

Interview Protocol

You are being asked to participate in this study because of your role as a GSA advisor within your high school. I am very interested in hearing about your perspective and experiences with advising this club. For example, I am interested to hear about the history of your GSA, the perceptions of the high school community concerning GSA activities, what it's like to be the advisor, as well as about the resources available to the GSA at the school. I have some questions planned; however I'd like them to serve more as a guide. Feel free to discuss any issue or topic without restraint as it fits with your role as GSA advisor. My goal is to obtain a complete picture of your experience.

Do you have any questions before we begin?

I'd like to first start the discussion talking about some background and history of the GSA at your school.

<u>Background</u>

1. Do you know when the GSA first began at your high school?

2. Why did the GSA get started?

3. A. [*If informant worked at school from inception of the GSA*] How was the formation of this club received by your:
Peers?
Administration?
Students?
Parents?

B. [*If informant was NOT present at inception*] Do you know how the formation of the GSA was received by:
Teachers?
Administration?

Students?
Parents?

4. Currently, what is the environment like in your school with homosexuality issues? Please describe how your school handles sexual orientation issues.

Now that you shared the history of the club, I'd like to next discuss with you your personal experience as an advisor.

Personal history

5. Have you ever been a club advisor before? If so, how has this experience as a GSA advisor compare to that other experience?

6. What prompted you to decide to become a GSA advisor?

7. What is it like to be a GSA advisor?

8. What role do you play with the GSA?

9. How has your sexual orientation identity affected your experience as a GSA advisor?

I'd like to next lead the discussion to talking about the resources and support that is available to you as a GSA advisor.

10. What would help you be a better advisor to this club? [Institutional changes, more resources...]?

11. Are there LGBT resources accessible to you and the GSA students at your school?

12. In what way has your school provided resources to help you be a successful GSA advisor?

13. Do you feel like your school administration supports you as an advisor to the GSA?

14. What has your relationship been like with peers/administration/students/parents since becoming a GSA advisor?

Now, I'd like to talk with you about the students that attend the club and the activities that they participate in.

GSA Activities

15. Could you talk to me a little bit about the students that attend the GSA meetings?

    A. What do they talk about?
    B. What do they do during GSA meetings?

16. How do you feel your GSA has impacted the school environment?

17. Is there anything that you think I should have asked, or would be important to know about GSAs that I didn't ask? Anything else that you would like to share?

Finally I'd like to ask some general questions about yourself and your school.

Demographics:

18. How long have you worked at the school?

19. Would you describe the school setting as rural, suburban, or urban?

20. SES of school?

21. Is specified sexual orientation harassment prohibited in school policy?

22. Education of LGBT issues in school?

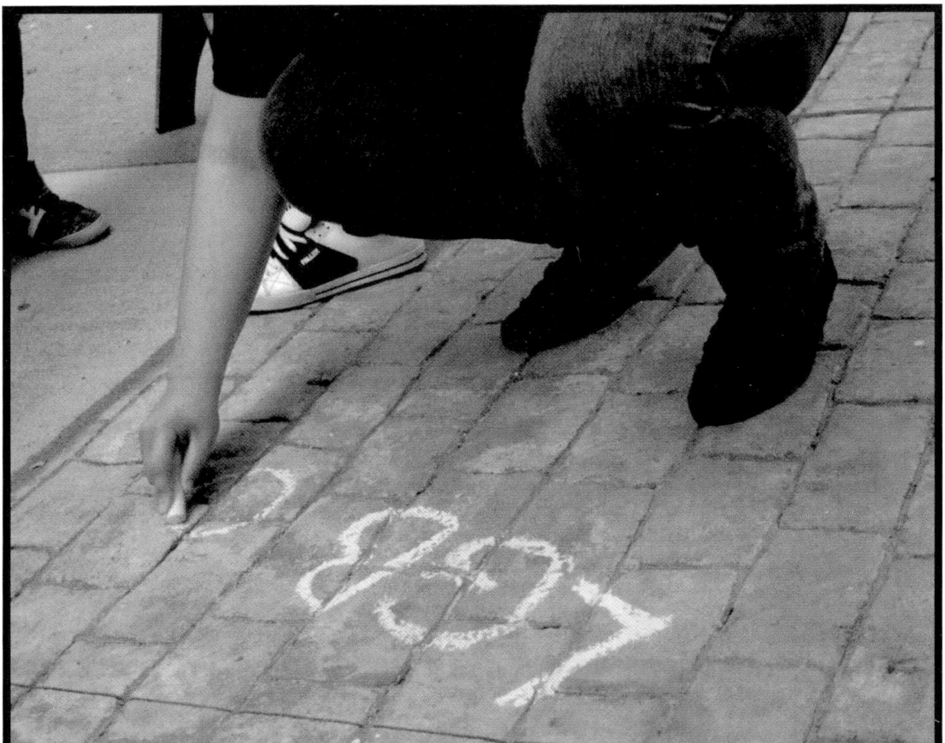

Chapter Three

Becoming an Ally: Straight Friends of LGBTQ High School Students

Darla Linville and David Lee Carlson

HIGH SCHOOL CAN be a time of struggle, a struggle to fit into the narrow spaces of fashion, gender expression, interests, and activities that constitute the realm of acceptable. Lesbian, gay, bisexual, transgendered, and queer or questioning (LGBTQ) students, as well as students with gender expressions outside the local definitions of feminine and masculine, often endure even more difficulties in high school social settings (Advocates for Children of New York, 2005; Friend, 1993, 1998; Gay Lesbian and Straight Education Network, 2005; Gibson, 1989; Human Rights Watch, 2001; Jackson & Hendrix, 2003; Leck, 2000; MacGillivray, 2000; Munoz-Plaza, Quinn, & Rounds, 2002; Nairn & Smith, 2003; Rasmussen, 2004; Sadowski, 2001; Smith, 2005; Szalacha, 2004). But what about their friends? What about the students who decide to take part in an allies group, such as a gay-straight alliance (GSA)? Or the friends who remain loyal after their friend comes out? What are the consequences and requirements for these straight allies in schools? What do they have to do to become the friends that their LGBTQ friends need? And, contrary perhaps to the expectations of schools and parents, what do straight friends gain from the process?

This chapter explores these questions in conversations with New York City high school students talking about the relationships between LGBTQ and straight young people in their schools. The conversations took place during a pilot research study in which students were asked about what it is like in their high schools for LGBTQ students. The young people in the study were New York City students-of-color from 6 high schools in 4 of the 5 boroughs. The 12 participants were in an after-school leadership program that met once a week for the entire school year. The program focused on social justice issues. Although they had somewhat different activist backgrounds than other New York City teens due to their participation in the social justice after-school group, in other ways they were quite typical. They ranged in age from 15 to 18, came from various ethnic backgrounds, and lived in diverse neighborhoods. Some qualified for financial assistance for school lunches based on their family income. Three of the 12 students self-identified as nonheterosexual, none were transgender, and 9 self-identified as straight. Four of the students were boys and 8 were girls.

While the pilot study was under way (Linville, 2008), other stories about friendships, relationships, negotiations of space and behavior, and identity wove themselves through the answers to the questions. Although students were not asked specifically about GSAs, friendship, or being an ally, in two focus groups the conversation turned repeatedly to these themes as students used the hour to reflect on how their relationships had been affected by one of their friends coming out or by coming out themselves. In these conversations, you will hear the voices of Michele,* Omar, and Angela who self-identify as straight, Annabelle who once self-identified as questioning but now self-identifies as straight, and Michael who self-identifies as gay. This chapter illustrates the ways students were thinking of themselves as friends in relationships with LGBTQ peers.

---

* Student names have been changed.

Theoretical Framework

Michel Foucault's concepts of friendship and ethics will be employed as an analytical framework through which to understand the students' words on ethically and aesthetically fashioning themselves as accepting and tolerant friends (Foucault, 1981/1997a, 1981/1997b, 1986). As an introduction to some of Foucault's ideas, we start here with the way Foucault examines relationship possibilities within the socially marginalized position of homosexuality in a 1981 interview entitled "Friendship as a Way of Life" (Foucault, 1981/1997b). In it he asks, "What relations, through homosexuality, can be established, invented, multiplied, and modulated?" (p. 135). In this way, Foucault understands that homosexuality is not just an individual identity that makes one deviant and abnormal, but a socially mediated position in which the sexual behaviors or attractions of some people come to be characterized as abnormal and Other (Miceli, 2005).

In these relations, each assertion of an unapologetic and unequivocal nonheterosexual identity expands the possibilities for everyone by failing to reiterate shame about nonnormative attractions and sexual behaviors. Foucault asserts that relationships between persons, outside of the heterosexual matrix and not limited to procreation, allow for many intimacies, affections, eroticisms, and loves that are unavailable to others who reject the possibility of nonheterosexual love. In these relations, emotional and physical needs that are often restricted to blood relations or spouses can be met by others with whom one shares an elaborated notion of friendship. Foucault proposes exploring the "multiplicity of relationships" (1981/1997b, p. 135), not limiting oneself to the binary choices of anonymous sex and lifelong, dependent relationships, but choosing instead the types of relations in which one wishes to engage within the possibilities of one's society. What then seems dangerous or unsettling about homosexuality is that it destabilizes the assumed goal of marriage and other socially and culturally sanctioned ways of being an adult.

For Foucault, each of us fashions a sexual self to ethically engage sexually and to meet our emotional and physical desires. These sexual selves are formed through a process that is both ethical and aesthetic. Ethically, we must measure ourselves against the rules and regulations of our social situation, the moral imperatives about sexuality that exist within our peer, religious, ethnic, cultural, racial, or gender groups. We decide which of these moral mandates is important to us, which we feel we must follow either because they resonate with our own desires or because the risks of not following them are too great. We decide what groups we will belong to, what friends we will have, what behaviors we will engage in, and what stories we will listen to and tell. Aesthetically, we also decide what parts of our physical presentation will represent our ethical decision to the rest of the world. For teens this may involve modest dress, bodybuilding, or eye-catching makeup. We decide what kind of a life we want to have, and we set out to build it in our intimate relationships. We search for others, both friends and lovers, who will help us nurture the qualities in ourselves that will help us be the person we want to be.

We'll talk more about the ways Foucault thinks we fashion ourselves as ethical persons following excerpts of the conversations presented below. In these conversations, young people discuss some of the decisions and negotiations that they engaged in to ethically and aesthetically fashion themselves as friends and allies of LGBTQ youth.

Questions, Answers, and Analysis

Interspersed between conversations in the focus groups will be thoughts on how to begin to answer the following questions: What is the effect of being an ally/friend on a straight student? How do straight students ethically fashion themselves? What are the aesthetics of being a friend/ally? What do joint LGBTQ and straight ally spaces in schools allow students to do? The conversations have been excerpted in large chunks from the focus group transcripts to allow the reader to see how meanings and understandings were negotiated within the group, how identities were formed, and how definitions of "allies" and "friendship," even when not so named, were refined and contested.

What is the effect of being an ally/friend on a straight student?

Conversation 1: Normalizing queerness within the friendship.

Michele:	But, like, I was saying to her, at our school, we kind of joke about it a little.
Darla:	How's that?
Michele:	Because it's like I was talking to our friend, and she was—remember the song she was singing? She's like, "I see balls everywhere." I was like, "Oh."
Annabelle:	"I see balls," and so we immediately thought, "Well, now you're on balls, right? Are you not afraid? Is there something there?" She was like, "No, I'm just singing."
Michele:	And it was a joke, so I was like, "So how's your—how's your boy, girl, boy friend?"
Annabelle:	And we're joking, but I think that, seriously, I don't know. I don't know. Frankly, we like her. I think because we know her and we knew her and everything, but I would—I don't think—
Michele:	Not everybody's accepting of it.
Annabelle:	Not everybody's accepting.
Darla:	At your school?
Michele:	At our school.
Annabelle:	Not everybody is accepting.
Michele:	Like, from what I can see, I see everybody accepted, but then the thing about our school, some people show you a different face, but behind you, they show you a different face.
Omar:	Definitely.
Michele:	So in front of her face it could be like, "Hey, hey, hey," but behind her it's just like, "Oh, my God. I can't believe she's, like, like a fag," or whatever, whatever, and they just want to talk about you behind your back, but as soon as you turn around, they're like, [sweet voice] "Hey, how you doing?"
Annabelle:	You know, we're all good, because I know in my—when I was talking to my friend the other day, and we were in a group playing basketball, and we were like, "Oh, well, what's-her-face, her name, came out, and she was, like, talking about there's a new expanded story," and then this boy came up. He's like, "Oh, well, she's really gay?" And we were like, "Yeah, she is." He's like, "Oh, snap. I didn't know she was," and he was saying a derogatory term, derogatory term towards her, and, you know, it was just like, you know, "Wow." You know, I don't know if that was a shock, but the fact that you could say that like that, it was just not cool, but we understood where he was coming from, though, be-

cause had we not known the person, the young lady, we would have probably said the same thing, too, you know, probably not in such a way, but we would have been thinking it, too.

In this conversation, Michele and Annabelle have to refashion themselves within their friendship—they need to make new choices about what they think and who they want to be in the friendship. Michele and Annabelle discuss their friend and the ways that they tease her about her sexuality. Yet they also tell us about how they each feel a little awkward about what this change in her has meant to their friendship, when they display confusion about who or what kind of person she is attracted to now. And they clearly point out that their affiliation with this girl, the maintenance of this friendship, adds a level of sensitivity to her situation that they might not have had otherwise.

First, Michele and Annabelle tell us about the ways their relationship with this friend has not changed in substantive ways. They can still include her in the banter about love and relationships that is common among friends, teasing her about who she is attracted to, about what features attract her, and expressing a teasing concern that her affections change too quickly for them to keep up with. As they might tease one another about boys and crushes, they tease her about her girlfriend, her seemingly wandering eyes, and possibly her singing. This is reassurance that her difference is not the kind of difference that would disrupt the intimacy of the friendship. Michele and Annabelle are reassured that their friend has not changed so much that they cannot poke fun at her about her relationships or use a lighthearted approach to express any discomfort. Their friend is reassured that her relationships do not need to be hidden from her friends out of shame on anyone's part. They can think of her in a love and sexual relationship with a woman, and she need not censor her speech or hide that part of her life from her friends. By approaching the conversation with playfulness, Annabelle and Michele reassure their friend that their relationship is resilient enough to absorb these changes.

As friends of a lesbian peer, however, Michele and Annabelle encounter challenges that they might not have otherwise encountered. As they talk with other students about their friend, and as they observe the interactions in their school, they are struck by the ways that their peers may seem accepting of LGBTQ students, but that the acceptance might not be very sincere. If they hear the gossip or hear other students say, "Oh, my God. I can't believe she's, like, like a fag," they have to decide how they will intervene in those conversations and if and how they will defend their friend's choices. They may be called upon to counter their peers' mistaken or stereotyping statements about LGBTQ students or homosexuality. They may feel they have to speak up to interrupt bullying or harassment occurring in the hallways, or to join in a conversation in a classroom if they feel that the comments may be silencing others. And, if they do feel compelled to interject themselves into these kinds of comments and incidents, they risk being labeled gay themselves. In the heteronormative sexuality regime, everyone's sexuality is under scrutiny and no proof is enough to definitively prove heterosexuality, but any deviation or suspicion is enough to label someone homosexual (Butler, 1990).

Annabelle and Michele seek role models and social spaces where they are invited to fashion themselves as persons accepting of differences, where they can engage with others about injustices that they feel and see and seek to find a more ethical way to be. They are required to confront their own prejudices and assumptions about their LGBTQ peers when they interact with their lesbian friend and talk to other peers about their lesbian friend. Annabelle says, "We understood where he was coming from, though, because had we not known the person, the young lady, we would have probably said the same thing, too, you know, probably not in such a way, but we would have been thinking it, too." She clarifies that the relationship they had with their lesbian friend discredits the prejudicial and hurtful comments expressed by other students in their school. They empathize with her and have built a history with her, spent time with her and created memories with her. They know that what the boy says is not true about their friend, but might not have known that if they hadn't had a previous relationship with her.

New information about her reshapes Annabelle and Michele's perspectives and forces them to refashion who they are within the friendship. That friendship is the basis on which they can build the next phase of their relationship, which includes this friend and her girlfriend. The identity that inspires hatred or discomfort in some of their classmates is understood by Michele and Annabelle as an act by their friend to fashion her sexual self. As their perspective on their friend changes, they learn new information about her and gain a greater appreciation of her. Their new knowledge provides Annabelle and Michele the opportunity for greater intimacy among friends.

Finally, Annabelle especially sees herself as both a queer ally and as someone who flourishes within the unclear, liminal spaces between friendship, love, desire, and romance that emerge when strict moral guidelines about proper sexual behavior are loosened. She does not express a current desire to be "bi-experienced" but allows for the possibility that she has felt herself to be "curious" at times and is comfortable allowing herself to feel her desires and consider for herself the best way to act on them. When she asserts elsewhere in the conversation "I could say that I was part of [the curious] group at one time," Annabelle practices a care of the self in which she fashions herself as a sexual subject who explores her desires and examines her life to ethically choose how she presents her sexuality and gender and to choose with whom she forms relationships. She will support her friend through both the pursuit of her lesbian desires and as a desiring subject capable of managing her desires. In doing so, Annabelle experiences the pleasures of transgressing boundaries of knowledge that may emerge through access to her friend's experiences in a relationship with a woman, the multiplied notions of love and friendship, and other pleasures, not necessarily bodily, that come from her relations with her queer friends and in her fashioning of herself as an ethical subject. By accepting her friend's desire to be a lesbian and to reveal an intimate part of herself, Annabelle clears the way to explore the otherness within herself and her community. It is the personal self-fashioning or continual refashioning of oneself that can alter both the political and ethical landscape. It is, in short, where both change and freedom occur.

How does the straight friend ethically fashion herself? What are the aesthetics of being a friend/ally?

Fashioning one's self as an ally, however, is more than just a matter of choosing to be friends with someone or choosing to attend an after-school meeting. Foucault describes discourses that create the categories in which human activity can be known. The categorization of sexuality into heterosexual (normal) and homosexual (abnormal or pathologized) limits subjects' knowledge of themselves and their desires. It is impossible for a subject to know himself or herself except through the discursive lens of the era and the culture (Foucault, 1973a, 1973b, 1977, 1978). However, within discourse, the subject can resist various subjections and can push the boundaries of possible positions. One is limited by the economic, political, and social conditions of the time and place in which one lives, but within that time and place one has choices about acceding to or resisting sexual and gender regulation (Foucault, 1981/1997, 1986). Foucault is often misunderstood to say that the structures—the economic, political, and social conditions of the time—constitute endless power that leaves no way out. Although in Foucault subjects are always confined by history or discourses that compel us to act in certain ways and human agency cannot escape the discursive network, agency does allow us to challenge the discursive limits and react in ways that change the terms of the discourse to some extent.

Foucault asks the following questions: What part of oneself does one alter or mold to make a particular power move within a certain space? What are the ways that one is invited or encouraged to be a certain subject in a certain space, and how does one negotiate those ways? What practices, activities, or power moves does one engage to be perceived as a certain subject? What kind of being does one want to become, or what goal does one have for oneself, to be a certain subject, and what power-resistance moves does one need to make in the everyday to become that being?

Allies fashion themselves, then, as friends of LGBTQ peers by engaging in these types of activities to make ethical and aesthetic decisions about themselves. They are not completely autonomous in these decisions, however. They cannot make these decisions without measuring the consequences on their social lives, economic standing (parents' reactions, for example), or their political power, which may be affected by being labeled a troublemaker in school. Neither are the allies completely independent of or completely determined by institutional or social powers; instead what we find in Foucault is a negotiation between the subject and these limits. Students' negotiations of the various knowledges they have about sexuality and gender—the official knowledges of school and sex education and their own experiences of sexuality and gender and friendship—engage them in the contestations of power and knowledge that animate Foucault's work.

Students in these conversations engage power and knowledge intersections to redefine the heteronormative expectations of schools and their peers. They exert power in institutional relations where they might be presumed to be powerless, because they have freedom to negotiate the power relationships. As long as states of domination do not exist, alternative discourses are possible (Foucault, 1981/1997a). In the relationship between everyday knowledge and institutional, formal knowledge, students are able to hear the experiences of their peers; listen to their own experiences of friendship, relationships, and desire; and advocate on behalf of the common humanity and right to exist in the spaces of schools. Thus, within spaces of power/knowledge relationships, the subjects of this study exceed, transgress, and resist certain lines of being adolescent, and by doing so, they practice their various forms of freedom.

Conversation 2: Making claims for social justice and acceptance.

Omar: Yeah, my last words would be people just have to stop being ignorant, and people have to get educated, and people have to stop letting little barriers cut into other people, because the day that we start, you know, we stop justice, and we start, you know, accusing people and start condemning people and start hurting people and stop letting them be free and let them do what they want is the day we start the road to Auschwitz right there. All you need is one person that is hurt or one person that is killed, and they're gay, by someone who doesn't believe in anything they have to do, and you're possibly . . . you cause riots, and you're gonna cause hatred, and people just need to accept each other's difference.

Annabelle: ... but my last word is basically people need to realize the beauty in everybody, whether you're gay, lesbian, questioning, or straight. I think we all need to see that we all are individuals, and it's okay, and there's nothing wrong with that, and as soon as you realize that, then we wouldn't even know. We wouldn't even call it lesbian, gay, or straight. We'd call that's Omar, that's Michele, and I'm Annabelle, you know, and that's it.

Omar and Annabelle here both reiterate their ethical stance about being friends of LGBTQ students. Omar's ethical stance is a rebellious stance in which he makes claims about justice for all and accepting differences. He references the recent topic of a school lesson on Auschwitz and incorporates the stance on civil rights, equality, justice, and acceptance that are frequently themes in the after-school program's workshop. In attending these workshops and affiliating himself with this group, he is fashioning himself as a social justice activist. He focuses on his beliefs, and his reactions to both gay boys and lesbians in his school, as well as the ideas about gender roles and limitations that he experienced in his family, to grapple with and ethically challenge prejudice. These beliefs may have led him to fear or revile his friend who is a gay boy. Instead, Omar chooses to confront the expectations that prior experiences and teachings gave him and to stand with his friend "who started up [the GSA] . . . and getting funding and stuff."

Omar sees his friend's needs for intimacy as equal to his own and prejudice against his friend's sexuality as a denial of that human need. Omar is creating new spaces of freedom for straight boys in his school by standing up for his friend, speaking out unabashedly about nonheterosexual sexualities, attending the GSA meetings, and also playing on the football team. He crosses the borders that students often cannot transgress—those that keep normative masculinity and heterosexuality on one side and homosexuality on the other, abnormal and less-valued, side. In short, Omar's relationship with his friend and his teammates demonstrates that allies fashion a rebellious stance that is motivated by empathy, a sense of fairness, and a push to live in spaces of possibilities.

Annabelle reiterates a theme she had talked about with Michele earlier in the conversation. They both insisted that sexuality and gender norms, although "real" and consequential in social, political, and economic ways, are unimportant or minor differences between people. Here she returns to this assertion, making two important points. The first is that "we all are individuals, and it's okay, and there's nothing wrong with that," meaning that we all "do" love, sexuality, and gender in slightly different ways and in relation with others who bring their own expectations, desires, and interpretations to our interactions. Second, she thinks ideal or possible future identity understandings will not be dependent on sexuality or gender expression. Sexuality and gender expression, then, would not define how others would interact with her, nor would it reveal to others the truth about her character, her abilities, or her morality.

Annabelle acknowledged the risks of claiming an LGBTQ identity earlier in the conversation when she says, "Once you proclaim yourself anything that separates you from the 'crowd,' you pretty much—not—you're pretty much putting yourself up, I think." Annabelle is performing a sophisticated cultural analysis in this summary by holding simultaneously the risks that LGBTQ youth (and adults) confront when claiming these identities and in understanding that these categories are socially constructed. Even more, she acknowledges that differing valuations of the categories mask the multiplicities of differences among people in the ways they negotiate their friendship, love, and sex relationships. She thinks critically about religious teachings when she says, "I mean, doesn't that kind of contradict itself when society comes around and twists the Lord's words and try to impose it or make it fit to the world as we know it now?" She uses her own experiences and those of her friends, as well as the teachings of her church on sexuality and on what it means to be a Christian person, as the ethical substance in which she makes decisions about the "rightness" of relationships. She is concerned to nurture good relationships with her friends and to understand which desires for love and sexuality are right for her. Hence, a characteristic of being an ally is to understand and contest the complex social systems that are so pervasive in schools and society.

Becoming an Ally

Conversation 3: Speaking out against prejudice and ignorance.

Angela:	Well, in my school, we like raising money for stuff. And the other day, they decided to raise money for the AIDS walk. In order to raise money, you had to dress up like the opposite sex and you pay money, which I found it really—
Michael:	Offensive.
Angela:	— not to that part. But it didn't relate to AIDS. So it was just like, "Okay." But then the following day at school there was a big sign that said, "Drag Day for AIDS." It offended so many people; everyone in the classrooms was talking about it. And basically, the message that was it was getting across to everyone was that, "Oh, all drag queens are gay."
	So you had to pay to be a drag, and then you were supporting AIDS. So what are you trying to say, that all drag kings—not everyone that dresses up like someone is gay, and not every gay person has AIDS. There's a lot of heterosexual people that have AIDS. The majority, since basically my school was building up the stereotype that all gay people have AIDS only.
Darla:	And do drag.
Angela:	Yeah.
Darla:	Um-hum, interesting. So was there an interesting conversation about it at your school then?
Angela:	Yeah, my whole Spanish, an hour we were talking about it. There was a person that was dressed up and they was just like, "We were just trying raise money." I was like, "Well, you send the wrong message across. You should have supported and not try to offend people." They were, "We're not trying to offend. We're trying to raise money." I was like, "But by dressing up, you're basically saying that all drags are gay and they have AIDS."
Darla:	Uh huh, conflating the issues.
Angela:	Yeah, and they're building up on stereotype, which I knew if a drag would come in, they would have been highly offended by that.

Foucault asks: What part of oneself does one alter or mold to make a particular power move within a certain space? What are the ways that one is invited or encouraged to be a certain subject in a certain space, and how does one negotiate those ways? What practices, activities, or power moves does one engage in to be perceived as a certain subject? What kind of being does one want to become, or what goal does one have for oneself, to be a certain subject, and what power-resistance moves does one need to make in the everyday to become that being?

Angela speaks powerfully to these questions in the ways that she confronts the students working to raise money for AIDS about stereotyping. It is not enough that they want to do good for a population that they deem worthy of help. Angela demands that to be an ally, to be considered a person working for the cause of AIDS or LGBTQ youth or those who participate in drag, one needs to understand the issues. An ally will understand that these issues often get conflated—in sex education literature, in popular media, in social services—and will be careful not to reinforce misconceptions in their words or deeds. Her perspective on these issues and their parameters is far more sophisticated than institutional understandings often are.

Angela thinks of herself as an ally, but does not consider many of the students working on this campaign to be allies because they have not educated themselves on the issues, or they don't care enough about the populations that they are representing and purporting to help to understand the differences between them. Her goal is to be a person who can speak about gender and sexuality issues with compassion and with an understanding of the concerns of students with LGBTQ identities in her school. Angela works on her attitudes, her preconceptions, and her knowledge to correct misconceptions and speak with authority in locations where other voices might be silenced. She accepts the responsibility of educating others with the knowledge that she has gained. She uses her power and knowledge to dismantle ignorance in her school. This characteristic of being an ally—to interrupt shallow or simplistic perspectives of LGBTQ persons and to speak out about the issues to her peers—is one that Angela strongly exhibits.

What do joint LGBTQ and straight ally spaces in schools allow students to do?

Conversation 4: Naming and creating spaces for queerness in schools.

Angela: I guess some part of my school they put a big impression that they do the day of silence, and a lot of people do it. But some people just do it, just not to talk—they don't feel like answering questions to teachers. But some people will be like, "Oh, I really am, like, I'm for the cause." . . . Yeah, I guess, like, stop, like, the derogatory terms that they use towards fags. I guess I would change that . . . I would definitely change the fag terms and the lesbian terms that people say to each other. Take accountable that people get offended by that.

Michael: [I'd change] a lot of things. *(Laughter)*

Darla: Go ahead. Make a list, Michael. *(Laughter)*

Michael: Well, I would like people in my school to be—'cause in [my school] people are slackers, and you know that's true . . . But in my school, we would set standards. 'Cause I'm part of SIA. That's like student government. We would set standards, but then nobody would be so committed to it that it would go through. So definitely more commitment so there can be like a gay/straight alliance at my school. But even if there was one, I don't think that many people would go. Just to the fact that nobody wants to be considered gay if they go there, 'cause they would lose their reputation in the school. I don't know. Right now the people that I hang—out of all my friends, I'm the only gay one. And I have a lot of friends and they're all straight. I'm the only gay one. So it would be cool if I found somebody gay, a guy that I could relate to. But it's not gonna happen any time soon.

Spaces in schools that provide opportunities for LGBTQ and straight youth to discuss issues of sexuality and gender may offer students a chance to make ethical decisions about becoming allies of LGBTQ youth. Through advocacy work in the school among teachers and students, straight and LGBTQ youth members of the GSA work to transform attitudes about sexuality and gender among the wider community of the school. This work in turn has been shown to make the school a safer environment for all students, regardless of their gender identity or sexuality (Gay Lesbian and Straight Education Network [GLSEN], 2005).

In the conversation above, Angela and Michael point out some of the different functions that GSAs can serve in schools for LGBTQ youth and for the larger school population. Their comments indicate both positive and negative effects that a GSA could have in their schools. In Angela's case, she is speaking about an existing club and what she has seen happen as a result of its existence. This club functions not just as a social or support group for students who identify as LGBTQ, but also as an advocacy group for change within the school (Miceli, 2005). Because of the group's political activities—the Day of Silence, LGBT History Month, and No Name Calling Week—it is very visible and involves more students in its activities than are official members of the club.

Some of the students who get involved in the advocacy campaigns really believe in the changes advocated by the GSA and participate to show their solidarity with the GSA members. Others, however, "just do it, just not to talk—they don't feel like answering questions to teachers." Angela observes that some students' ideas and attitudes are not changed by the advocacy work of the GSA, they just go along with the action for the excitement and disruption that it brings to the school day. So although the school is generally a positive environment for LGBTQ youth and is characterized as very open, very tolerant, and safe for all students by Angela, she still observes students who do not believe in the model of acceptance and the social change put forth by the activist members of the GSAs.

In Michael's comments, we see a more reserved expectation about what a GSA could accomplish in his school. Michael would welcome the social aspect of the club, the opportunity it would provide to meet another gay boy with whom he could share experiences and who he "could relate to." Although he is not certain that the GSA could offer that kind of social and support experience, he would value such a result. He does not feel that kind of support in his current social network and tenuously holds an expectation that providing the space in his school might provide opportunities for connections he seeks. All of his friends at school are straight, and Michael expresses his dismay at the kind of censoring of his own speech that happens in order not to alienate his friends. He states, "Yeah, 'cause you don't want to give off that—I don't want to give the other person, 'Oh yeah. Don't say this and this and this,' 'cause I'm that. So I think that they're gonna feel like, 'Oh, we can't say these things around him, so let's just not even hang out with him.'" A supportive space like a GSA would provide him the opportunity to be as unguarded in his speech as he imagines his friends to be and a place to protest the language and actions of others. It would be a space in which to seek empathetic listeners who understand his point of view and who do not think he is asking too much when he asks his friends not to speak disparagingly about LGBTQ persons in his presence, or at all.

Michael is skeptical about the value of a GSA to change the overall acceptance level of the school for LGBTQ youth or its ability to produce allies among the non-LGBTQ population of the school. He acknowledges that this productive capacity works in Angela's school, but he is afraid that the strong homophobic tendencies in his school would keep students from joining the group as allies, because of the worry they would "lose their reputation." What appears as apathy elsewhere in his descriptions of his school might be described in this situation as the inertia of heterosexism that would prohibit heterosexual students from challenging the taken-for-granted superiority and advantage of heterosexuality. Michael imagines that most students in his school will not be able to make the rebellious stance of Omar or the informed stance of Angela to fashion themselves as allies. He claims, "I think the unsafe space is school. The safe space is out of school to me." For Michael, the changes he can envision for his school do not mitigate the overwhelming sense of heteronormativity that he feels pervades most students' attitudes.

Like Michael, Mary Louise Rasmussen (2006) expresses some doubt about the good that GSAs and other clubs might provide to LGBTQ students in schools. She describes spaces in schools that are defined as serving LGBTQ students and as for LGBTQ students as *heterotopic* (Foucault & Miskowiec, 1986) in Foucault's terminology. By *heterotopic*, Foucault means these are spaces of "deviation" (p. 25), where those who are not considered normal are placed by society. Foucault cites prisons and psychiatric hospitals as examples. An example of heterotopic space in schools is one to which a person is relegated involuntarily or to which it looks like there is free and voluntary entrance, but certain rules or codes must be followed to be allowed to be there. The space, which seems like an entrance, is itself an exclusion (Rasmussen, 2006).

In Rasmussen's description, this heterotopia could include LGBTQ students being excluded from spaces in schools even without declaring themselves LGBTQ, based on the assumptions that other students make about them. Also, students who are nonheterosexual and nongender-conforming but who do not conform to the standards of lesbian, gay, bisexual, transgender, or queer identities may be excluded from the spaces that are created by schools to protect them. As GLSEN materials state, being inclusive of bisexual and transgender students requires more than adding those words to the banner. Bi and trans students (and adults) often feel left out of lesbian and gay organizations. Additionally, school administrators or teachers who decide that LGBTQ students are a "disruption" to the order or discipline of the school or that queer students' behavior is "inappropriate" or puts them in danger may choose to remove the student to a more safe environment. This kind of "safety transfer," which Rasmussen mentions and which students may experience in New York City high schools, abdicates responsibility for addressing heterosexism in the schools and removes the student against whom malice or violence is directed. LGBTQ students are then quietly excluded from their regular schools in the name of their "protection." The political moves based on identity that gain students "safe spaces" in schools also work to control their gender expression and sexuality and to confine them to certain understandings of their desires and their subjectivities.

One argument against these spatial identity labels in schools is that they enforce an essential definition on the sexuality of students. In other words, there is an assumption that students who are LGBTQ are different in a way that they cannot change—they are born that way or otherwise essentially gay and Other. The qualification for protection by schools from harassment, bullying, and name-calling often requires that students must claim the "naturalness" of their queerness. Frequently the LGBTQ community is charged with demanding a label as well, not trusting someone who is experimenting, unwilling to call himself gay, or moving between categories. Schools reflect this prejudice, dismissing student desires as either displays of inappropriate or deviant sexuality or inevitable and something that the student cannot help being. LGBTQ students must be served by the school in some way, but in the current structure, the deviance and pathology become located in the body of the student, not in the school or the heterosexual students. Thus, heterotopic spaces also fail to counter the heterosexism in schools. They leave intact the construction of heterosexual as normal and homosexual as deviant other. The problem is identified, and if it cannot be concealed or normalized by the LGBTQ students, then the student is removed from sight for her inappropriate behavior. Although school boards and administrations have embraced GSAs as the answer to the problems of harassment and homophobia, LGBTQ students and their allies encourage us to look more closely at the attitudes and behaviors of all students when seeking to increase acceptance and integration of nonheterosexual and nongender-conforming youth.

Conclusion: Who Is an Ally?

Many definitions of *allies* and *friends* emerge from these conversations, together with a range of attitudes and activism that students use to represent what they mean by these terms. In fact, students do not use the term *ally* to speak of themselves or others in their schools. It is a term from the GSA literature that we have imposed on their conversations. We think it fits and is more precise for the experiences they are describing than the more ambiguous term *friend*. But within students' language is the possibility for a friend to be an educated activist who speaks out for LGBTQ students' rights in schools and also for the friend who agrees not to use the term *fag* in the presence of his gay friend and to remain loyal after it becomes public knowledge that his friend is gay. This latter stance may appear very passive on the spectrum of allies' attitudes, but it may be a profoundly courageous stance within the social and political climate of the school.

If we follow Foucault's thinking on power and knowledge, we can see that there is not one universal definition of a good ally or friend that can be imposed on every situation. Every relationship is a negotiation of power, a request that needs be met, an acquiescence to desires of self and other, an interaction that takes place within the structures that set limits on the roles that each person plays. So, too, in the relations of allies and LGBTQ students is a give and take of power, a negotiation of how much each person will bend to stay in the friendship, and a recognition of the larger social, political, and economic forces that bear on each of the participants.

These conversations provide us with several different examples of fashioning oneself as an ally. There are friends who change their own definitions of relationship, friendship, and love. Michele and Annabelle refashion the parameters of their friendship with their friend who comes out as a lesbian by changing their language and expectations about her attractions and love interests to include "her" as well as "him." Additionally, Annabelle examines her own choices and agency to understand her own desires. She engages in a critical dialogue with both her church and her culture about right and wrong in terms of love and sexuality. Michele and Annabelle use their knowledge of their friend and their friendship to reexamine previous ideas and fashion ethical selves both as friends and as sexual selves in their own love relationships.

In another instance, we see a rebellious stance that pushes back the boundaries of heteronormative masculinity. Omar engages in locker-room banter and behavior with his teammates in a space in which he judges it difficult or impossible for queerness to exist in his school. At the same time, he is not bound by that hypermasculine and homophobic culture and can also move in the spaces of the gay-straight alliance, working with his friend to secure funding and promote the club among both LGBTQ and straight students. Omar rebels against limitations that he finds contrary to his desire to continue a friendship with a gay boy. Although he does not claim to be experimenting with his own sexuality, he is making discursive space for himself and others to try on sexuality to see what fits best.

There are also friends that demand an educated and activist ally stance. Angela is most vocal about delimiting between those who are really allies—informed, intentional, and outspoken—and those who are just going along because it is the socially acceptable thing in their school. She makes many demands on potential allies: that they understand the context of the activism they undertake, that they be sensitive to the language used by the LGBTQ community about itself, and that they speak out to their peers to correct misperceptions about LGBTQ people. She pushes the rest of the focus group to demand more of their peers and to ask for more justice for LGBTQ youth in their schools. She believes that speaking out about these issues will contribute to a better school atmosphere for all students and that student activism is necessary to change the school climate. Angela deploys her knowledge as power to disrupt stereotypes and misconceptions and to push for justice.

Foucault's analysis of power involves looking at the day-to-day interactions of individuals on the personal, relational level. Although Foucault did not provide a method to practice freedom, what we learn from these students is that, as one practices being an ally, one is practicing freedom not just for oneself but for everyone else as well. This is precisely how Foucault can be useful. School administrators and teachers can create spaces where these practices of freedom can take place. Classrooms where teachers present information about nonnormative gender identities and diverse sexualities, where varied and multicultural nonheterosexual lives are portrayed—in literature, history, and science, as well as sex education—provide spaces for students to become educated about LGBTQ issues. These are places where the voices of contemporary LGBTQ activists can be heard and current debates about identity can be reviewed—not to ossify these identities and arguments or to present the "correct" information, but to give the bodies struggling with these identities and desires a little breathing room in the classroom. Actions and conversations that include LGBTQ voices and issues can make students feel that they are legitimate participants in the school setting. As part of the educational mission to teach students how to participate in a democratic society, school administrators and teachers must create opportunities for both those who would be oppressors to examine their privilege and those who would be oppressed to express themselves and see themselves represented in positive ways. Including opportunities for students to be allies across differences in sexuality and gender expression works to fulfill that mission.

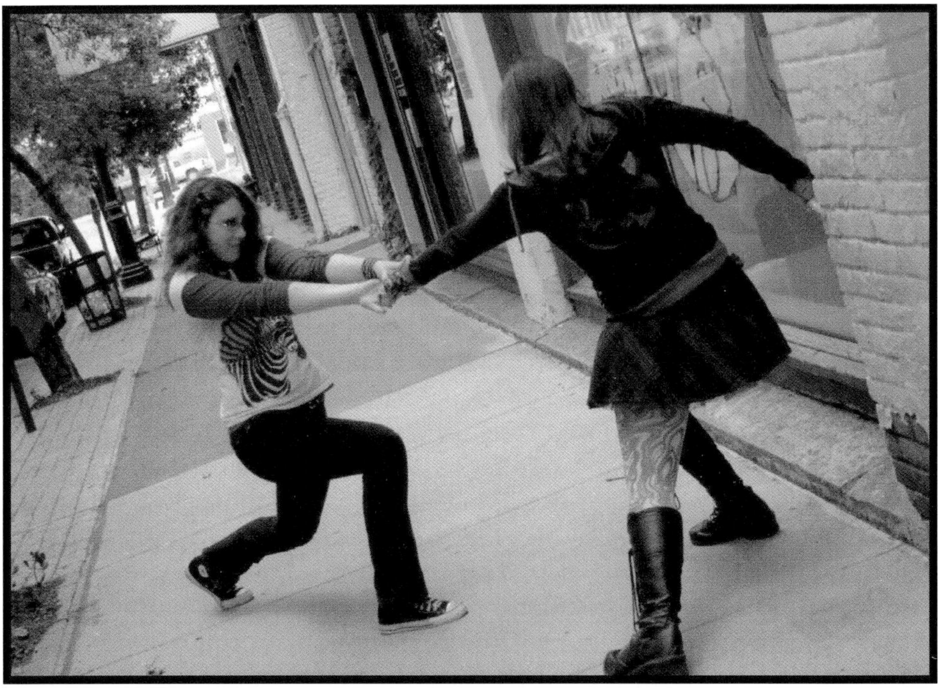

Chapter Four

Attitudinal Ambivalence in the Developmental Contexts of LGB Adolescents

Sean G. Massey

THE QUESTION OF whether and to what extent there has been progress in combating antihomosexual prejudice is discussed throughout this volume and reflects a debate that extends throughout public opinion research (Correl, 1999) and gay and lesbian psychology. The work of scholars such as Herek (2000, 2003), Herek and Capitanio (1996), Meyer (2003), D'Augelli (1998), and others illuminates the prevalence and consequences of the victimization of lesbian, gay, bisexual, and transgendered (LGBT) youth. More recently, however, scholars such as Savin-Williams (2005) have argued that these discussions seriously exaggerate the negative experiences of LGBT youth, and that these youth are faring far better than they have in past and better than predicted by current scholars in the field.

Many of the claims made from both sides of these debates, were based on findings gathered through the use of case and focus group methodologies or studies of predominantly adult samples. Idiographic approaches are valuable in that they allow for the voices of participants to be heard in ways and in more detail than would be possible through the use of a more nomothetic approach. It is also true that adult samples can provide clues into the possible experiences of youth. However, neither approach allows for a conclusive answer to the question: Which is it, progress or marginalization?

For example, from his many interviews with gay youth from around the country, Savin-Williams argues that most are doing quite well and are not experiencing the hostile and violent moments described by the bulk of gay-affirmative scholars. However, other data, including some collected by the author of this chapter, suggest that many LGBT youth continue to experience the soul-killing isolation, judgments from family, ostracization from peers, lack of resources and attention from teachers and institutions, lack of educational opportunities, and lack of materials that adequately describe their lives (D'Augelli, 1998; Bochenek & Brown, 2001; D'Augelli, Hershberger, & Pilkington, 2001; Bertram & Massey, 2007; Cooper-Nichols & Bowleg, this book; Joyce, O'Neil, & McWhirter, this book). The existence of these counter stories does not mean that youth aren't also thriving as Savin-Williams suggests, but it does make the point that there is work still to be done.

As has been pointed out elsewhere, the particular developmental challenges facing adolescents cut across a number of different life domains, but the search for identity and self-understanding is a dominant theme for many youth (Graber & Archibald, 2001). For LGBT youth, the identity issues shared with heterosexual youth are compounded by issues of developing a sexual identity in the face of a heterosexist world—albeit one that has changed dramatically over the past half-century since the beginning of the modern gay liberation movement, but one that nevertheless still presents LBGT youth with many of the challenges described above.

The task of gay identity formation has been described and critiqued elsewhere (Troiden, 1979, 1989; Cass, 1979; Rotheram-Borus & Langabeer, 2001). The goal of this chapter is not to reexamine these models or to question the notion that progress has been made. What it will do, however, is to offer a set of examples, drawn from stories collected by the author for journalistic purposes, that paints a particular picture of the challenges these youth face living in a relatively progressive city in Central Texas and in a more conservative town in Upstate New York. These stories describe a context of growing support *and* continued hostility, a social world in which sexual prejudice is both personal and institutional, and a place where the possibility of anti-gay violence is still a cause for unease. These stories will be followed by an exploration of anti-homosexual prejudice research and a new conceptualization of anti-homosexual prejudice that allows for a more nuanced assessment of the increasingly ambivalent context of LGB adolescent lives. As part of this discussion, a new multidimensional measure, created by the author, will be presented that not only allows the possibility of ambivalent attitudes, but also operationalizes positive attitudes.

Could It Happen Here?

While working parttime as a freelance journalist for the major local daily newspaper in Austin, Texas, a city of approximately 1.2 million people, I had the opportunity to collaborate with a longtime friend and colleague on the first major study of quality of life and feelings of safety and satisfaction for LGB residents. This collaboration raised a number of provocative questions about the similarities and differences between social science research and journalism—a set of questions discussed in more detail elsewhere (Massey, under review).

One of the projects that resulted from this venture into journalism was our work on focus group reactions to a local production of *The Laramie Project*, a play created by the Tectonic Theater Company that chronicled the reaction of residents of Laramie, Wyoming, to the murder of gay college student Matthew Shepard (Massey, 2002). The newspaper had arranged for a group of high school students and a group of adults to watch the play and participate afterward in a series of focus group discussions. The discussions were initiated by a set of questions adapted from remarks made by residents of Laramie, Wyoming, claiming that the sort of violence demonstrated in the murder of Shepard couldn't happen in a town like Laramie. Each group was asked, "Could this sort of thing happen here [in Austin]? Are we that sort of people?"

Reactions to this question ranged from diagnosing Shepard's murderers, Aaron McKinney and Russell Henderson, as sociopaths to blaming the homophobic social context surrounding those involved in the incident. The Austin participants described both the progressive nature of the town and yet an ongoing possibility of anti-gay violence and hostility.

Patrick (17, white male): Hate is just a completely natural human emotion. It's a pretty crappy one and there is nothing you can do to change it. It's always going to be in [your] range of emotions and the best thing you can do is try to fight it.

David (17, Latino): Growing up as a little kid, you are taught to hate certain types of people, and it goes on throughout life. But it starts when you are a kid.

Helena (17, white female): You can't really compare Austin to any other city. Especially in Texas because it's such a melting pot. The community is an accepting, nurturing, free-spirited type of place. So it's really not like any other town.

Jackson (19, white male): That's what we want to think. I would say on a daily basis I encounter at least a little bit of homophobia. I think it could easily happen in Austin. If you have x-amount of homophobia, and have a mix of circumstances, why not?

Patrick: I was on the [main] drag the other night and I saw two men holding hands. It was perfectly fine over there. But that's a more accepting side of town than where I'm from. I think it totally depends on what side of town you are on.

When asked about their educational institutions, members of both groups described their high school as a place where gay and lesbian youth are continually teased and hassled.

Helena: You couldn't really be openly gay at [my high school]. I mean a lot of people would be comfortable with it, but there are teenagers who would be so turned off by things that cause them to question their own image and the person they are trying to be.

One of the adult participants, Dana (40, female massage therapist), described her observations of ongoing harassment of a variety of youth and an unwillingness of teachers and administrators to intervene: "I do a lot of work in a local high school. And this is a good, blue-ribbon school. I see girls being sexually harassed, grabbed. I see weaker smaller boys being picked on and harassed in front of teachers, physically threatened. Teachers don't do anything. They just say, 'kids are going to be kids.' And if you teach that to people, that's the most basic intolerance."

> Helena: We all sound like disillusioned youth. We all hope in this room that we can change, that we can see Billy Bob turn into a really cool, understanding guy. But as kids we've seen things day to day, we see that kind of stuff every day and that stuff affects us, and sometimes we think the future is full of crap. But we do have faith.
>
> T.J. (17, white male): I guess I'm an idealist. I think we can make a difference. We've come a long way. We're never going to have a totally egalitarian society, but we might come close. We always have something to work toward.

Most students thought viewing the play and discussing its implications were helpful. One student, David (17, Latino), who was a self-identified "homophobic," suggested that watching the play and participating in the discussion afterward made a difference in how he thought about things.

> I want to say some things so you get the homophobic viewpoint on things. It seems like the terms people use, you know, "that's so gay!" (in a derogatory tone) and stuff, that hurts them more than I realized. I use that word far more than I should. I really took from this that that hurts people and I really shouldn't do it.

Throughout these interviews, participants described both the town and schools as risky places for LGBT youth. Schools were sites of anti-gay harassment, and some teachers had failed to provide the sorts of protection and support these youth had come to expect. In some areas in this progressive town, gay people could hold hands and walk together without fear; yet in other areas, the risk of doing so was clear. The message provided by these insiders did indeed suggest that progress had occurred and that there was hope for positive change. At the same time, however, these youth were clearly aware that risks remained and that the threat of violence and harassment was very real for LGBT youth.

Discussions with an LGBT Youth Group

A second collaborative project involved a large-scale survey published in the local newspaper that explored the local LGBT community's feelings of satisfaction and safety in Austin, as well as the heterosexual community's attitudes toward their LGBT neighbors (Barnes & Massey, 2001). The results of this survey were analyzed together with the findings from a series of face-to-face views and focus groups with local residents discussing their experiences living in Austin. One such interview was conducted with a group of gay and lesbian youth at a local organization that offered support, education, and social opportunities for LGBT youth. The interview centered around the 2003 *Lawrence v. Texas* decision by the U.S. Supreme Court decriminalizing sodomy throughout the country. Texas was one of the states that had a specifically anti-gay sodomy law on the books, and the state had a reputation for enforcing the law from time to time. Again, the youth interviewed highlighted both the progress and the challenges they continue to face.

> Steven (18, white male): I saw [the U.S. Supreme Court ruling] on MSNBC . . . on TV. I called [the support organization] to find out if it was true. I expected it, but I didn't believe it when I heard it. I had shivers when I heard—I didn't know what to do. I had goose bumps. I had to run around the entire apartment. I didn't know who to call.
>
> Susie (15, white female): I thought, "I'm LEGAL!" Called my friends . . . I was at my father's house, so I ran around . . . I saw it on TV . . . I had to be all normal with them. Then I ran down and called my friends. I was ecstatic. I'd never felt happier. I was jumping up and down. That day couldn't get any better. Nothing bad would ruin my day!
>
> Franklin (15, white male): I was sitting down playing video games. I got a call from a friend from [the support organization] who said, "Gay sex is legal!" I called Susie to confirm it. I was happy, because I want to go into the air force. It's going to make it better for the government. It'll make it better in the military. It's going to take away the "Don't Ask Don't Tell" policy. It made me really happy!

When asked how the sodomy laws had influenced their lives, each saw the law as affecting their lives both directly and indirectly:

> Steven: The people who hate gays, all the anti-gay laws just give them a reason to do it.
>
> Susie: Yeah, it gives them a reason.

Attitudinal Ambivalence 117

> Franklin: I was just pissed off. If straight people can have sex, why can't I have it? How can there be a law that can say something about the privacy of your own home?
>
> Susie: It's no one's business!
>
> Franklin: How are they going to enforce this anyway?
>
> Susie: Yeah, but that got me paranoid. Like, if you go on a date, someone is going to call the cops.
>
> Steven: How can they keep you from making love to the one you are in love with? In high school, they said being gay is wrong—athletes, the Christian people, even the school principal. I wanted to start the gay/straight alliance in school. She hated the fact that I was trying to start a group. She told me that . . . that she was disgusted with my lifestyle. I got sponsors for the club. But by the time it got started she said it was too late and that I had to wait until next year. But I graduated!
>
> Susie: It was like—I can't walk down the hall with my best friend without someone saying something. Eventually I just said yeah to try to get them off our backs. But it just got worse.
>
> Franklin: I had trouble with people using the Bible against me. I'm not really out. But the word got out anyway. A lot of people thought I was. Now that I'm letting people in, they're saying, "That's wrong!," using the Bible.

These youth described the *Lawrence v. Texas* decision by the U.S. Supreme Court as a remarkable achievement, and one that had positive implications for their lives. They demonstrated a remarkable understanding of the far-reaching implications of the previous sodomy laws and the benefits of limitations of the ruling.

> Franklin: [The sodomy ruling] will make a little difference here, but a big difference nationally. Yeah, it's legal now, but they didn't do anything with it before.
>
> Susie: I think it will make a big difference here because this is the capital; this is where the bills are passed. But I agree that it will make a bigger difference nationally. There are two sides. Sometimes you got both people who are supportive and people who are not because Austin is very diverse. My close friends who I hang out with are great about it [according to Susie there are about 2000 students in her high school], but other people are not.

Franklin: I think it is going to make people who are for gay marriage more active and it will make the folks who are opposed more active too. Austin is way good. Austin is great. The city I'm from, they didn't have [a support group] or anything like this. Everybody here seems to be more accepting than where I'm from.

Steven: I went to a rural school right outside of Austin. There were about 400 people in my high school. Very closed-minded people. Most of the teachers were very supportive, but the principal and many of the students were not—in a big way!

The attitudinal context that these youth describe ranges from supportive to hostile. They are aware that there is a need for cautious optimism and strategic choices regarding when to come out, who to talk to, and a dependence on a community of supportive friends. When asked what was next, what was left to do, these youth outlined a number of areas where work was still needed.

Franklin: I think it should be illegal for kids in our schools to discriminate against ethnicity or sexual orientation. And gender identity too—if a chick wants to be called him or dude—if they specifically want to be called that, they should.

Steven: I can't believe that they let sex come before marriage. All these people are so morally high—and they said go out there and have sex but don't get married! And you can still get fired from your job because we are gay. I know someone . . .

Franklin: I would like to get legally married. If I come out, the military would have a problem with that. I want to join the air force.

Adolescence and Attitude Functions

The interviews summarized above describe a developmental context full of ambivalent messages. Positive changes have occurred: homosexuality has been decriminalized, support groups and GSAs are available to many, and gay marriage and military service are both possibilities that are within their imagined futures. At the same time, schools still allow anti-gay bullying and harassment to continue, parents are not seen as allies, and experiencing anti-gay violence on the streets is still a possibility. These changes, and the issues resistant to change, suggest that the social world in which these youth are developing is dramatically inconsistent.

The measures that social psychologists have traditionally had available to assess public opinion of lesbian and gay youth (Herek, 1984; Kite & Deaux, 1986) are limited to a unidimensional view of antihomosexual prejudice, that is, one that does not consider ambivalent attitudes. Herek's (1984) Attitudes Toward Lesbians and Gay Men (ATLG) Scale assesses prejudice ranging from overt hostility to benign tolerance. But the notion that attitudes can be multidimensional or can extend beyond tolerance to acceptance, and even valuing, has not been adequately operationalized by these existing measures (Massey, 2009).

This section of the chapter will offer theoretical support for the idea of a multidimensional measure of antihomosexual prejudice and will review literature that explores antihomosexual prejudice among adolescents. Finally, it will discuss a new multidimensional measure, created by the author, that not only allows the possibility of ambivalent attitudes, but also operationalizes potentially positive attitudes.

Herek (1986, 1987) introduced the first formal theory connecting heterosexuals' attitudes toward gay men and lesbians to the earlier functionalist attitude theories of Katz (1960). In his neofunctional approach to attitudes, Herek suggested that attitudes serve experiential-schematic, ego-defensive, social-expressive and value-expressive functions. Through a series of studies with undergraduates, Herek (1987) demonstrated that participants' evaluations of gay men and lesbians were based on several different factors, including previous experiences or interactions with gay and lesbian people (experiential-schematic), feelings of revulsion or disgust (ego-defensive), concerns about the opinions and respect of others (social-expressive), and the need to express their beliefs and core values (value-expressive).

Most existing unidimensional measures of antihomosexual prejudice, however, do not allow for the exploration of distinct influence of these separate functions (Hegarty & Massey, 2006; Massey, 2009). This limitation has implications for predicting potential attitudinal changes and limits the possibility of assessing attitudinal ambivalence in adolescence. Whereas attitudes serving either a value-expressive and ego-defensive function are considered fairly immutable and resistant to intervention, attitudes serving experiential or social-expressive functions have been found to be more flexible.

As has been stated earlier, adolescence represents a time of intense awareness of one's social status and growing concern about one's place in relationship to peers and others outside of one's family (Graber & Archibald, 2005). This period of growth likely results in increasing attention to the social-expressive and value-expressive functions served by the attitudes one holds.

Although a wealth of research dating back to the 1960s assessing the prevalence and correlates of antihomosexual prejudice exists within the social psychological literature (Wallace, Peters, & Morgan, 1967; Dunbar, Brown, & Amoroso, 1973; Kite, 1994; Herek, 1987, 1988, 1994; Herek & Capitanio, 1999; Herek & Glunt, 1993), most has been collected on college-age students and very little explores the attitudes of younger adolescents (Horn, 2006). This absence is perplexing given the amount of research, discussed earlier in this chapter and by other authors in this book, identifying the challenges faced by high-school–aged LGBT youth and the potential negative consequences of experiencing these challenges at this time in human development.

Horn (2006) conducted a study that explored the attitudes toward homosexuality of 10th graders, 12th graders, and college-aged youth from the midwestern United States. Students completed a self-report questionnaire that assessed their beliefs and attitudes about gay and lesbian students, their comfort interacting with gay and lesbian students, and their feelings about how gay and lesbian students are treated in their school. Overall, students' attitudes and the subsequent indications of behaviors were more favorable than expected. Differences were found in the predicted direction regarding the age of respondents, with younger adolescent respondents expressing greater levels of prejudice than older adolescents. Horn found that younger adolescents (10th graders) were more uncomfortable interacting with gay people than the older ones (12th graders and college students). Similarly, 10th graders were more likely than were 12th graders and college students to judge the exclusion of same-gendered gay or lesbian peers as acceptable behavior. The reason given for the discrimination was that it affirmed social norms. At the same time, age differences were not found for the belief that homosexuality was morally wrong. Horn points out that social cognitive developmental research (Fishbein, 2002) suggests that prejudice increases during middle adolescence because of the social cognitive limitations of that age. Across all groups, boys were more averse than girls were.

Horn ends with a call for further research exploring the developmental shifts in attitudes toward gay men and lesbians. She also argues for the use of multiple measures to better assess the complexity and corresponding independent shifts in attitudes from early adolescence to emerging adulthood.

Polymorphous Prejudice: A Multidimensional Measure

The growing complexity in social and political discourse around the status of sexual minorities, as discussed in the interviews presented earlier in this chapter and as suggested by the findings in Horn's study, underscores the need for new psychometric approaches that assess the multiple facets of sexual prejudice. In addition, because current research focuses almost exclusively on the prevalence of prejudicial attitudes or the willingness to interact with gay or lesbian peers, it fails to consider the implications of progress that has been made, the growing number of positive images of same-sex sexuality, and the availability of favorable representations of gay and lesbian lives.

Research by this author has found not only that attitudes are multidimensional, but also that it is possible and useful to assess attitudinal variance beyond simple tolerance, to include favorable and even positive beliefs about gay men and lesbians in our measures (Massey, 2009). A 7-factor model was developed to assess heterosexuals' attitudes and beliefs about gay men and lesbians. The measure includes the following factors:

- Traditional Heterosexism: the likelihood to see gay people as immoral, sinful, or perverted and the belief that they should be denied certain rights and privileges

- Denial of Continued Discrimination: the belief that discrimination against gay people is no longer a problem, that gay people have equal opportunities for advancement, and that claims of discrimination are unwarranted
- Aversion Toward Gay Men and Lesbians: an affective reaction including the need to avoid contact, discomfort with possible contact, and criticisms of gender performance
- Value Gay Progress: a belief grounded in pro-diversity values, such as the belief that the accomplishments of the gay movement enhance society or that homosexuality represents a special quality that should be encouraged
- Resist Heteronormativity: a feeling of discomfort with traditional ascribed sex and gender roles and behaviors, the need to resist them, the belief that sex and gender transcend a simple binary definition, and an awareness of and discomfort with the privileges that come from being heterosexual in heteronormative world
- Positive Beliefs: the endorsement of a variety of positive characteristics or unique insights that are a consequence of either being gay or lesbian or being positioned on the margins of heteronormative society

Unidimensional measures of sexual prejudice (such as Herek's ATLG) that assess attitudes along a hostile-tolerance dimension seem to best explain the dimension of moral condemnation of sexual prejudice. As Horn's findings suggest, traditional heterosexism may be the least reactant to developmental attitudinal shifts. Attitudinal measures that tap into feelings of aversion may be more susceptible to emerging gender role conflicts and the social-expressive needs of adolescents.

It is also possible that the Value Gay Progress, Resist Heteronormativity, and Positive Beliefs subscales, which account for favorable evaluations of gay men and lesbians, will be able to provide additional insight into the complexity of adolescent attitudes. Adolescents may be willing to express pro-diversity values and praise the accomplishments of the gay and lesbian movements. Some may see these accomplishments as enhancing society. Others may be critical of the expectation of heterosexual society, may resist traditional ascribed sex and gender roles and behaviors, and/or may believe that sex and gender are fluid concepts with which one can be playful. It is also likely that many will associate a variety of positive characteristics with gay men or lesbians and see this group as having something valuable to offer.

Conclusion

The stories the youth in this chapter tell are stories of hopeful progress and, at the same time, a continued awareness that their lives are filled with encounters with heterosexism and antihomosexual prejudice. Hope comes from significant advances that have been made in terms of depathologizing and decriminalizing homosexuality, advances that have been made in terms of civil rights and family law, and progress that can be seen in the affirming policies and curricula that are available in some schools. Cynicism, however, is also understandable. Although the media has filled a previous vacuum with images of LGBT lives, it has not always been in useful and positive ways. Negative messages are also present and come from peers, school administrators, parents, and a society in which institutionalized heterosexism continues in the armed forces and employment protections, and in marriage and family laws that are allowed to vary from state to state.

Many of these youth demonstrate a willingness to confront these injustices and are resilient to the challenges they face. Some would argue that researchers, educators, and other human services professionals have overstated the challenges faced by LGBT youth. However, as the words of the youth in this chapter point out, the need is still there. Hearing only the stories of progress could have potentially devastating consequences for ongoing advocacy projects, the development of school-based programming, and public policy and funding decisions related to LGBT youth. Educators, counselors, and other youth advocates must continue to listen closely to both the messages of progress and the messages of marginalization.

Researchers must partner in this effort with their education and human services colleagues. The theories and instruments researchers develop constrain the sorts of questions that can be asked and the tools available to understand what we observe. Qualitative methods tell us that LBGT youth are powerful examples of resilience and thriving. These youth are aware that progress has been made, and yet, they continue to encounter ongoing heterosexism. Sometimes the differences they experience are a matter of what they are doing, whom they are talking with, or where they live. Looking for attitudinal shifts along a single hostile-tolerant dimension will ultimately obscure the complexity that exists. More subtle measures must be created allowing researchers to fine-tune our ability to assess the attitudinal ambivalence defining the context in which LGBT adolescents are living and developing.

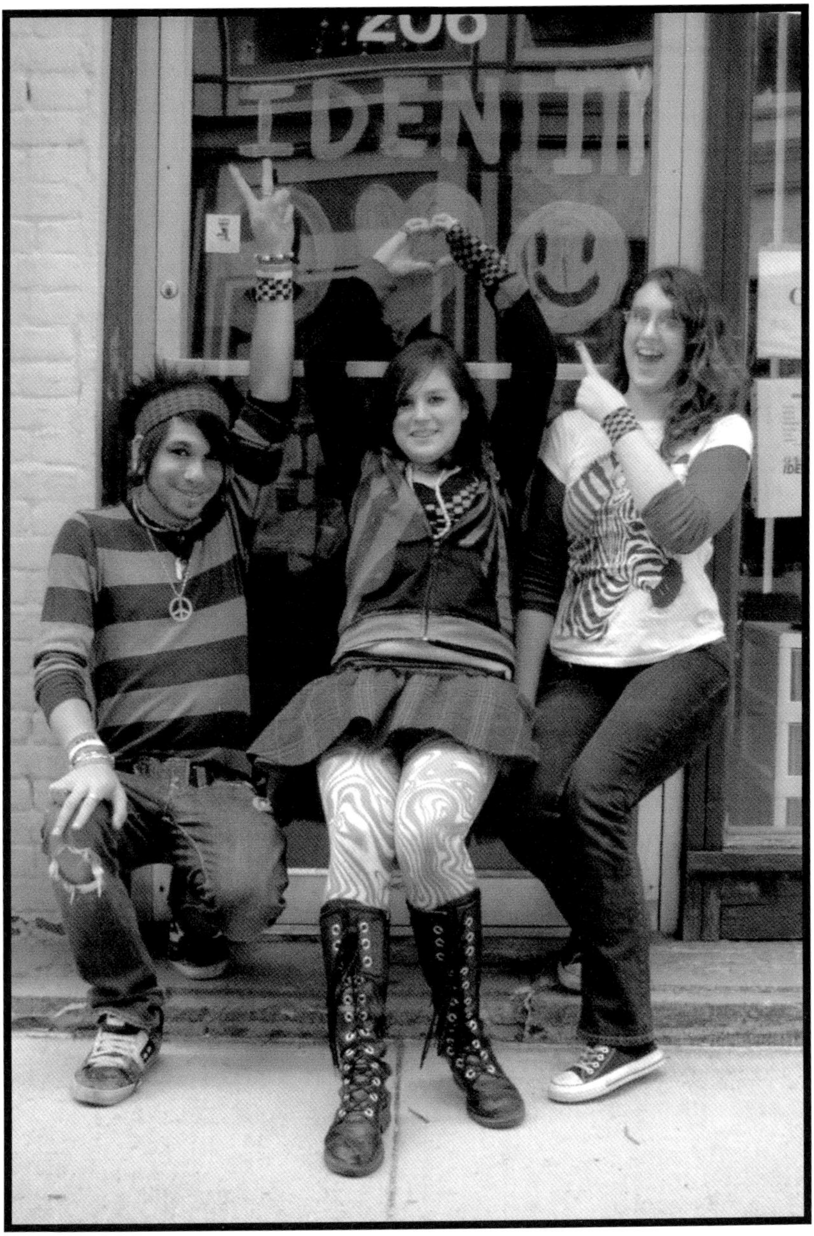

Chapter Five

Aspirations, Inspirations, and Obstacles: LGBTQ Youth and Processes of Career Development

Jeneka Ann Joyce, Maya Elin O'Neil, and Ellen Hawley McWhirter

JACKSON IS A 16-year-old sophomore in high school who, for the past 3 months, has attended a mandatory, after-school study hall for students who are struggling to maintain passing grades. Gina is a volunteer who aids the students in getting back on track academically through advising, tutoring, and student advocacy. For the past few days, Gina has been noticing Jackson's listless behavior and inattentiveness throughout the study hall. She pulls Jackson aside and states her observations. He looks down, shuffles his feet, and mumbles something under his breath.

"You are not in trouble or anything, Jackson. I am concerned and was wondering if you would like to talk with me about anything going on about school or home." Jackson looks at Gina and sighs.

"My mom lost her job again and we really need some money. I'm stressed about it because, you know, I'm old enough get a job now and I actually found a good weekend job through this guy I know." Gina learned that Jackson was struggling with the decision of whether or not to take the job because the manager of the store would frequently make jokes about gay men. "It's not like I'm gay or anything, but it makes me uncomfortable to hear that stuff."

Jackson looks down and says, "I guess, I thought that I might be, but you know, I don't really know anyway."

Although this is a fictional example, the intersection of employment, education, sexual orientation, and cultural background affects youth on a daily basis. As counselors, teachers, and other education or human services professionals, being informed about how these issues impact youth and understanding the cultural and contextual complexities they face will increase our ability to support their educational and career development.

In this chapter, we summarize and expand on the previous research related to lesbian, gay, bisexual, transgendered, and questioning (LGBTQ) youth and vocational processes. First, we clarify the terminology that we use in this chapter. *Sexual minority adolescents* are those individuals who experience same-sex sexuality, such as same-sex attraction, same-sex behavior, and/or individuals who claim an identity as gay, lesbian, or bisexual (Savin-Williams, 2001). We acknowledge the many differences between LGBTQ youth. We use terminology proposed by the Human Rights Campaign Foundation (HRC) and others (HRC, n.d., 2004) by using the umbrella terms of *transgender* and *gender variant* interchangeably to refer to individuals who identify as minorities in terms of gender identity or individuals who express their gender in unconventional ways by current U.S. sociocultural standards. We use the term *LGBTQ* as an umbrella term that includes all the aforementioned groups. Finally, we use the terms *career* and *vocational* interchangeably. In the first section of this chapter, we outline current perspectives within vocational psychology and address potential contextual challenges that LGBTQ adolescents may encounter. Next, we summarize theories of career development and specific vocational and educational concerns salient to LGBTQ adolescents. Then, we give an overview of 2 career development theories and use these as the basis for providing specific recommendations for facilitating the career development of LGBTQ adolescents.

Current Perspectives in the Field

The vast majority of early career and vocational research was based on the experiences of young, able-bodied, white, middle-class men, and it was infused with Western values such as individualism and autonomy (Peterson & González, 2005; Blustein, McWhirter, & Perry, 2005). Scholars have consistently critiqued the applicability of career development processes to other groups such as ethnic minorities, poor and working-class persons, sexual minorities, women, and individuals with disabilities. More recent vocational research identifies the needs of underserved populations and the contexts that influence education and work (Blustein et al., 2002; Blustein, 2007). Blustein and colleagues (2005) argue that "the potential of vocational psychology to improve the education and working lives of all people—not just the college-bound or college-educated—is enhanced by assuming an activist social justice agenda" (143). An activist social justice agenda focuses on the contextual challenges of individuals and addresses educational and vocational issues both individually and institutionally. Similar to Blustein et al. (2005), we define vocational psychology broadly as the "academic and nonacademic skills, knowledge, interests, choice, and behaviors that are acquired before, during, and after entry into the workforce" (143).

An emerging body of literature directly addresses the vocational needs of sexual minorities (Fassinger, 1996; Morrow, Gore, & Campbell, 1996; Croteau, Anderson, Distefano, & Kampa-Kokesch, 2000; Chung, 1996) and individuals who identify as transgender or gender variant (O'Neil, McWhirter, & Cerezo, 2008). Gender variant and sexual-minority individuals face unique challenges in life and within the workforce due to homophobia, heterosexism, gender bias, and other types of discrimination (Fassinger, 2000). Negotiating a stigmatized identity is challenging at any age. However, during adolescence, varying aspects of identity, including sexual identity, become particularly important (Patterson, 1995). Adolescents must not only come to terms with an emerging sexual identity, but also simultaneously make decisions about classes, school effort, and behavior that influence their vocational trajectories. Although a good deal of research captures the struggles of sexual-minority adolescents (e.g., D'Augelli, 2002; Savin-Williams, 1995; Savin-Williams, 1994; Grossman & Kerner, 1998; Brent, 1995), research on the dynamic interplay between sexual identity development and career development is just beginning (Fassinger, 2000; Nauta, Saucier, & Woodard, 2001; Schmidt & Nilsson, 2006). Very little research attends to the career development needs of individuals who identify as gender variant or transgender (Chung, 2003; O'Neil, McWhirter, & Cerezo, 2008). Individuals who identify as gender variant or transgender may experience identity challenges, discrimination, and oppression as do lesbians, gays, and bisexuals, but it is clear that they also negotiate unique stressors, concerns, and challenges (Chung, 2003; Diamond, 2002; O'Neil, McWhirter, & Cerezo, 2008). Researchers have inadequately addressed the vocational needs of transgender individuals, and more research is needed.

Challenges on the Margins for LGBTQ Adolescents

Residing in a homophobic society, sexual-minority adolescents may experience distinctive stressors directly related to same-sex attraction, sexual behavior, and sexual identity (e.g., Meyer, 1995; Fassinger, 2000; Savin-Williams, 1994). Persistent stressors for sexual-minority adolescents such as coming out to others, being victimized for their sexual orientation or attractions, or being "outed" (having one's sexual orientation revealed to others without permission) often compound normative adolescent concerns. Similar to sexual-minority youth, transgender youth experience many of the same stressors, and in addition, they are frequently faced with an even greater stigma and lack of understanding about issues pertaining to gender identities (HRC, n.d.).

Sexual minorities are presumed to move through stages of development that begin with the realization of same-sex attraction and confusion regarding feelings of being "different," subsequent exploration and experimentation, and eventual self-labeling, disclosure to others, and pride in one's sexual identity (Cass, 1979; Troiden, 1988). Initial stages that typically begin during adolescence may be fraught with confusion, self-deprecation, and possibly social isolation (Mohr & Fassinger, 2000; Troiden, 1988). Many sexual-minority adolescents experience social isolation, fear, and further emotional distress in both school and home contexts (Grossman & Kerner, 1998). Martin and Hetrick (1988) found that sexual-minority youth who chose to seek counseling services often voiced a lack of support from friends and social alienation as the most difficult concerns in their lives. Although identity development models have been helpful in guiding research and describing processes of sexual identity development, recent research supports a broader conceptualization of identity development that does not progress in stages, but that reflects the different developmental trajectories of sexual-minority youth (e.g., Diamond, 2003; Savin-Williams, 2001). We found no identity development models for transgender youth in the literature. It has been suggested, however, that these adolescents experience similar contextually based challenges and developmental processes as sexual-minority youth and youth who experience discrimination based on minority identities (HRC, n.d.).

Psychosocial outcomes for sexual-minority youth such as quitting school, committing crime, and running away from home are strongly correlated with incidents of physical and verbal abuse from both peers and family members. Social marginalization and stigmatization may lead to avoidant coping strategies such as substance use and abuse, risky sexual behavior, and quitting school (Fassinger, 2000). Therefore, it is not surprising that, in comparison to heterosexual peers, sexual-minority adolescents are more susceptible to substance abuse and/or dependence, depression, suicidal thoughts, and suicide (Fergusson, Horwood, & Beautrais, 1999; Hunter, Rosario, & Rotheram-Borus, 1993; Brent, 1995). Although few practitioners and researchers would argue that LGBTQ adolescents have the potential to face distinctive psychosocial adversity, the effects of the adversity may vary in intensity based on factors such as gender, ethnicity, the availability and nature of social support, local political climate, coping ability, and self-esteem. Variations in personal characteristics and environmental contexts likely affect adolescent socioemotional, academic, and behavioral outcomes; therefore, the existence of a "typical" trajectory for sexual-minority adolescents is unlikely (Diamond, 2003).

Theories of Career Development

Case Example

Rachel is a 14-year-old freshman in high school and has consistently played sports throughout her life. She earned all-league soccer honors in middle school and has thought about the idea of becoming a professional soccer player or coach in the future. She recently asked her parents for permission to join the school's soccer team. Rachel's parents told her that now that she was in high school, she needed to stop acting like a boy and being influenced by all the "boyish girls" on the soccer team. They are pressuring her to wear very feminine clothing and to join her church's youth group, and they frequently ask her about dating. Rachel believes her parents are terrified that she is a lesbian and that they will only escalate their efforts if she shares that she is questioning her sexual orientation.

Sexual-minority adolescents often face impediments to exploring who they are, what they enjoy, and what they want for themselves and their lives. Adolescent developmental expectations within U.S. sociocultural norms include the ability to transition to secondary school, learn the academic and life skills necessary for college and/or work, form close friendships and romantic relationships, and become involved in extracurricular activities (Masten & Coatsworth, 1998). Successful negotiation of these tasks builds a foundation for youth as they pursue future work and/or educational opportunities.

Donald Super's (1990) life span, life-space theory of career development emphasizes that career development occurs across the life span and that vocational decisions and choices represent an implementation of self-concept. In Super's theory, self-concept is somewhat fluid and encompasses all aspects of self, including sexual and work identities. Super acknowledges the dynamic interplay among biological, psychological, and social factors involved in career choice and development, and highlights how societal variables such as family, school, social policy, and peer groupings interact with psychological variables such as values, interests, personalities, and skills to impact career development (Super,

1990). In the above example, Rachel's engagement in a particular set of extracurricular activities was contingent on parental approval and expectation. Rachel received specific messages regarding gender role expectations from her parents. These parental expectations may influence the activities that Rachel chooses to pursue in the future and her ideas surrounding "appropriate" female activities or even career pursuits. In this way, social variables affect how individuals form their values and interests and also how individuals develop specific skill sets. Gender identity development, sexual identity development, and career development cannot be evaluated outside a person's individual context because of the interplay between contextual influences and supports on development.

Super (1990) stated that individuals move through 5 developmental stages: growth, exploration, establishment, maintenance, and disengagement. The successful resolution of developmental tasks during each stage enables individuals to function effectively within their life roles. Life roles change over time, and for adolescents, they typically include roles of child, student, and sometimes worker. The developmental stage corresponding with adolescence is *exploration*, and the associated tasks include exploration and identification of interests and values and successful coping with environmental demands (e.g., school, work, family relationships, and responsibilities). This stage also includes learning academic and work-related skills such as time management, carrying out multi-step projects, and effective group work. Super defines a person's career maturity as his or her readiness to take on the developmental tasks of each stage of development (Super, 1990).

LGBTQ adolescents in overtly homophobic school and family environments may for safety reasons have to dedicate more energy to hiding their interests and values than to exploring them, and their skill development may be hindered if, for example, they hesitate to engage in group projects for fear of being outed or shamed. One of the authors worked with a gay client, "Charlie," who attended and completed medical school because this was what was expected of him by his family. Before pursuing medical school, he had not engaged in career exploration. He courageously stopped the trajectory expected and reinforced by others in his life and, with the aid of a counselor, began asking the questions, "Who am I?" and "How do I really want to dedicate my life's energy?" Rachel, in the case example that opened this section, will need some support as she navigates family expectations and relationships and her own unique skills and interests to avoid ending up in a similar situation as Charlie. Rachel may choose to forgo a career that aligns with her values and interests in favor of career pursuits that are aligned with traditional gender roles and with her family expectations. It is also possible for Rachel to show her parents the opportunities that her soccer pursuits can provide, including athletic scholarships, meaningful leadership opportunities, and building a strong work ethic. Supportive adults can help youth identify ways that their interests are similar to and different from cultural and family expectations. Counselors may be able to help clients navigate and integrate these personal, cultural, and family values, goals, and expectations.

Another career development model, Lent, Brown, and Hackett's (1994) Social Cognitive Career Theory (SCCT), specifically addresses contextual influences and social-cognitive variables within career development. Similar to Super's model, SCCT assumes that individuals are active agents within their environments and that there is an active interplay among individuals, their environments, and their behaviors. These 2 theories differ in scope and purpose, however. While Super's theory is intended to describe career development over the lifetime, SCCT focuses specifically on how career and academic interests are shaped and result in career and educational accomplishments and outcomes.

Lent et al. (1994) propose that person inputs (such as birth-assigned sex, race/ethnicity, and genetic factors) as well as background contextual influences (such as socioeconomic status and school quality) combine to influence individuals' learning experiences. Learning experiences in turn affect self-efficacy expectations (confidence in ability to perform specific tasks like pass a math test) and outcome expectations (beliefs about what will happen after performing a task or engaging in a behavior: "If I ace the math test, I'll be very proud" or "I'll be made fun of"). Self-efficacy and outcome expectations influence the development of personal interests ("I like math"), which are translated to goals ("I'll study

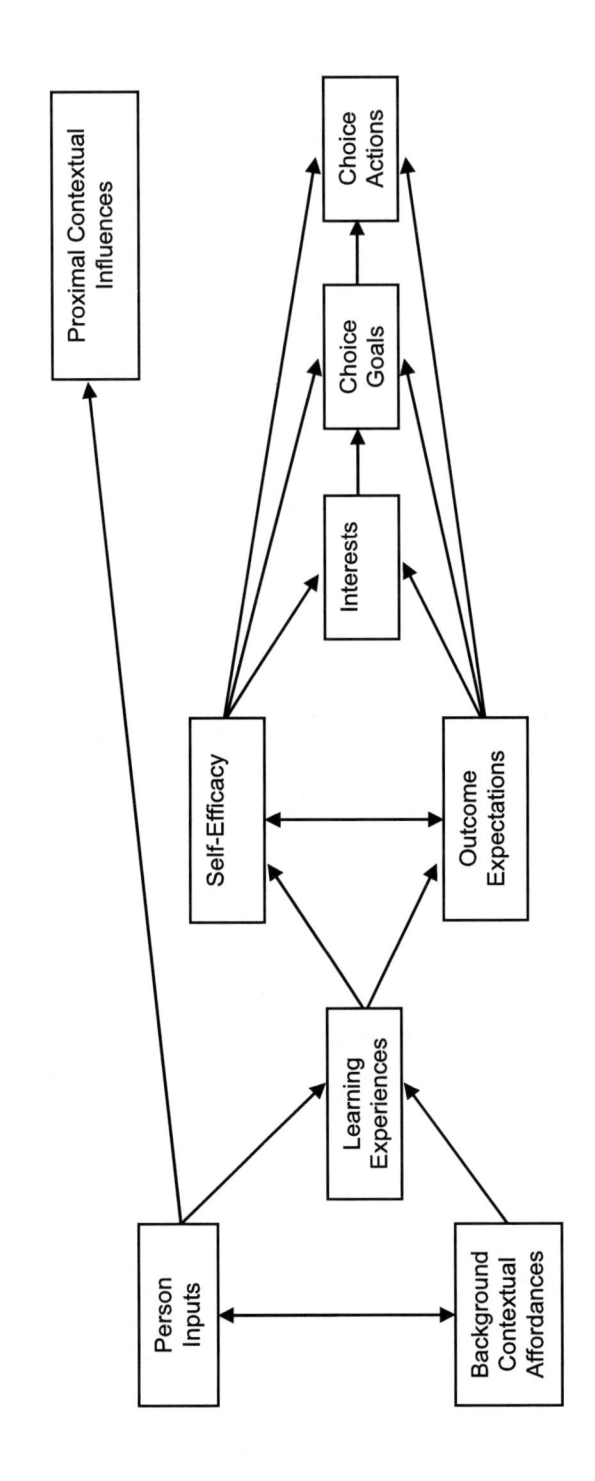

Figure 1. Lent, Brown, & Hackett's (1994) Social Cognitive Career Theory

math in college") and goals into actions ("I'll become a math major"). However, this process is also influenced by contextual supports and barriers, which may reinforce or alter this trajectory.

SCCT acknowledges the role of real and/or perceived contextual barriers in how interests are translated into academic and career-related goals and how these goals are eventually enacted (Lent et al., 2000). LGBTQ adolescents might not pursue an interest in teaching at the elementary or secondary school level, for example, due to perceptions that they will be outed, prevented from entering the profession, or have to live a closeted life. In the following section, we discuss specific vocational concerns from the perspectives of Super's life-span life space theory and SCCT.

Specific Vocational Concerns for LGBTQ Adolescent

Case Example

Sam is a 17-year-old high school student whose birth-assigned sex was female but who now uses male pronouns, binds his chest, and has presented as male in school and other contexts for the past two years. Sam has been volunteering as a Web site manager for his local LGBTQ youth resource center for over a year. He takes computer science and math classes at his high school and has been mentored by one of his teachers who is helping him apply for college. Due to his family's limited financial resources and their limited support of Sam since he came out as transgender, Sam's teacher is assisting him with scholarship applications. She has provided him with many scholarship applications and feels that the best hope for him would be to apply for a prestigious "Women in Computer Science" scholarship. She is tentative when approaching Sam about this scholarship, although she gets frustrated when he refuses to apply for it, stating, "I'm not a woman, so I don't qualify for it." She explains that he has experienced discrimination similar to what women in computer science face, but he remains adamant in his refusal to apply for this award.

Potential career development barriers for LGBTQ adolescents include lack of guidance (Nauta, Saucier, & Woodard, 2001); lack of role models to broaden career exploration, allow for reality testing, and assist in later career adjustment (Fassinger, 1996); and gender-stereotyped environments that may limit the development of interests (Morrow, Gore, & Campbell, 1996). Additionally, the work of Morrow, Gore, and Campbell (1996) and, more recently, the research conducted by Schmidt and Nilsson (2006) suggest that sexual identity confusion and conflict may hinder or delay the career development process for sexual-minority adolescents. Morrow et al. (1996) point out that values for safety within the workplace may supersede the influence of interests in determining the career choices of gay and lesbian individuals.

Schmidt and Nilsson (2006) studied the relationship between "internal psychological resources devoted to recognizing oneself as lesbian, gay, or bisexual, social support, and career development" (26). They found that sexual-minority youth who expended greater psychological energy in the realm of sexual identity development struggled with adolescent career developmental tasks such as career exploration. Adolescents who struggled with sexual identity development placed greater energy in understanding that portion of their identities to the exclusion of other developmental tasks. Schmidt and Nilsson (2006) suggest that when working with LGB youth, practitioners take into account both career and sexual identity development and address how individuals are coping with simultaneous developmental processes. We caution reliance on similar recommendations when working with transgender adolescents because of the lack of research. It has been suggested that both gender identity concerns and vocational concerns be considered when working with transgender clients, regardless of age (O'Neil, McWhirter, & Cerezo, 2008). One issue that is particularly salient for gender-variant youth is verbal, physical, or sexual harassment. In many educational and vocational contexts, gender-identity related "humor" is viewed as acceptable despite gender-variant youth experiencing it as a form of harassment. Educational and human service professionals need to be familiar with local and state laws that serve to protect gender-variant individuals from harassment in school and work contexts. These are examples of the some vocational concerns that may be experienced by transgender youth. However, more research on particular topics such as the influence of harassment on career-related self-efficacy and outcome expectations and strategies for improving school and work environments for gender-variant individuals is needed.

Recommendations for Practitioners Working in Educational Contexts

This section offers specific recommendations for professionals working with LGBTQ youth in school settings, focusing on environmental factors and the individual vocational needs of these populations. Social barriers such as homophobia and other forms of discrimination may adversely affect career and academic choices and outcome expectations. Contextual barriers and the absence of support may interfere with career maturity and the timely resolution of adolescent vocational tasks (Morrow et al., 1996; Schmidt & Nilsson, 2006; Nauta et al., 2001). These impediments have the potential to greatly impact future academic and career opportunities and subsequent access to resources in society. Career interventions that acknowledge structural and individual factors are important, and school-based career development efforts that address contextual and systemic impediments as well as providing individual guidance will provide for greater changes and contribute to prevention of career and educational problems for LGBTQ youth in the long run.

Creating supportive environments for LGBQT youth. Sexual orientation and gender identity are highly divisive topics, and not all teachers, parents, or administrators will agree that "special services" or targeted interventions for this population are necessary or even desirable. The climate of schools may be aversive to both LGBTQ teachers and students. Within school settings, fear, victimization, and non-disclosure can be normative (Fassinger, 2000). In addition, some may argue that the population of sexual minorities in schools is too small to warrant the use of highly valuable resources. In light of these possible barriers, it is important for practitioners to collaborate with and educate schools, communities, and districts about the lives and concerns of LGBTQ young people, including safety issues, factors that impede their optimal healthy development, and the consequences of failure to improve school climates for them.

Assessing the school, district, and community climate and resources can help practitioners identify community allies and potential advocacy activities to aid in the fostering of more positive school climates for LGBTQ students. The appendix suggests questions to aid in the assessment process. In addition, practitioners may also find helpful Chesir-Teran's (2003) comprehensive assessment of school-level processes, which includes measurement of the effects of heterosexism in schools. Results of such assessments can be shared in the context of a district's mission and responsibilities, including the protection of students and the provision of healthy learning environments. Practices to enhance the climate for LGBTQ adolescents may include professional development training for school staff on topics such as LGBTQ challenges, how to improve classroom climate for LGBTQ students, how to respond effectively to hostility or exclusion directed at LGBTQ students, demystifying LGBTQ individuals, and how to support student identity development even when some identities may conflict with the values of the staff member. Practitioners can also work with school and district administrators to implement practices that decrease the incidences of discrimination and harassment based on presumed sexual orientation and gender identity.

Ettner (1999) and Carroll and Gilroy (2002) propose that, when working with transgender clients, practitioners should strive to create a trans-positive environment; their recommendations can be applied to working with youth in educational contexts, and similar recommendations can be applied to working with sexual-minority youth as well. When working directly with LGBTQ adolescents, regular acknowledgment of LGBTQ concerns can depathologize the topic. Services tailored for LGBTQ students should be advertised using a variety of outreach strategies due to the stigma of sexual and gender minority identities/experiences. Similarly, practitioners should critically examine their beliefs and biases and how these affect their interactions with students and coworkers. Finally, it is necessary to create and enact interventions that address both identity and career/educational development. This allows practitioners the flexibility to address personal and educational concerns of LGBTQ youth that may include managing a stigmatized identity, isolation from peers and family, depression, and questions regarding sexual and gender identities, while also imparting valuable skills and strategies for career exploration processes.

Addressing ethical considerations. Some potential risks or special considerations should be accounted for when working with LGBTQ adolescents. Practitioners must actively evaluate ethical considerations pertaining to confidentiality and informed consent. Several contextual factors and values may complicate eliciting parental cooperation. Adolescents may not wish to reveal their possible sexual or gender minority status to anyone, especially parents, because of homophobic attitudes and biased behaviors. Parental knowledge concerning a child's questioning of his or her sexual or gender identity may be beneficial for the child because the parents may be able to offer support and consistent monitoring to ensure healthy and safe decisions. Research has shown that parental emotional support/involvement and support from prosocial adults serve as vital components of healthy adolescent development (Savin-Williams, 2001). Social support helps to foster healthy outcomes for youth and has been correlated with lower levels of internalized homophobia and higher levels of sexual identity disclosure and expression (Jordan & Deluty, 1998). On the other hand, the consequences of requiring that parents be informed about youth participation in career interventions may not lead to positive experiences of adult support if parents react negatively about their child's participation in LGBTQ-related activities. A qualitative investigation conducted by Muñoz-Plaza, Quinn, and Rounds (2002) found that a sample of LGBT high school adolescents experienced peers and non-family adults to be more supportive than family members, and most participants did not disclose their sexual orientation to their parents while in high school. Adolescents may fear that disclosing their sexual orientation could lead to family estrangement. The limitations of confidentiality would have to be discussed with participants, and practitioners should follow the ethical guidelines of their profession.

Using theory and research-based practices. We recommend that school-based career intervention programs be grounded in career theory and consist of materials that are gay-affirmative and gender fair. Both SCCT and Super's life-span, life-space career development theory take into account the contextual influences or barriers that may constrain agency, choice, the development of interests, and notions of self. Ideally, interventions will address contextual factors at the district and school levels (e.g., policies, practices, and climate), and also student-level factors (e.g., self-efficacy expectations, goals, exploration behavior, and identity development). Focusing on both the individual and the environment serves as an attempt to combat the effects of oppression based on same-sex sexuality (Morrow et al., 1996) and gender variance.

The role of the practitioner is to assess needs, support student development of self-concept, teach decision-making skills, provide occupational information, help facilitate career planning, and advocate for the psychosocial well-being of LGBTQ adolescents. Structured group intervention should include materials, supports, and activities that are specifically tailored to address the unique issues that LGBTQ adolescents may face, such as social isolation, sexual identity confusion, low self-esteem and self-efficacy, constricted interests, and low career maturity.

Brown and Krane (2000) conducted a meta-analysis of effective career intervention practices and recommended 5 sessions as optimal and identified the elements most often associated with positive career development outcomes. Following their recommendations for length (5 sessions) and content, we now describe a possible career intervention for LGBTQ adolescents. Potential goals of a career intervention for LGBTQ adolescents may be as follows:

1. Create a supportive and safe space for LGBTQ adolescents to explore self-concept and career development and help adolescents build support networks that will facilitate their abilities to pursue their career aspirations (Brown & Krane, 2000).
2. Develop healthy, active coping skills and resilience.

3. Highlight objective and/or perceived contextual barriers that may interfere with the career development of LGBTQ individuals.
4. Build self-efficacy expectations for LGBTQ adolescents and expand their range of career options.
5. Ensure that LGBTQ adolescents are exposed to gay, lesbian, bisexual, and transgender prosocial adult role models.

Interventions should not only provide socioemotional support for adolescents as they struggle with questions of identity and intersecting relationships with family, peers, and significant others, but also guide LGBTQ adolescents through career exploratory activities and help build tangible skill sets to navigate the world of work and/or higher education. Objectives could include the following: Participants will have a greater level of support, a more positive self-concept, and higher self-efficacy and outcome expectations. Participants will also be able to articulate barriers that they may encounter as they enter the world of work and possible strategies to navigate those barriers.

Each group intervention session might be 1.5 hours long. The purpose of the first two sessions is to lay ground rules for confidentiality, build trust and rapport in the group, and address possible impediments to career development including sexual identity confusion and lack of social support (Schmidt & Nilsson, 2006). The discussions should be facilitated at a developmentally appropriate level and allow youth to explore their confusion and ask questions about aspects of their identity. The first two sessions highlight the mechanisms of identity development and the role of homophobia and heterosexism within conceptions of identity. Participants explore what it means to experience same-sex sexuality or gender-variant identities in the context of their multiple roles such as child and student. Intersections of gender, race/ethnicity, and other cultural identities should also be acknowledged and validated. Participants are asked to examine their fears, support systems, and coping strategies. Gay and lesbian identity development models are discussed, and the facilitator shares community resources that support LBGTQ adolescents. Additionally, participants link private aspects of self, such as sexual orientation and gender identity, with the world of work. By the end of the second session, participants would have completed interest and values inventories such as the Strong Interest Inventory (Donnay, Morris, Schaubhut, & Thompson, 2005).

The third session has three primary objectives derived from Brown and Krane (2000): 1) provide individualized interpretation and feedback from career assessments, 2) provide updated information on the requirements and likely consequences of considered career paths, and 3) provide participants with the opportunity to explore what a safe work and/or academic setting would look like for LGBTQ individuals, including how to investigate nondiscrimination policies within organizations. Congruent with the developmental task of exploration, the third session allows students to explore interests and values and also to become more familiar with available resources that allow adolescents to better prepare for higher education or the workforce. Participants learn how to locate jobs that could be perceived as incongruent for LGBTQ individuals and engage in discussion related to these constrictions. Participants are asked to bring their academic class schedules and analyze how their current academic preparation aligns with possible careers of interest. This session provides resources on different strategies to assess LGBTQ-affirmative regions of the country and LGBTQ-affirmative communities within universities and workplaces.

The purpose of the fourth session is to expose participants to LGBTQ role models as a means of building self-efficacy expectations. Role models should represent diverse ability, gender, ethnic/cultural, and religious groups present within the classroom (Nauta, Saucier, & Woodard, 2001). Community role models will discuss their careers, including their career development process, the real-life implications of being "out" on the job, and how sexual identity and/or gender identity is managed on the job. The fourth session would also connect youth with resources such as LGBTQ affirmative organizations that offer mentoring opportunities. This session also explores possible externships in businesses owned and operated by LGBTQ community members.

Based on initial exploratory activities regarding self and work, the fifth session culminates by allowing the participants to clarify in writing career and life goals (Brown & Krane, 2000). All participants must incorporate specific attributes of different work contexts that are perceived as safe for LGBTQ individuals and how those work contexts align with their interests and values. If work contexts are deemed unsafe, participants identify strategies to manage identity while remaining fulfilled at work (Chung, 2001). Participants identify the advantages and disadvantages of "being in the closet." Participants identify future academic courses that will contribute to the development of appropriate skills for their intended job.

Practitioners may choose to measure the effectiveness of this or other career interventions for LGBTQ youth by assessing career maturity, career self-efficacy expectations, goals, and other targets prior to the intervention and after the completion of the intervention. Qualitative feedback can also be solicited from students to gauge program effectiveness.

Challenging heterosexual norms through innovative curricula. Schools have the responsibility to promote acceptance of diverse individuals, and vocational curricula have the potential to assist in the creation of an LGBTQ-affirmative school environment by making diversity and inclusion explicit. Adolescents do not always self-identify as gay, lesbian, or bisexual even if they engage in same-sex behaviors (Diamond, 2000), and the stigma of same-sex sexuality and/or gender variance may keep individuals in the closet. Career services, therefore, must be available for broader audiences so as to reach "closeted" or questioning students and reduce the stigma associated with LGBTQ identities.

Plausible objectives of a curriculum-based class could be as follows: (1) explore self-concept and individual diversity within the group, (2) highlight the effects of diversity within the workplace, (3) explore academic and workplace policies and policy implications for diverse populations such as sexual or gender minorities, (4) challenge stereotypes by providing role models of varying sexual orientations and gender identities, and (5) explore specific strategies to ally with LGBTQ communities and advocate for individuals within the diverse workplace. Specific outcomes could include participants' ability to articulate the role of diversity in their lives and in today's workplace, the effects of discrimination and stigma in the workplace, and strategies to combat discrimination and provide support for marginalized groups. Participants will demonstrate competency in self-exploration and understanding the intersections between private and public aspects of self (Fassinger, 2000). This type of curriculum allows students the opportunity to better understand the impact of discrimination and stigma for marginalized persons and how to ally with these communities.

Conclusion

LGBTQ adolescents face significant challenges as they engage in the simultaneous tasks of identity development and career development. These challenges may include sexual harassment, peer victimization, family and/or community rejection, and/or violence. Other challenges include lack of attention to their unique concerns, reduced self-efficacy and outcome expectations, delayed career maturity due to unwelcoming family and school environments, and lack of guidance in negotiating these and other challenges. These challenges may contribute to diminished psychological and maladaptive coping strategies for some LGBTQ adolescents. In addition, low levels of social support and higher levels of inner sexual or gender identity conflict will further complicate their efforts to accomplish the career development tasks of adolescence. Practitioners and researchers have an obligation to address oppressive forces within schools and within the greater society. Contextual social supports and resources may serve to redirect adolescent energy into other realms of their identity, while continually exploring the impact of sexual and gender identity within their lives. Interventions should seek to support, educate, and provide resources for LGBTQ adolescents, as well as the families and schools within which they reside. According to Morrow, Gore, and Campbell, "Society can only benefit as professionals confront barriers to career development and lesbian and gay people are encouraged to contribute their abilities, interests, and energies to endeavors consistent with their capabilities and desires" (Morrow, Gore, & Campbell, 1996, 148). We extend this to include all LGBTQ adolescents. They have innumerable strengths and contributions to offer our communities, if we can increase their wellbeing in their families and schools, promote their integration and self-exploration, and facilitate their exploration and goal achievement. It is not simply the Jacksons, Rachels, Charlies, and Sams who benefit, but all young people and, indeed, all of us who will benefit.

APPENDIX

Phase 1: Creating the Conditions for Change

Objectives
- Consider the general demographics of the school and school district
- Assess career education resources and curriculum
- Assess school climate
- Assess community resources

Outcomes
After a thorough evaluation of the school, district, and community, the interventionist would have a general idea of areas of support and possible collaboration and also targeted efforts for advocacy.

Targeted Questions for Evaluation

Consider General Demographics
- What percentages of students are of varying ethnicities? Socioeconomic background? Sex?
- How many students drop out of school per year? Why? What is the graduation rate for the school? What percentages of students attend higher education institutions (four-year universities, community colleges)? What percentages of students attend vocational colleges?
- What percentages of students go directly to work after graduation?

Assess Career Education Resources and Curriculum
- What career resources are already available? Do career resources contain up-to-date information on the requirements and likely consequences of considered career paths (Brown & Krane, 2000)?
- Is the career education curriculum gay-affirmative and gender-fair?

- What grade-levels are provided with career guidance? Are there particular courses that students are required to take in career education? If not, are electives available?
- Does the school have guidance counselor(s)? What is the caseload for the person(s)?

Assess District and School Climate
- Is sexual orientation a protected status for teachers and administrators in the district?
- Does the school have any "out" teachers or administrators?
- Are hiring practices of the district gay-affirmative?
- Are domestic partner benefits available for gay, lesbian, and bisexual couples?
- Is training available for teachers and administrators surrounding issues of multiple forms of diversity?
- Are there specific policies that guard against discrimination and harassment of students based on sexual orientation?
- What are current disciplinary actions if the policy is violated?
- Are these policies reinforced? How are these policies reinforced?
- Do students have the option to participate in gay/straight alliances? If so, what is the make-up of the group? Is the group active?
- How do teachers support diversity within their classrooms? Stickers? Conversations? Course content?
- What resources are available in the school that address the needs of GLB youth (books, magazines, other materials)?

Assess Community Resources
- Are there any local community-based support groups for issues pertaining to GLB identities? What local clubs are available for youth?
- Are there chapters of national organizations within the community such as Parents and Friends of Lesbians and Gays (PFLAG) or Gay and Lesbian Parents Coalition International?
- What political figures in the area support the basic rights of GLB communities?

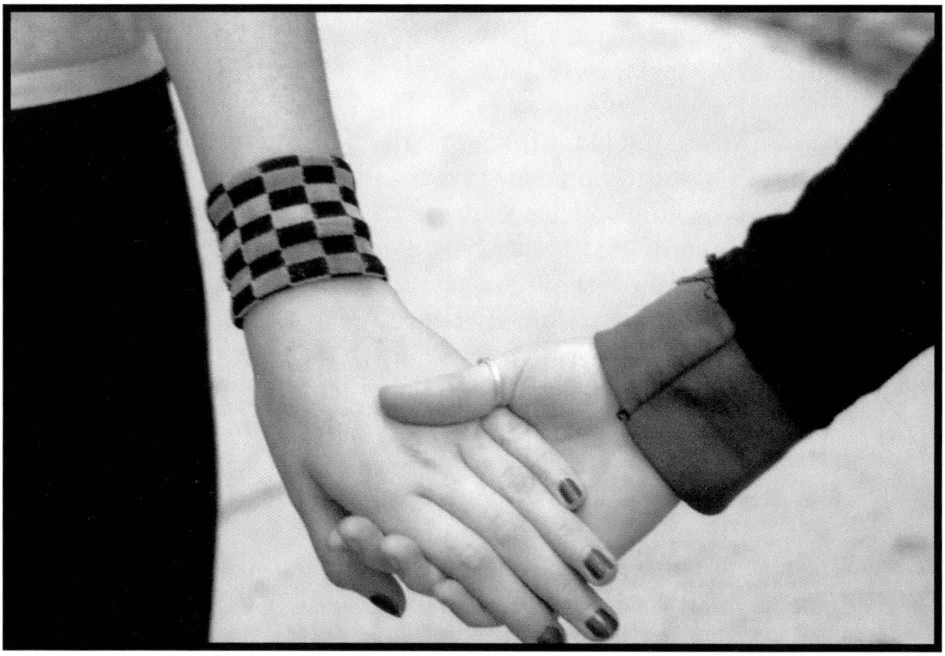

Chapter Six

Working with LGBTQ Youth with Disabilities: How Special Educators Can Reconceptualize CEC Standards

Thomas Scott Duke

HOMOPHOBIA IS CHARACTERIZED by the fear, loathing, and/or hatred of lesbian, gay, bisexual, transgendered, and queer (LGBTQ) individuals. *Heterosexism* is characterized by the belief that *only* heterosexuality is good, healthy, and "normal" and the assumption that LGBTQ individuals are inferior to heterosexuals (Sears, 1996). *Ablism* is characterized by the fear, loathing, contempt, pity, and/or hatred of individuals with disabilities, the belief that *only* people *without* disabilities are competent, healthy, and "normal" and the assumption that people *with* disabilities are inferior to people *without* disabilities (Abberly, 1987; Brown, 2003).

McIntosh (1992) argued that privilege has been and continues to be a powerful force in creating and maintaining hegemonic social structures. She suggested that oppression can be best understood and explained as a concomitant of privilege. Social structures that contribute to *racism* maintain white privilege through the oppression of people of color (Trask, 1999). Social structures that contribute to *sexism* maintain male privilege through the oppression of women (Bornstein, 1994). Social structures that contribute to *homophobia* and *heterosexism* maintain heterosexual privilege through the oppression of LGBTQ individuals (Pharr, 1998). Social structures that contribute to *ablism* maintain "able-bodied" privilege through the oppression of persons with disabilities (Abberley, 1987; Brown, 2003).

Harley, Nowak, Gassaway, and Savage (2001) observed that LGBTQ people with disabilities come from diverse cultural and linguistic communities, have a wide range of abilities and disabilities, and represent multiple sexual orientations and gender identities/expressions. Harley et al. described LGBTQ individuals with disabilities as "multiple cultural minorities" who experience multiple forms of oppression. *Most* LGBTQ individuals with disabilities are subjected to forms of oppression rooted in homophobia, heterosexism, *and* ablism. *Many* LGBTQ individuals with disabilities are *also* subjected to forms of oppression rooted in racism, sexism, and classism (Kosciw, 2004; Pharr, 1998).

Schools as Sites of Oppression

The African American, lesbian, feminist scholar Barbara Smith (1999) described schools as "virtual cauldrons of homophobic sentiment." She noted "everything from the graffiti in the bathrooms and the put-downs yelled on the playground to the heterosexist bias of most texts [and other learning materials] and the firing of teachers on no other basis than that they are not heterosexual" (114) creates learning environments hostile to LGBTQ students, parents, and teachers. This hostility reinforces and reproduces the homophobia and heterosexism that pervade contemporary U.S. society and contributes to the oppression of LGBTQ individuals.

LGBTQ youth are routinely subjected to harassment, contempt, and acts of violence in school settings. They are debased, degraded, and dehumanized on a daily basis. Many LGBTQ youth don't feel safe in the schools. They feel isolated, marginalized, lonely, and afraid (Gay, Lesbian, & Straight Education Network 2005; Kosciw, 2004; Mallon & DeCrescenzo, 2006; Sears, 1987, 2003). These negative school experiences have devastating effects on LGBTQ youth. They experience alarmingly high rates of suicide, substance abuse, family problems, homelessness, and negative school outcomes (Remafedi, 1994; Remafedi, Farrow, &

Deisher, 1991). Savin-Williams (1994) argued that verbal and physical abuse in school settings contribute to high rates of substance abuse, prostitution, suicide, homelessness, and school failure among lesbian, gay male, and bisexual youth; it should be noted, however, that this same author later critiqued the research on sexual minority youth and concluded that such research often emphasizes pathology and negative outcomes while ignoring the remarkable resiliency of many LGBTQ adolescents and young adults (Savin-Williams, 2001).

While the school experiences of (nondisabled) LGBTQ students have been under-documented (Kosciw, 2004), the lives and experiences of LGBTQ youth *with* disabilities have been virtually ignored. At present, only a handful of articles describe the experiences of LGBTQ adolescents and young adults with disabilities (Blanchett, 2002; Harley et al., 2002; Thompson, 2002; Thompson, Bryson, & De Castelle, 2001). LGBTQ individuals with disabilities have been marginalized and ignored by the academic, special education, and social services establishments. Social justice demands that academics, educators, and social service providers generate and disseminate knowledge about the lives and experiences of LGBTQ youth with disabilities.

The Council for Exceptional Children (CEC) Standards

The Council for Exceptional Children (CEC) is an international professional organization that seeks to improve educational outcomes for individuals with disabilities. The CEC (2003) developed a set of professional standards for special educators. The *CEC Knowledge and Skill Standards* represent the knowledge and skill base that all special education teachers must possess if they are to provide safe, effective, and respectful school-based services to students with disabilities and their families. This knowledge and skill base is organized around 10 broad standards.

- Standard 1, *Foundations,* outlines what every special educator should know about the philosophical, historical, and legal issues that form the foundations of special education.

- Standard 2, *Development and Characteristics of Learners,* describes what special educators need to know about the growth and development of typical and atypical learners.
- Standard 3, *Individual Learning Differences,* identifies the knowledge that special educators must possess if they are to demonstrate an understanding of the effects that disabilities can have on an individual's learning in school and throughout life.
- Standard 4, *Instructional Strategies,* delineates the skills special educators need to develop and implement evidence-based instructional strategies and offer individualized instruction to students with disabilities.
- Standard 5, *Learning Environments and Social Interactions,* outlines the knowledge and skills special educators must possess if they are to create learning environments for individuals with disabilities that foster cultural understanding, safety, emotional well-being, and positive social interactions.
- Standard 6, *Language,* describes what every special educator needs to know about typical and atypical language development and the ways in which disabilities can interact with an individual's experience with and use of language.
- Standard 7, *Instructional Planning,* delineates the skills special educators need to develop long-range individualized instructional plans anchored in both general and special curricula.
- Standard 8, *Assessment,* identifies the knowledge and skills special educators must possess if they are to use the results of formal and informal assessments to develop, implement, and evaluate effective, responsible, and culturally responsive services for individuals with disabilities.
- Standard 9, *Professional and Ethical Practice,* offers special educators a set of professional and ethical guidelines that should inform all aspects of their work with students, families, and colleagues.
- Standard 10, *Collaboration,* delineates the knowledge and skills special educators must possess if they are to collaborate routinely and effectively with individuals with disabilities, families, other educators, related service providers, and per-

sonnel from community service agencies in culturally responsive ways (Council for Exceptional Children, 2003).

Embedded within the 10 broad CEC standards are 126 *common core competencies*. Many of these competencies address issues of cultural and linguistic diversity, but only *one* of the 126 competencies explicitly addresses sexual orientation. Standard 9, *Professional and Ethical Practice*, Common Core Skill 6 (CC9S6) requires special educators to "demonstrate sensitivity for the culture, language, religion, gender, disability, socio-economic status, and sexual orientation of individuals" (Council for Exceptional Children, 2003, 59). However, additional competencies can (and, in my opinion, *should*) be interpreted broadly so that concepts of *culture* and *diversity* are understood to encompass sexual orientation and gender identity/expression. Competencies that lend themselves to this sort of expansive, inclusive, and LGBTQ-friendly (re)interpretation include:

- Standard 1, *Foundations*, Common Core Knowledge 9 (CC1K9), which requires special educators to recognize the "impact of the dominant culture on shaping schools and the individuals who study and work in them" (54)
- Standard 1, *Foundations*, Common Core Knowledge 10 (CC1K10), which requires special educators to recognize the "potential impact of differences in values, languages, and customs that can exist between the home and school" (54)
- Standard 5, *Learning Environments and Social Interactions*, Common Core Skill 5 (CC5S1), which requires special educators to "create a safe, equitable, positive, and supportive learning environment in which diversities are valued" (56)
- Standard 9, *Professional and Ethical Practice*, Common Core Knowledge 1 (CC9K1), which requires special educators to critically examine any "personal cultural biases and differences that affect one's teaching" (59)
- Standard 10, *Collaboration*, Common Core Knowledge 1 (CC10K1), which requires special educators to "foster respectful and beneficial relationships between families and professionals" (59)

Problematizing the CEC Standards

Critical theorists study the phenomena of privilege and oppression in social institutions to transform these institutions and emancipate the oppressed (Morrow & Brown, 1994). Critical theorists in the field of education have argued schools can become public institutions where knowledge forms and values are taught for the purpose of educating young people for democratic empowerment, resistance, and hope, rather than for the purposes of conformity, subjugation, and assimilation (Freire, 1970, 1974; hooks, 2003; Kincheloe, 2003; Lather, 1991). In recent years, critical theory has interacted with poststructuralist, postmodern, cultural studies, queer, disability rights, and feminist discourses. This interaction, or blending of discourses, has allowed the relationships between knowledge and power to be examined from the perspectives of historically marginalized groups, including women, people of color, indigenous peoples, the poor, LGBTQ individuals, people with disabilities, and people living with human immunodeficiency virus/acquired immune deficiency syndrome (HIV/AIDS) (Anzaldua, 1999; Bornstein, 1994; Brown, 2003; Denny, 1994; Lather & Smithies, 1997; Pharr, 1998; Smith, 1999; Trask, 1999).

Thompson et al. (2001) explored the theoretical and practical constraints of identity formation for LGBTQ individuals with disabilities. Thompson et al. argued that neither disability theorists nor queer theorists have adequately described, examined, or accounted for the complex identities of LGBTQ people with disabilities. Thompson et al. suggested that a blending of (queer, disability, and other) discourses and perspectives might provide a more comprehensive approach to the development and implementation of effective, culturally responsive, and socially just services for LGBTQ people with disabilities.

The postmodern thinker Michel Foucault (1926–1984) believed that *truth* is a human invention and "possibly even a Western illusion" (Cannella, 1997, 13). He suggested that knowledge, reality, and truth are constructed by human beings, through language, in multiple forms that are forever changing. Foucault was interested in exploring the relationships between power, knowledge, and language (which he called *discourse*). He believed that knowledge constructs gain legitimacy when they are accepted as objective reality, or truth, by those who have the power to impose their values, beliefs, and understandings about the nature of reality on other human beings. The knowledge constructs of those with power are used to dominate other members of society. Modern narratives are knowledge constructs that mask the acquisition and maintenance of power (Foucault, 1980).

Foucault (1980) believed that discourse simultaneously creates knowledge and limits alternative knowledge forms. He problematized (i.e., critically examined) the discourses that are used to justify various social institutions, including psychiatry, medicine, the human sciences, and the prison system, and he demonstrated how these discourses have allowed certain groups to gain power over others. Foucault asked:

> What knowledges have been excluded [from these discourses]? Whose knowledge has been disqualified as beneath our hierarchical systems? Whose truths have been hidden through our rhetorical methods? How have particular groups gained control over others through the construction of discourse knowledges and truths? (Cannella, 1997, 13–14)

In the contemporary United States, heterosexuals have the power to impose their (mostly heterosexist and often homophobic) values, beliefs, and understanding about human sexuality on *all* members of society. These (mostly heterosexist and often homophobic) knowledge constructs have been accepted as objective reality, or truth, by a significant segment of the U.S. population. These knowledge constructs are embedded within the curricula, policies, and practices of most public schools and special education programs. These knowledge constructs are also embedded within the *CEC Knowledge and Skill Standards.*

Increased social justice and equality for all human beings require that all forms of knowledge be examined critically from the perspectives of oppressed peoples (Kincheloe, 2003). The CEC (2003) claims that the *Knowledge and Skill Standards,* which guide and inform most university-based special education teacher preparation programs in the United States and, therefore, profoundly influence the education and training of most special educators, "represent the knowledge and skill base that [special education] professionals entering practice or assuming advanced roles should possess to practice safely and effectively" (xi). Social justice, therefore, demands that special educators who work with LGBTQ youth with disabilities, LGBTQ parents and their children, and/or LGBTQ colleagues critically examine the *CEC Knowledge and Skill Standards* from the perspectives of LGBTQ people (that is, from a *queer* perspective).

A number of educators have used interrogative methods developed by Foucault (1980) to reveal systems of privilege and oppression hidden within the discourses surrounding their respective fields. Skrtic (1995a, 1995b, 1995c, 1995d, 1995e), for example, problematized the discourse and knowledge traditions that have that have influenced and justified the field of special education. Silin (1995) critically examined the "silence" (or *lack* of discourse) surrounding HIV/AIDS in U.S. schools and classrooms. Cannella (1997) interrogated "the power relations that have been constructed within the patriarchal value structure that is the institution of [early childhood] education" (163). Cannella asked:

> What knowledge has been hidden within the discourse on developmental psychology? Whose knowledge is disqualified as we construct notions of "childhood"? How is the exclusion and control of younger human beings, subjugated cultures, or subdominant groups like females hidden in the forms of discourse that we use? (15)

If special educators, university-based teacher educators, and researchers were to problematize the field of special education from a queer perspective, they would contribute to the development of a discourse that recognizes and empowers LGBTQ youth with disabilities, LGBTQ parents and their children, and LGBTQ special educators and related service providers. At present, however, such a discourse remains latent and unrealized, existing only in the realm of possibility.

The knowledge constructs embedded within the *CEC Knowledge and Skill Standards* and the discourse and knowledge traditions surrounding these standards, have yet to be critically examined from a queer perspective. This chapter represents, in part, my attempt to blend critical, queer, disability rights, and feminist discourses for the purpose of problematizing (i.e., critically examining) the *CEC Knowledge and Skill Standards*. The work of critical theorist, activist, and educator Paulo Friere (1970, 1974); disability rights activist, historian, and poet Steven Brown (2003); disability rights activist and educator Norman Kunc (1992); third-wave feminist, lesbian activist, and educator Suzanne Pharr (1998); and gender theorist, playwright, and "gender outlaw" Kate Bornstein (1994), who writes from the perspective of "an S/M transsexual lesbian, ex-cult member, femme top and sometimes bottom shaman" (143) have profoundly informed my attempt to problematize (and reconceptualize) the *CEC Knowledge and Skill Standards* in ways that acknowledge and address the lives of LGBTQ youth with disabilities, LGBTQ parents and their children, and LGBTQ special educators and related service providers.

Critical examination involves the location of knowledge forms that have been excluded and/or disqualified as beneath hierarchical systems (Foucault, 1980). I, therefore, attempted to locate knowledge forms (related to the experiences of LGBTQ youth with disabilities, LGBTQ parents and their children, and the LGBTQ school-based professionals that serve them) that have been *excluded* from the *CEC Knowledge and Skill Standards*. It wasn't hard to do. As previously noted, only *one* of the 126 competencies embedded within the CEC standards *explicitly* addresses sexual orientation. *None* of the competencies explicitly address gender identity or gender expression. The exclusion of knowledge forms related to the lives and experiences of LGBTQ individuals with disabilities from the *CEC Knowledge and Skill Standards* might lead one to assume that special educators do not need to know (or care) very much about sexual orientation or gender identity/expression to engage in safe and effective practice with LGBTQ youth with disabilities, LGBTQ parents and their children, and LGBTQ colleagues.

Reconceptualizing the CEC Competencies

Sawieki (1991) argued "it is politically irresponsible to radically question existing theoretical political options without taking any responsibility for the impact that such critique will have and without offering any alternative" (99). That is to say, "Deconstruction without reconstruction is an act of irresponsibility" (Putnam, quoted by Appleby, 1994, 234). It is not enough simply to critique the *CEC Knowledge and Skill Standards*. Social justice demands that special educators also *reconceptualize* these standards. The remainder of this chapter suggests ways that special educators who work with LGBTQ youth with disabilities, LGBTQ parents and their children, and LGBTQ colleagues might reconceptualize the CEC "diversity" competencies to challenge school-based homophobia and heterosexism.

Standard 1: Foundations, CC1K9

Impact of the dominant culture on shaping schools and the individuals who study and work in them.

Special educators who wish to challenge school-based homophobia and heterosexism and create classrooms, programs, and schools that welcome and support LGBTQ youth with disabilities, LGBTQ parents and their children, and LGBTQ colleagues might reconceptualize CC1K9 as follows:

Impact of the dominant [homophobic and heterosexist] culture on shaping schools and the individuals who study and work in them.

The dominant culture in the United States is both homophobic and heterosexist. Most public schools (and school-based special education programs) reinforce and reproduce the (homophobic and heterosexist) values of the dominant (heterosexual) culture. School-based homophobia and heterosexism damage LGBTQ youth with disabilities, LGBTQ educators, and students with disabilities who have LGBTQ parents (Fox, 2007; Sears, 1996; Smith, 1999).

The Gay, Lesbian, and Straight Education Network (GLSEN) (2005) commissioned a nationwide survey of LGBTQ youth who attended public schools in the United States. Two thirds of the students who participated in this survey had been subjected to verbal abuse and/or physical violence in school settings. Mallon and DeCrescenzo (2006), Remafedi (1994), Sears (1987, 2003), and others have described the intense loneliness and isolation of LGBTQ youth.

Remafedi et al. (1991) conducted a study of 150 gay and lesbian youth in Minneapolis, Minnesota. More than 30% of the youth who participated in this study attempted suicide at least once as a teenager. Almost half of the youth who attempted suicide reported multiple suicide attempts. Remafedi et al. found disproportionately high rates of substance abuse, homelessness, prostitution, family problems, and negative school outcomes among gay and lesbian youth. Young men with "feminine gender role characteristics" were the most likely to engage in self-destructive behaviors (e.g., suicide and substance abuse) and the most likely to experience family problems, homelessness, and negative school outcomes. Remafedi et al. concluded that homophobia (in the schools and in the broader culture) contributes to the misery (and the deaths) of gay and lesbian youth.

Casper, Cuffaro, Schultz, Silin, and Wickens (1996), Corbett (1993), and Harbeck (1992) noted that positive representations of LGBTQ people are usually excluded from the (heterosexist) school curricula. Fox (2007), Powell (2003), and Swartz (2003) recommend that educators infuse LGBTQ issues into the school curricula through the use of literature (written for children and young adults) that explores the lives of LGBTQ individuals. Swartz observed that

> Looking at families, friendships, and relationships critically with regard to the ways in which concepts are passed on through culture can continue on into the ways in which love, friendship, and concepts of family become limited in scope in cultures constructed to privilege binary oppositions. Students can begin to understand the ways in which narrow conceptions not only limit our humanity but also create stereotypes, prejudice, racism, sexism, and homophobia. (p. 11)

Special educators can collaborate with regular classroom teachers who teach students with and without disabilities in inclusive classroom settings to develop lessons based on literature that explores the lives of LGBTQ people. Special educators can help regular classroom teachers adapt and modify these lessons so that students with a wide range of abilities, disabilities, and developmental levels can actively participate in all aspects of each learning activity.

Duke (2007) reviewed the professional and empirical literature on gay and lesbian teachers who work in public school settings. He found that:

1. Public schools in the United States are sites of institutional homophobia.
2. State and federal laws that discriminate against gay and lesbian teachers and other school-based professionals contribute to homophobia in the schools.
3. Many gay and lesbian educators are "closeted" at work because they fear losing their jobs.
4. Gay and lesbian youth, therefore, often lack positive (gay and lesbian) adult role models.
5. Gay and lesbian educators, gay and lesbian students, and students with gay and lesbian parents are verbally abused in school settings.
6. Many gay and lesbian students are violently assaulted in school settings.
7. Many gay and lesbian educators feel empowered when they "come out" at work.
8. The presence of "out and proud" gay and lesbian educators in the schools can create learning environments where gay and lesbian students feel welcome and safe.

Corbett (1993) noted, "There are untold numbers of homosexual . . . [school-based] professionals—most of whom live in fear that they will be discovered, labeled as perverts or pedophiles, and summarily fired—or worse" (30). Special educators can contribute to the development of school environments that welcome and value LGBTQ professionals. When LGBTQ educators feel safe, secure, and supported (and when they believe that they won't be fired for "coming out" at school), they can serve as powerful, positive role models for LGBTQ youth with disabilities.

A number of authors have identified strategies that teachers and administrators can use to create classrooms, programs, and schools that welcome and support LGBTQ youth, LGBTQ parents and their children, and LGBTQ colleagues (Carter, 1998; Corbett, 1993; Fox, 2007; Lamme & Lamme, 2002; Ryan & Martin, 2000). These strategies are delineated in Table 1. Special educators and related service providers can use these strategies to address the "impact of the dominant [homophobic and heterosexist] culture on shaping schools and the individuals who study and work in them" (Council for Exceptional Children, 2003, 54).

Standard 1: Foundations, CC1K10

Potential impact of differences in values, languages, and customs that can exist between the home and school.

Special educators who wish to challenge school-based homophobia and heterosexism and create classrooms, programs, and schools that welcome and support LGBTQ youth with disabilities, LGBTQ parents and their children, and LGBTQ colleagues might reconceptualize CC1K10 as follows:

Potential impact of differences in values . . . and customs that can exist between the [LGBTQ] home and [heterosexist] school.

Millions of children in the United States have LGBTQ parents (Stacey & Biblarz, 2001; Patterson, 1995), and many students with disabilities live in households headed by LGBTQ individuals. Some LGBTQ parents remain "in the closet" because they fear that they, or their children, will not be treated with dignity and respect by teachers, administrators, and other school-based professionals. Other LGBTQ parents do not disclose their sexual orientations and/or gender identities/expressions because they fear violence, job loss, loss of child custody, and/or the myriad other forms of (legal and illegal) discrimination that LGBTQ people commonly encounter. Families headed by LGBTQ parents are, therefore, often invisible and underserved by the public school and special education systems (Casper, Schultz, & Wickens, 1992; Casper et al., 1996; Corbett, 1993; Lamme & Lamme, 2002; Ryan & Martin, 2000; Wickens, 1993).

Table 1

Strategies to Challenge School-Based Homophobia and Heterosexism

- Engage in honest self-reflection to examine and clarify any anti-LGBTQ biases that might affect your teaching and/or your relationships with LGBTQ students, parents, and colleagues.
- Learn more about the lives of LGBTQ people in the contemporary United States (including the discrimination they commonly encounter and their ongoing struggle for legal recognition and equality).
- Infuse LGBTQ issues into the curriculum through the use of high-quality literature that explores the lives of LGBTQ individuals.
- Use antibias curricula and other curricula that explicitly address issues important to the LGBTQ community.
- Use affirming and inclusive language when speaking about gender and sexuality.
- Challenge all homophobic comments made by students, staff, and parents.
- Do not allow anti-LGBTQ bullying.
- Celebrate diversity and teach respect for *all* people.
- Make explicit curricular connections between homophobia and other forms of social oppression (e.g., racism, sexism, ablism, classism).
- Position the LGBTQ liberation movement within the broader struggle for social justice and human rights.
- Display gay-friendly icons and symbols (e.g., rainbow flags, upside-down pink triangles). Members of the LGBTQ community know what these icons and symbols mean.
- Include positive representations of LGBTQ individuals and their families in your classroom, program, and school (e.g., display posters of two women with children—or two men with children—LGBTQ parents and their children will understand that such posters mean "two moms" or "two dads").
- Develop (and enforce) nondiscrimination and nonharassment policies in your classroom, program, and school.

Continued on next page

Table 1 *(Continued)*

- Offer in-service workshops and other professional development opportunities that help school-based professionals strengthen their antibias practices.
- Use staff and parent meetings as opportunities to explore myths, fears, and conflicting views about gender expression/identity, sexuality, and LGBTQ individuals.
- Understand how federal, state, and local laws protect (or discriminate against) LGBTQ parents.
- Appreciate and acknowledge the courage it takes for LGBTQ parents to "come out" in school settings. Understand that many LGBTQ parents are afraid to "come out" because of the very real possibility that they, or their children, will be subjected to harassment, contempt, physical violence, and other forms of (legal and illegal) discrimination.
- Use inclusive language in all verbal and written communication with parents.
- Understand how federal, state, and local laws protect (or discriminate against) LGBTQ teachers and related service providers.
- Appreciate and acknowledge the courage it takes for LGBTQ teachers to "come out" in school settings. Understand that many LGBTQ teachers are afraid to "come out" because of the very real possibility that they might be harassed, treated with contempt, accused of pedophilia, and/or fired.
- Encourage colleagues to engage in community-based activism and school-based inquiry.

According to a recent Gallup poll, many Americans (49%) do *not* believe that homosexual relations are morally acceptable; however, most LGBTQ parents raise their children to believe that homosexual relations *are* morally acceptable. This same poll found that a majority of Americans (53%) do *not* believe that same-sex marriages should be legally valid; most LGBTQ parents, however, raise their children to believe that same-sex unions are just as valid as heterosexual marriages and should, therefore, entitle same-sex partners to the identical (and myriad) benefits, rights, and protections that flow from legally recognized (heterosexual) marriages in the United States (Saad, 2007).

Many teachers, administrators, and other school-based professionals are uncomfortable with (or hostile to) curricula, policies, and practices that acknowledge the lives, values, and aspirations of LGBTQ parents and their children (Carter, 1998; Casper et al., 1992, 1996; Corbett, 1993; Powell, 2003; Wickens, 1993). Fox (2007) noted that this discomfort (and hostility) "plays out in numerous ways . . . in our school communities by the [knowledge] forms we produce, the books that children read, how we address the letters we send home, the posters we display in the hallways and classrooms, what we decide to talk about and teach our children," what we choose *not* to talk about and teach, and all other aspects of the school experience (278). Fox argued that most LGBTQ parents are painfully aware that schools refuse to recognize (or represent) their lives and values and that the "heteronormativity of the schools may prevent [LGBTQ parents] from being involved or participating" (278).

Students with disabilities who have LGBTQ parents have every right to have their parents' values respected (and represented) in their schools and special education programs. Carter (1998), Corbett (1993), Fox (2007), Lamme and Lamme (2002), Ryan and Martin (2000), and others have identified strategies that school-based professionals can use to create classrooms, programs, and schools that recognize and represent the values of LGBTQ parents. These strategies are delineated in Table 1. Special educators and related service providers can use these strategies to address "differences in values . . . and customs that can exist between the [LGBTQ] home and [heterosexist] school" (Council for Exceptional Children, 2003, 54).

Standard 5: Learning Environments and Social Interactions, CC5S1

Create a safe, equitable, positive, and supportive learning environment in which diversities are valued.

Special educators who wish to challenge school-based homophobia and heterosexism and create classrooms, programs, and schools that welcome and support LGBTQ youth with disabilities, LGBTQ parents and their children, and LGBTQ colleagues might reconceptualize CC5S1 as follows:

Create a safe, equitable, positive, and supportive learning environment in which . . . [LGBTQ individuals] . . . are valued.

Critical consciousness is characterized by the ability to recognize, acknowledge, and take action against the multiple forms of oppression that contribute to social, political, and economic injustice (Freire, 1970, 1974). bell hooks (2003), Bornstein (1994), Lather (1986), Pharr (1998), Smith (1999), Trask (1999), and many others have argued that the subjugation of oppressed peoples (e.g., LGBTQ people, people with disabilities, people of color, indigenous peoples, women, the poor) is so all-pervasive that the oppressed are often unaware of their own degradation. Freire described the failure to recognize one's own oppression as a form of *false consciousness* (or a *lack* of critical consciousness). When the awareness of oppression (i.e., *critical consciousness*) begins, so, too, begins the struggle for liberation.

In his book *Movie Stars and Sensuous Scars: Essays on the Journey from Disability Shame to Disability Pride,* the disability rights activist, historian, and poet Steven Brown (2003) chronicled his journey from *disability shame* (i.e., false consciousness) to *disability pride* (i.e., critical consciousness). Brown wrote:

> People with disabilities have forged a group identity. We share a common history of oppression and a common bond of resilience. We generate our music, literature, and other expressions of our lives and culture, infused from our experience of disability. Most importantly, we are proud of ourselves as people with disabilities. We claim our disabilities with pride as part of our identity. (80–81)

I found Brown's story compelling because it mirrored my own (lifelong) journey from *gay shame* (i.e., false consciousness) to *gay pride* (i.e., critical consciousness). I am an "openly gay" professor of special education at a state university in Alaska who spent 9 years teaching adolescents with emotional and behavioral disorders at pubic schools in New York City's Harlem community and on Molokai, a mostly rural island in the Hawaiian archipelago. I have come to believe that my *real* work as a special educator is to empower young people to make the journey from fear, shame, self-loathing, and passivity (i.e., false consciousness) to hope, pride, self-respect, self-advocacy, and social and political action (i.e., critical consciousness). I have also come to believe that students from historically oppressed groups (e.g., LGBTQ youth with disabilities) are more likely to develop critical consciousness in "safe . . . and supportive learning environment[s] in which diversities are valued" (Council for Exceptional Children, 2003, 56). It's a no-brainer, really; when students feel safe and respected—and when they feel that their teachers and peers care about them—they are better able to learn (Noddings, 1992).

The developmental psychologist Abraham Maslow (1970), in his discussion of the hierarchy of human needs, explained that *safety* (e.g., security, stability, and freedom from fear) and *belonging* (e.g., love and acceptance from family, friends, life partners, and colleagues) are essential and prerequisite human needs that must be met before an individual can achieve a sense of *self-esteem* (e.g., achievement, self-respect, and self-worth) and *self-actualization* (e.g., creativity, fulfillment, and the development of innate talents). The disability rights activist and educator Norman Kunc (1992) reconceptualized Maslow's hierarchy of needs from a disability rights perspective. Kunc argued that our present educational system has *inverted* Maslow's hierarchy so that "belonging has been transformed from an unconditional need and right of all people to something that must be earned, something that can be achieved only by the 'best' of us" (37). According to Kunc, students with disabilities are required to *earn* the right to belong to and be accepted by their school communities (often, through the mastery of academic subject matter and/or through the demonstration of "normal," and therefore, "appropriate" social behaviors). Kunc expressed alarm at the severity of the social problems that plague so many of our youth. He identified an "epidemic of self-hatred" in our society and schools, an epidemic that he attributed, in large part, to the *inversion* of Maslow's hierarchy of needs (37). He wrote:

> Academic averages are plummeting, the drop-out rate is increasing, and teen pregnancy is becoming a major social concern. Teenage suicide is increasing at an exponential rate and now has become the second leading cause of adolescent death in the United States and Canada. Extreme violence, drug dependency, gangs, anorexia nervosa, and depression among students have risen to the point that these problems now are perceived almost as an expected part of high school culture. [These] . . . are the symptoms of a society in which self-hatred has become an epidemic. Feelings of personal inadequacy have become so common in our schools and our culture that we have begun to assume that it is part of the nature of being human. It is certainly questionable whether our society will be able to survive if this self-hatred is allowed to flourish. (37–38)

Many LGBTQ youth with disabilities will *never* "earn" the right to belong to their schools and communities (although many desperately want to). Furthermore, many schools create learning environments that are overtly hostile (homophobic, heterosexist, and ablist) to LGBTQ youth and unwelcoming to students with disabilities. These hostile school environments make it difficult for many LGBTQ youth with disabilities to meet an even more essential and basic human need—the need to feel safe, secure, and free from fear—a need that Maslow (1970) argued must be met before one can begin to experience a sense of belonging and acceptance. Special educators who "create . . . safe, equitable, positive, and supportive learning environment[s] in which . . . [LGBTQ individuals] . . . are valued" develop classrooms, programs, and schools where LGBTQ youth with disabilities can begin their (lifelong) journeys from *safety* (and freedom from fear) to *belonging*, from *belonging* (and acceptance by teachers and peers) to *self-esteem*, and from *self-esteem* (and self-acceptance) to *self-actualization* (and critical consciousness) (Council for Exceptional Children, 2003, 56). *These* special educators develop classrooms, programs, and schools that become *incubators* for social justice, critical consciousness, and LGBTQ liberation.

Standard 9: Professional and Ethical Practice, CC9K1

Personal cultural biases and differences that affect one's teaching.

Special educators who wish to challenge school-based homophobia and heterosexism and create classrooms, programs, and schools that welcome and support LGBTQ youth with disabilities, LGBTQ parents and their children, and LGBTQ colleagues might reconceptualize CC9K1 as follows:

Personal . . . [anti-LGBTQ and heterosexist] biases . . . that affect one's teaching.

Educators who benefit most from systems of privilege (e.g., white privilege, male privilege, heterosexual privilege, able-bodied privilege, class privilege) often fail to recognize or acknowledge the oppression of students, parents, and colleagues because "the phenomenon of privilege cannot be recognized within the American ideology of meritocracy" (McIntosh, 1997, 224). Freire (1970, 1974) described the failure to recognize the oppression of others as a form of *false consciousness* (i.e., a *lack* of critical consciousness). Teachers, administrators, and related services personnel who *lack* critical consciousness frequently fail to recognize and acknowledge their own cultural biases; such educators mindlessly contribute to systems of privilege and oppression in educational settings by imposing their personal values, beliefs, and biases on students, parents, and colleagues. *Critically conscious* educators recognize and acknowledge "personal cultural biases and differences that affect . . . [their] teaching" and make every effort to avoid reinforcing and reproducing systems of privilege and oppression based on race, gender, sexual orientation, ability and disability, socioeconomic status, religion (or lack thereof), age, health, language, or national origin (Council for Exceptional Children, 2003, 59).

Skrtic (1995c) explained that *all* human beings, including (LGBTQ *and* heterosexual) special educators, are caught in multiple webs of power, multiple systems of privilege and oppression. Public schools (and school-based special education programs) in the contemporary United States often reinforce and reproduce systems of privilege and oppression based on anti-LGBTQ and heterosexist biases (Smith, 1999). Common anti-LGBTQ and heterosexist biases include homophobia, biphobia, transphobia, internalized homophobia, internalized biphobia, internalized transphobia, heterosexism, cultural heterosexism, and psychological heterosexism. As previously noted, *homophobia* is characterized by the fear, loathing, and/or hatred of gay men and lesbian women (Pharr, 1998). *Biphobia* is characterized by the fear, loathing, and/or hatred of bisexual individuals (Hutchins & Kaahumanu, 1991). *Transphobia* is characterized by the fear, loathing, and/or hatred of transgender individuals (Denny, 1994). Gay men and lesbian women who *internalize* homophobia, bisexuals who *internalize* biphobia, and transgender individuals who *internalize* transphobia frequently struggle with intense feelings of denial, self-loathing, fear of discovery, and/or extreme discomfort with other LGBTQ individuals. As previously noted, *heterosexism* is characterized by the belief that *only* heterosexuality is good, healthy, and "normal" and the assumption that LGBTQ individuals are inferior to heterosexuals (Sears, 1996). *Cultural heterosexism* (or heteronormativity) denies, denigrates, and/or stigmatizes nonheterosexuality in cultural institutions (e.g., public schools and school-based special education programs). *Psychological heterosexism* occurs when an individual internalizes a heteronormative worldview and develops anti-LGBTQ prejudices (Herek, 1990). Special educators who work with LGBTQ youth with disabilities, LGBTQ parents and their children, and LGBTQ colleagues should engage in ongoing (and honest) self-reflection to examine the impact of "personal . . . [anti-LGBTQ and heterosexist] biases . . . that affect [their] teaching" (Council for Exceptional Children, 2003, 59).

Standard 9: Professional and Ethical Practice, CC9S6

Demonstrate sensitivity for the culture, language, religion, gender, disability, socioeconomic status, and sexual orientation of individuals.

This competency *explicitly* addresses sexual orientation. The CEC's decision to adopt this competency was, initially, a source of controversy among CEC members. Some members of the CEC were opposed to the adoption of this competency because it explicitly acknowledges the lives and experiences of lesbian, gay, and bisexual individuals with disabilities; lesbian, gay, and bisexual parents; and lesbian, gay, and bisexual special educators and related service providers. The leadership of the CEC made a courageous (and socially just) decision when they decided to include this competency in the *Knowledge and Skill Standards*.

Unfortunately, this competency does *not* address the lives and experiences of transgender youth with disabilities, transgender parents and their children, and transgender educators. Sexual orientation is *not* synonymous with gender identity and/or gender expression. Some transgender individuals consider themselves to be *heterosexual;* other transgender people consider themselves to be *bisexual;* still others describe themselves as *gay* or *lesbian* (Bornstein, 1994). Transgender youth are especially vulnerable to verbal and physical abuse in school settings and negative school outcomes (GLSEN, 2005; Mallon & DeCrescenzo, 2006). Special educators who wish to challenge the school-based oppression of transgender people and create classrooms, programs, and schools that welcome transgender youth with disabilities, transgender parents and their children, and transgender colleagues might reconceptualize this competency as follows:

Demonstrate sensitivity for the culture, language, religion, gender, disability, socioeconomic status, and sexual orientation of [LGBTQ] individuals.

Special education teachers who actually try to *implement* this competency by creating classrooms and curricula that acknowledge and affirm the lives and experiences of LGBTQ people will no doubt encounter resistance from unsympathetic administrators, school boards, parents, and colleagues. These educators *do* have legal rights, as do LGBTQ students with disabilities and LGBTQ parents. Special educators who encounter such resistance should seek the support and counsel of nonprofit organizations that advocate for and support members of the LGBTQ community and their allies. I strongly recommend two such organizations: Parents,

Families, and Friends of Lesbians and Gays (PFLAG) and the GLSEN.

PFLAG is a national nonprofit organization with more than 200,000 members and supporters that "promotes the health and well-being" of LGBT individuals "and their families and friends" through support, education, and advocacy (http://community.pflag.org/, July 6, 2008). PFLAG has more than 500 chapters located in all 50 states. Special educators can learn more about PFLAG's advocacy efforts, support services, and educational programs by visiting the PFLAG Web site (www.pflag.org).

GLSEN is "the leading national education organization focused on ensuring safe schools for ALL students . . . regardless of sexual orientation or gender identity/expression" (http://www.glsen.org/, July 6, 2008). There are currently more than 40 accredited local GLSEN chapters in the United States. Special educators can obtain information about GLSEN's educational resources, public policy agenda, student organizing programs, and development initiatives by visiting the GLSEN website (www.glsen.org).

Standard 10: Collaboration, CC10K1

Foster respectful and beneficial relationships between families and professionals.

Special educators who wish to challenge school-based homophobia and heterosexism and create classrooms, programs, and schools that welcome and support LGBTQ youth with disabilities, LGBTQ parents and their children, and LGBTQ colleagues might reconceptualize CC1K9 as follows:

Foster respectful and beneficial relationships . . . [with LGBTQ parents and LGBTQ colleagues].

Federal laws require special educators, administrators, and related service providers to collaborate actively with students with disabilities and their families to develop individualized education programs, transition plans, and other special education services (Americans with Disabilities Act of 1990, PL 101-336; Individuals with Disabilities Education Act of 1990, PL 101-476; Individuals with Disabilities Education Act Amendments of 1997, PL 105-17). Thayer-Bacon and Brown (1995) noted collaborators need to feel safe to speak and to believe that their voices will be heard and their efforts valued. These authors suggested that individuals who collaborate in school settings characterized by diversity must understand the impact of history on oppressed groups. To include the voices and perspectives of each person participating in the collaborative process and to benefit fully from the contributions that he or she might bring to the collaborative effort, team members must consider the possible impact of historical (and contemporary) forms of oppression (e.g., racism, sexism, classism, ablism, homophobia, and heterosexism) on individual team members (Duke, 2004). Collaborators should realize that historical (and contemporary) forms of oppression might silence and/or marginalize individual team members and cause them to feel invisible, unheard, and afraid. Special educators, administrators, and related service providers who collaborate with LGBTQ parents and LGBTQ colleagues should be mindful that these collaborations are taking place within school settings that almost certainly reinforce and reproduce the homophobia and heterosexism that pervade contemporary U.S. society (Fox, 2007; Sears, 1987, 1996, 2003; Smith, 1999). School-based professionals should be aware that many LGBTQ individuals feel a level of discomfort, distrust, fear, and/or hostility toward public schools (and school-based special education programs) because these institutions have been, and continue to be, sites of homophobic and heterosexist oppression.

Carter (1998), Corbett (1993), Fox (2007), Lamme and Lamme (2002), Ryan and Martin (2000), and others have identified strategies that school-based professionals can use to challenge homophobia and heterosexism. These strategies are delineated in Table 1. Special educators, administrators, and related service providers can employ many of these strategies to "foster respectful and beneficial [collaborative] relationships" with LGBTQ parents and LGBTQ colleagues (Council for Exceptional Children, 2003, 59).

Conclusion

Skrtic (2005) argued that a dramatic increase in student diversity, coupled with the extensive bureaucratization of U.S. public education in the first half of the twentieth century, resulted in the construction of a special education system that pathologizes students with disabilities and labels disproportionate numbers of poor and minority students as "mentally deficient" or "severely emotionally disturbed." He explained that school organizations are

> Standardized, nonadaptable structures that must screen out diversity by forcing students with unconventional needs out of the system. And because ... [schools] are public bureaucracies charged with serving all students, special education emerges as a legitimating device, an institutional practice that, in effect, shifts the blame for school failure to students through medicalizing and objectifying discourses, while reducing the uncertainty of student diversity by containing it through exclusionary practices. (149–150)

Skrtic urged special educators to reconceptualize their work with students and families as part of the broader struggle for social justice and human rights and to engage actively in inclusive practices that recognize and affirm—rather than *pathologize*—the diversity of their students.

The *CEC Knowledge and Skills Standards* affirm the value of diversity and require special educators to consider multiple forms of diversity as they develop and implement instructional services for students with disabilities. The CEC standards repeatedly acknowledge, and thereby *legitimize,* culture, language, and disability as appropriate topics for professional discourse. *Other* forms of diversity, including sexual orientation and gender identity/expression, remain taboo and have been marginalized or excluded from the professional discourse that surrounds the field of special education. Special educators who wish to challenge school-based homophobia and heterosexism and create classrooms, programs, and schools that welcome and support LGBTQ youth with disabilities, LGBTQ parents and their children, and LGBTQ colleagues can reconceptualize the CEC standards so that concepts of *culture* and *diversity* are understood to encompass sexual orientation and gender identity/expression.

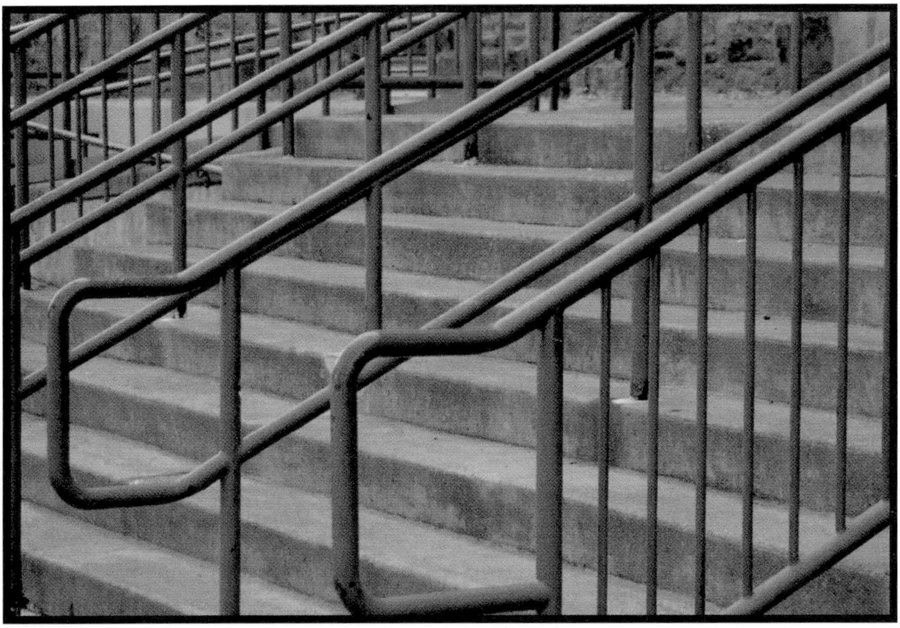

Chapter Seven

School for the Self: Examining the Role of Educational Settings in Identity Development among Gay, Bisexual, and Questioning Male Youth of Color

Omar B. Jamil and Gary W. Harper

ADOLESCENCE IS A developmental time period marked by multiple transitions, when youth are undergoing the physical changes of puberty while at the same time trying to develop an integrated sense of self. Unfortunately, during this process when youth are learning about and growing comfortable with their identity, they may also be subject to harassment and isolation if they are different from their peers. These negative experiences, along with other stressors of adolescence, can make the process of identity development challenging.

Psychological research describes the development of individual identity as the gradual movement toward becoming an adult who is integrated into society, and it involves, among other things, determining one's life goals and aspirations (Erikson, 1980). In addition to this type of development, sometimes referred to as ego identity development (Erikson, 1980), individuals who belong to minority groups must also develop their sense of identity as it relates to their minority group membership. Youth who identify with various ethnic minority groups or who identify as sexual minorities must also develop a sense of ethnic and/or sexual identity. But how do youth develop these sometimes conflicting multiple identities?

Prominent models of ethnic and sexual identity development share similar elements and suggest that identity development is typically prompted by a particular event, either negative (e.g., experiencing racism) or positive (e.g., having a romantic attraction to a person of the same sex). After this initial stage prompting awareness of one's identity, the individual engages in a process of exploration within his or her community, which may involve a withdrawal from the larger dominant community. During this process, an individual may view his or her group as better than the dominant group, but over time, people integrate their sexual or ethnic identity with their overall identity. This general process of identity development has been discussed in the literature as occurring both in linear stages (Cass, 1979; Cross, 1978; Kim, 1981; Phinney, 1989; Troiden, 1989) and in nonlinear phases (Atkinson, Morten, & Sue, 1979; Helms, 1990; Smith, 1991). However, the above theories all apply singularly to either sexual *or* ethnic identity development, and none have specifically explored the process of identity development as it occurs for individuals who are members of both sexual and ethnic minority communities.

In examining the research on sexual and ethnic identity development, one cannot simply apply the research that has focused on either sexual or ethnic identity to individuals who identify as both sexual and ethnic minorities. On the one hand, racism within the gay community may present a barrier to sexual identity development, because a person will not feel comforted and welcome in his or her own sexuality due to exclusion from elements within the gay community (Diaz, 1998; Harper, Jernewall, & Zea, 2004; Martinez & Sullivan, 1998). Similarly, heterosexism in ethnic minority communities may prevent ethnic identity development, whereby youth cannot feel totally comfortable in their ethnic identity due to intolerance and exclusion by their own ethnic group members (Chung & Katayama, 1998; Montiero & Fuqua, 1994; Parks, 2001; Tremble, Schneider, & Appathurai, 1989). Additionally, while many ethnic minority youth learn about their ethnic culture's established history, traditions, practices, and communities from their parents, they typically do not receive similar types of information about "gay culture." Therefore, these youth often learn about "gay culture" and its accompanying language, rituals, symbols, and culturally normative behaviors and practices through nonfamilial adults, peers, mass media, and the Internet (Harper, 2007).

It is clear that research on sexual and ethnic identity development may not be wholly applicable for sexual minority youth of color due to their unique life circumstances. Consequently, it is not only important to understand the distinct experiences of sexual and ethnic minority youth, but it is also necessary to reexamine the theoretical ways in which youth are understood to better accommodate for their unique experiences. From a critical constructivist theoretical perspective, the unique multiplicity of identities for gay and bisexual youth of color requires a reinterpretation of how identity development is socially constructed and defined, thereby challenging current stage models of ethnic and sexual identity. Additionally, critical constructivist theorists would examine the contexts within which identity development occurs, as well as the socially constructed nature of the labels used to define their identities. From this dearth of applicable research to sexual and ethnic minority youth and the suggestions posed from a critical theory perspective, there is a clear need to understand the specific processes that these youth undertake to develop both their sexual and ethnic identities. How do youth develop their ethnicity when they cannot feel entirely comfortable in their ethnic community due to homophobia and heterosexism? How do youth develop their sense of sexual identity when racism in the gay community marginalizes and isolates them further?

Research on how individuals develop their sense of adult identity suggests that youth learn from their immediate surroundings, which involve informal mentoring by significant adults in their lives, as well as through peers (Erikson, 1980; Marcia, 1966). This form of mentorship and learning has become an integral part of adult identity development, and as a result, most individuals eventually develop a positive and healthy sense of adult identity. But how do sexual minority youth of color do this when they are navigating multiple processes of identity development without clear supportive communities or institutions? What institutions do they access to assist them with developing a positive and integrated sense of self? What roles do current educational institutions, both formal and informal, have in the development of ethnic and sexual identity?

Exploring Important Institutions: Our Methods

To examine the role of educational institutions in the multiple identity development processes of gay/bisexual/questioning (GBQ) male adolescents of color, data originated from a qualitative exploration of the specific processes by which youth developed their sexual and ethnic identities. We conducted interviews with GBQ-identified Latino and African American male youth living in the Chicago metropolitan area as part of a larger study focused on issues of identity, sexuality, substance use, and sexual behaviors among GBQ male youth.

We recruited a total of 97 GBQ male youth between the ages of 15 and 22 through a diverse array of lesbian-, gay-, bisexual-, and transgender- (LGBT-) focused support organizations and community agencies. After screening for eligibility, we administered a quantitative survey to all participants, assessing demographic factors, sexual identity, ethnic identity, sexual behaviors, and substance use. Because the analyses presented here focused on issues of multiple identity development processes for GBQ youth of color, we considered only the 22 interviews with youth who reported both a mono-ethnic identity as either African American or Latino and a sexual identity as gay, bisexual, or questioning.

The sample of 12 Latino participants included 9 Mexican/Mexican American individuals, 2 Puerto Rican adolescents, and 1 who was of both Puerto Rican and Mexican ancestry. Among the Latino participants, 7 self-identified as gay, 4 self-identified as bisexual, and 1 self-identified as questioning. Of the 10 African American participants, 6 self-identified as gay, 3 self-identified as bisexual, and 1 self-identified as questioning. We derived all demographic information listed above from the quantitative measure where youth selected one from a list of options to describe their identities.

The in-depth qualitative interview explored 4 aspects of the participants' identities: masculine identity, ethnic identity, sexual identity, and an integrated identity—but the data reported here originated from sections of the interview that focused on ethnic and sexual identity (see the appendix). Phenomenological and constructivist frameworks commensurate with queer theory guided the creation of the semistructured interview protocol. Thus, for each identity, participants were asked to define and describe their identity using their own words and conceptualizations, and then they were guided through an in-depth exploration of factors that have influenced each specific identity development (e.g., community connections and facilitators/supports). Because we did not impose predetermined heteronormative sexuality and ethnicity labels on the participants, the youth provided responses that were less culturally bound.

Learning from Youths' Stories: Our Analysis

Because we were seeking to learn about the lived experiences of GBQ male adolescents of color with regard to their sexual and ethnic identities, our analysis used a psychological phenomenological framework (Creswell, 1998; Patton, 1990). This allowed us to learn about the sociocultural behaviors, language, roles, and interactions within a culture-sharing group and to focus on individual and shared experiences and meanings given to those experiences. By understanding each individual's experiences, the researcher can determine the larger framework to describe the structure, or "essence," of the phenomenon (Schutz, 1970). The analysis was also influenced by our constructivist approach to having participants define and describe their sexuality and ethnicity using their own terms and conceptualizations. The analysis for this chapter solely focused on the educational and other institutional factors and supports used by participants in the development of their sexual and ethnic identities.

After the participants were interviewed, the transcripts were analyzed and additional codes were created and/or clarified based on our phenomenological framework. Initial a priori codes were created (such as "identity awareness," "identity connection," and "identity comfort") that were grounded in identified core concepts from literature concerning sexual and ethnic identity development. We created pattern codes to connect subsequent concepts under larger headings within each transcript; then we identified consistent patterns in meaning, concepts, and themes across all interviews (Creswell, 1998; Miles & Huberman, 1994). Given the phenomenological and constructivist frameworks that guided our data collection and analysis, we sought to represent different voices and ensure that conceptual "outliers" were not silenced by the average or dominant perspective by presenting all voiced themes instead of only those that were endorsed by a majority of participants.

To ensure the quality and ecological validity of the interview data, we enacted several credibility checks. These involved member-checking individual interviews (after half of the interviews were conducted) and focus groups (after all interviews were conducted) with youth whereby findings were presented and feedback was solicited, as well as feedback interviews with adult "experts" who had ample experience working with GBQ youth.

Finding Youths' Identities: Our Results

In examining the narratives of their sexual and ethnic identity development processes, specifically the use of supports in the development process, it was clear that youth used not only identified educational contexts such as schools, but also other environments and settings to learn about their sexual and ethnic identity. As a result, "educational contexts" will be discussed in a broader sense as settings in which learning occurred. From our analysis of the many types of educational contexts used by youth in their identity development process, 4 primary findings emerged.

The first finding was that youth developed their multiple identities concurrently but with limited interaction throughout the processes. Second, school settings served as contexts and facilitators of ethnic and sexual identity development. Community-based organizations (CBOs) also were instrumental in the development of sexual and ethnic identity development. Finally, informal educational contexts such as family, peers, and cultural events were also important in the development and continued connections across one's identities and communities

Development of Multiple Identities Concurrently during Adolescence

Overall, we found that youth were often developing their sexual and ethnic identities concurrently. This is made evident by examining the time periods during which their first awareness of sexual and ethnic identities occurred, which typically took place during the junior high and high school years. For example, in the following quote, a 19-year-old Latino youth identifies his first awareness of ethnic identity:

> I first realized that I was Mexican when my freshman year of high school at International Night . . . one of the Spanish dances I saw, I just watched these people and look at them and say, wow, that is so awesome! And that just got me started on it [the investigation of his identity].

The same participant, in a later portion of the interview, describes how he became aware of his sexual identity:

> Well, around that time (high school) I thought I was bisexual and I still claimed to be bisexual, until my senior year in high school. It wasn't until around January, I think it was, I said, forget it. I'm gay. I'm not gonna be ashamed of it anymore. There's no point in being ashamed of it. I . . . this was after having as many friends as I did who were gay, going to several gay events, I had gone to Pride that year, that was my first year going to the Pride Parade, 2003.

Although the majority of youth reported that they engaged their ethnic and sexual identity development processes postpuberty, some youth indicated that their ethnic identity development started during elementary school. In addition, youth stated that the process of identity development was one that involved exploration and reflection, and therefore this process spanned several months to several years. By considering these two points in tandem, we can hypothesize that the mutual overlap between the two identity development processes exists for most youth. Further, this suggests that for many youth, there are moments when they are developing their sense of ethnicity in relation to their sexuality and vice versa.

We also found that youth, in the process of sexual and ethnic identity development, did not specifically benefit or become emboldened by previously experiencing other forms of oppression. This result contradicts findings in prior research, such as the work of Russell and Truong (2001), who suggested that one reason why sexual minority people of color are not significantly affected by the acknowledgment and development of their sexual identity is because they were inoculated to oppression by previously experiencing it during the development of their ethnic identity. The assumption is that youth learn how to navigate ethnic marginalization and oppression and will be able to apply those skills when later confronted with heterosexism and homophobia. Dube and Savin-Williams (1999) used this reasoning to explain differences in academic achievement scores in relation to sexual identity development milestones. They found that white sexual minority youth had significantly higher fluctuations in their grade point average (often negative) compared to their Latino, African American, and Asian American counterparts, whose scores overall stayed consistent throughout development.

Interestingly, although youth in our study engaged in multiple identity development processes that often overlapped, they did not specifically reference another identity development process when describing each process. Youth who may have developed their sense of ethnicity prior to developing their identity as a GBQ male did not talk about enacting any of the steps used in their ethnic identity process while developing their sexual identity. Analyses suggested that cross-referencing of identity development did not occur for these youth because sexual and ethnic identity development involved two very different processes.

Overall, the process of developing ethnic identity involved "owning" their predetermined ethnic identity label, which was transmitted through their parents and other members of their ethnic group, including community members. Developing sexual identity, on the other hand, involved a process of developing an appropriate label to describe their non-heterosexual sexual identity and later disclosing that identity to others. During this process, youth often did not have access to GBQ-specific resources, and as a result, they had to develop their sexual identity on their own without much outside assistance.

Youth, therefore, developed their sexual identity through a very individualized process—one that was often invisible to their parents. The invisibility of this search was paramount for youth, because many feared expulsion from their parents' household merely for their same-sex sexual desires or attractions. Among youth of color, more than 30 percent reported in the quantitative survey in our larger study that they had been kicked out of their homes by their parents for at least one night due to their sexual orientation.

During the process of sexual identity exploration, youth developed a complex understanding of their own sexual and romantic attractions and eventually identified a label that would best encapsulate their identity. Although most youth in our study identified themselves as "gay," some adopted other labels in the qualitative interview in addition to "bisexual" or "questioning," including "trade" and "queer." The following quote of a 19-year-old African American male who first identified himself as "questioning" illustrates the nuances of identity labeling.

> Very secretive about . . . okay, wow, secret. Nobody don't really don't know that hey, you're like that. That's why people in the world will, that's why gay male or gay female they call me trade. You know what trade is? Trade is another way of saying that okay, he's gay but he doesn't play as gay. Or he's bisexual, but not really bisexual. Same thing for a female, trade. They're like trading off. That's what it is.

Along with the label, youth also provided a specific definition to describe what their identity label meant, with definitions of the same label varying across participants.

Due to the very different pathways to identity development, one public (ethnic identity development) and one private (sexual identity development), youth did not use the same resources or processes in one area of development while going through the other. For example, due to negative cultural views regarding same-sex attracted individuals, youth typically could not use their immediate family members in the development of their sexual identity as they may have done during the process of ethnic identity velopment. Conversely, youth could simply develop their ethnic identity through speaking with family members and peers and did not have to resort to the use of secretive and/or impersonal resources such as the Internet or community agencies as they did with their sexual identity.

Role of Schools as Facilitators to Identity Development

As indicated in the previous section, youth simultaneously developed their sexual and ethnic identities accessing different overall processes. In addition, youth may use the same resource in the development of their sexual or ethnic identity in very different ways. Although youth may actively pursue resources in the development of their identities, such as going to agencies or reading materials, they also learn and draw on the strengths of the institutions in their immediate environment. Because adolescents are engaged in the school environment for more than 30 to 40 hours a week, many found elements in this educational environment that facilitated the development of their identities.

With regard to ethnic identity, participants stated that their school served as a venue where they learned about their own cultural history. A majority of our Latino participants grew up in primarily Latino neighborhoods, and therefore most of their classmates were ethnically similar. As a result, learning about their cultural history and heritage was part of the school's history curriculum. This also occurred through acknowledging and celebrating ethnic-specific holidays and festivals. One participant's teacher directly challenged him to learn more about his ethnic identity and tutored him in his ethnic history.

Although many of our African American participants attended school with primarily African American peers, they typically did not express that their ethnicity or culture was integrated or discussed in the school environment. One participant did, however, note that his teachers informed him of potential career options to end the cycle of poverty endemic in his ethnic community.

School for the Self

The previous points illustrate how ethnically similar classmates and supportive teachers can foster an educational environment that promotes ethnic identity development through teaching about culture and heritage. However, participants also learned from experiences with ethnically dissimilar peers. First, some participants found that cultural exchange events not only made them proud of their own ethnic group, but also encouraged tolerance and appreciation of other ethnic groups, a sentiment that was echoed throughout the school curriculum. This appreciation of other ethnic groups has been noted by ethnic identity theorists (Atkinson, Morten, & Sue, 1979; Cross, 1978; Helms, 1990) as being integral to the development of an integrated sense of identity, because one must balance valuing his or her ethnic community as well the numerical majority (white) community. Additionally, youth indicated that being in schools or classrooms where they were an ethnic minority facilitated their sense of being an "other" and prompted the development of their own minority identity. This experience of being the "other" was not primarily negative and often required participants to reflect on the differences between their own ethnicity and the ethnicity of those youth surrounding them. However, some participants had the negative experience of social marginalization, whereby they could not bond with their classmates, either due to a lack of shared features or interests or because of overt rejection. The following quote by a 17-year-old Latino illustrates his experience of trying to connect with white peers:

> I think that, well, even recently when I went into high school freshman year, I had all these honors classes with all these like white kids and, like, I did not find their humor funny at all. And I was there, not laughing at their jokes, and I felt different. I felt weird, and then I realized that, you know what, I have different beliefs than these people do. I have different ways of thinking, different ways of what I find funny or not.

Some youth also used school-based, ethnic-specific social groups to find camaraderie among ethnically similar peers, to learn about their ethnic culture and heritage, or to celebrate ethnic-specific holidays and traditions. Although the activities of these groups were not predominantly focused on ethnicity or culture, participants mentioned enjoying being in the company of their peers in these school groups. Therefore, they became a space where youth could celebrate their culture by reinterpreting traditions in a more youth-oriented fashion, which increased motivation to value and maintain their culture. Also, youth felt as though their ethnically similar peers understood the struggles they experienced in the school setting, and they did not have to explain their culture or their ethnic-specific experiences to them. Although a school-based setting provided a formal and structured environment for ethnic identity facilitation, participants found that their ethnically similar peers also provided this same type of support.

Previous research on the process of ethnic identity development does not specifically attend to the roles that the school setting and the educational system may play in the development of ethnic identity, but it does identify a stage of active search that youth enter upon becoming aware of their ethnic identity (Atkinson, Morten, & Sue, 1979; Cross, 1978; Helms, 1990; Kim, 1981). As the previous quote suggests, other research addresses "eye-opening" moments that initiate identity development. This is contained in the stage called Encounter in the theories of Cross (1978) and Helms (1990), and Awakening to Social Political Awareness in Kim's (1981) theory of identity development.

The school environment also assisted youth in developing their sexual identities, although the types of support varied across participants. Due to heterosexism prevalent in today's society, many school environments were not venues where LGBT topics were included in school curriculum. Despite years of movement toward the attainment of rights for LGBT individuals, discussing LGBT topics in schools was still viewed as taboo by our participants. Additionally, many participants stated that the school environment was a venue where individuals would be harassed because of their perceived sexual orientation. A few participants, however, noted that teachers who identified as heterosexuals had provided support by either directly challenging other students who made heterosexist remarks or supporting the GBQ student individually after class.

Despite the heterosexist environment, however, some youth were able to view their schools as venues that would assist them with developing their sexuality. For example, some youth used

School for the Self

school-based social groups to find camaraderie and support with other LGBT peers. A few of the youth who used such groups did not specifically identify as LGBT before entering the group, but rather developed their sense of self with regard to their sexuality through participation in the group. For participants who were in college, some also used school-based organizations, primarily as a means of building a community within a college environment. One participant, a 22-year-old Latino, decided to create a social group at his college campus to connect with other LGB-identified students.

> Um, I think one of the interesting things was I didn't really have a direct connection to the [gay] community. So I decided to create one when I went to [college name]. I was active in a couple of organizations and then I became president of student government, and one of the perks of being president is that you get to approve or deny any organization, so I was like, hey, I'm gonna create a gay club. So I founded the [name of organization] on campus...
> So [for the first meeting] I ordered one pizza, I posted flyers and sat back and watched people pour in, we had like, close to 20 people showed up at that meeting and it was really good as far as getting to know people and networking and just talking ... I think it worked out very well.

In addition to accessing groups within the school or university setting, youth also identified older adults who were LGBT who served as role models. Two participants noted that learning that a teacher was gay-identified helped them normalize the idea of being gay. Both participants varied in the level of interaction with these teachers, but the mere presence of a role model who was LGBT enabled the youth to realize that being gay or bisexual was not necessarily different from being heterosexual, and that individuals who are LGBT-identified can live satisfying lives as adults. One 19-year-old Latino participant disclosed his sexuality to a track and field teacher, who later privately disclosed his sexuality and became a source for advice:

> We didn't know, like, their [teachers at his school] business or anything . . ., like we didn't, like, I didn't know he [teacher] was gay . . . until like, until after . . . when um, because I happened to be dating someone in my school at that time, and he had, . . . he had mentioned it to him that we were dating. And then he was like, oh . . . so then that's when he started

to feel more comfortable and he told us about his partner. So, and then I would go up to him for advice. I think I did that like maybe three times, couple of times.

Similar to ethnic identity development, participants also indicated initial awareness of their sexuality in the school setting. All participants became aware of their sexual orientation through simply being cognizant of their same-sex sexual and romantic attractions. Many of these instances of awareness—of noticing that they were attracted to members of the same sex—occurred in the school setting, whether that was during class, in gym, or in after-school activities. Our findings are consistent with theories of sexual identity development which state that part of development involves immersion and identification with one's sexual identity community, although previous theories assumed that individuals engage in this process once they have completed college (Cass, 1979; Coleman, 1982; Troiden, 1989).

The Roles of Community-Based Organizations in Identity Development

The previous section detailed how youth developed their sexual and ethnic identities through their school educational settings where they spent a majority of time learning and socializing with other youth. Youth also stated that they used an array of community agencies that facilitated the development of their sexual and ethnic identities. It should be noted here that youth were primarily recruited for this study through community-based organizations (CBOs). These organizations offered a range of services, with some providing a "drop in" center and others hosting educational activities through programming that focused on pertinent life issues. As facilitators of identity development, there were a variety of ways in which these community-based organizations (CBOs) were helpful.

Ethnic-specific CBOs (predominantly heterosexual) were described as playing a facilitative role in youth's ethnic identity development. Participants stated that they felt empowered by staff members with college degrees who belonged to their ethnic group. One particular agency strongly encouraged its members to pursue advanced degrees and careers, and participants stated that they enjoyed visiting college campuses while at the same time learning about their culture. Participants also benefited from the supportive and accepting environments created by CBO staff and participants. One 18-year-old Latino participant stated that he preferred and found more support in a primarily heterosexual Latino CBO compared to an ethnically/racially mixed LGBT CBO.

> [In CBO A-GBQ Agency], where it's nothing but African American and white people over there . . . So I fit in, but it's kind of awkward around them. And if I find Hispanic LGBT men around, in [CBO B-Latino Agency], well, the people who I talk to there, they're really accepting and so I feel like I can openly talk to them about practically anything.

Participants also identified religious institutions as facilitating their ethnic identity. They described religious institutions as being a social center where the diversity of members of their ethnic group congregate and connect with one another. In religious institutions, celebrations were observed specific to their ethnic and religious cultural traditions, such as Kwanzaa, which a 19-year-old African American youth describes here.

> I supposed, um, back when I went to church, that was a really big influence. Because they had annual Kwanzaa celebrations and it was an all-black church, there were just, it was kind of a, it just had the gamut of black culture in it just from like the really well educated and not so much, it had everyone that I had seen up to that point, the different aspects of my culture all just in one place every Sunday. And so I think that really made a big difference.

Previous literature on ethnic identity development does not specifically state that youth would use CBOs per se. However, theories acknowledge that youth go through a period of immersion and learning about their identity through a variety of sources before fully integrating ethnicity into their larger holistic identity (Atkinson, Morten, & Sue, 1979; Cross, 1978; Helms, 1990; Phinney, 1989; Troiden, 1989).

Participants also identified organizations that served the needs of LGBT youth as being supportive in the development of their sexual identity. Youth primarily identified CBOs as providing meaningful connections within their LGBT community during initial stages of identity development. Through these community agencies, they were able to develop and identify with a sexual orientation label. Additionally, they were better able to understand what that identity would entail. Youth learned through their peers, staff members, and guest speakers what life is like for a sexual minority person. For example, youth were instructed what to expect and how to manage heterosexism by the larger dominant communities. In addition, youth learned about current issues in LGBT politics and news and other relevant information that may be pertinent to their current developmental age group or that may be important issues to consider as they grow older.

Participants also learned how they could successfully navigate gay, white, and ethnic communities as a GBQ individual. Youth would learn what being in the gay community meant, and how to connect safely with other sexual minority individuals in the gay community. They also learned ways to traverse their potentially heterosexist ethnic communities by discussing how and to whom to disclose their sexuality, as well as how to handle conflicts that arise due to heterosexism. In addition, they gained self-confidence, garnered support, and met other friends who fostered new connections with the gay community. A 19-year-old African American youth noted:

> Yeah, first, after I started going to like say for instance groups like [GBQ Group] or anything like that, you started to fit in like, hey, this culture is funny, to me it's like, it's culture. This culture is funny and man, I love to be a part of this, this is funny.

By facilitating and engaging in discussions of sex and sexuality, participants also stated that other youth and staff members in these organizations were able to help them normalize being GBQ. They fostered discussions and identified positive aspects of their sexual identities and communities, including an understanding of GBQ history. Youth identified staff as being positive role models—staff who often talked about their personal lives and gave the participants insight into how their lives can be "normal" despite being a sexual minority. Additionally, the space created in the organization enabled the youth to be themselves without worry of reprimand from a heterosexist society, even if temporarily. The following quote from an 18-year-old African American male illustrates this concept:

> Just the fact that I could come there and be myself. Which I found out later wasn't really different from the person that I thought was so fake and phony. I was just accepting of myself when I was there, and then not accepting as soon as I left. But when I was there I felt comfortable just to think, yeah, oh, my gosh, hey, I can look at guys and not be afraid. Yeay!

Informal Educational Contexts

In this study, it was clear that youth were continually learning as they traversed their multiple communities of membership. They learned about and became more comfortable with their sexual and ethnic identities through these informal educational contexts, such as impromptu and valuable interactions with other individuals. Many developmental theorists have emphasized that connection to and participation in elements of either a sexual or ethnic identity community is integral to successful identity development (Atkinson, Morten, & Sue, 1979; Cross, 1978; Helms, 1990; Phinney, 1989; Smith, 1991).

First, participants identified members of their immediate and extended family as facilitators of their ethnic identity development. Family members were seen as transmitters of culture by teaching language skills, cultural elements (e.g., food and dance), and generalized concepts of how to be a member of their ethnic group (e.g., how to be "Mexican"). Additionally, participants stated that their family reminded them to be constantly aware of their ethnic identity (e.g., "never forget you're a Puerto Rican"), and instilled within them a sense of pride in their ethnic identity.

To break free from the social marginalization and oppression faced by communities of color, family members also encouraged the participants to pursue an education, to be goal-oriented, and to persevere in life. The following quote from a 22-year-old African American participant illustrates the transmission of these goals and how they reverberated within the school setting.

> And then it's like my, my two uncles, they very much, like my uncle, he very much, my older uncle, he very much taught me like the teachers in school. So I mean, the very much teachers and all, Malcolm X, Martin

Luther King, stuff like that. And he very much taught me other stuff that was in the school, too. I'd say he played a positive role in my life.

Participants identified peers as facilitative in the development of their ethnic identity. Peers transmitted cultural elements (e.g., ethnic-specific music and food) and traditions (participation in cultural-specific events) and also were described as imbuing youth, including this 19-year-old Latino male, with a sense of pride and appreciation for his ethnic identity.

> [Interviewer] Like do all your friends sort of help you learn things about being Mexican?
> [Youth] Not so much learn, but I guess appreciate the fact that I am Mexican.

Next, many participants indicated finding support for their sexual identity development from heterosexually identified peers, both males and females. Most of these peers were individuals from their schools, who were also members of their ethnic group.

Participants also identified LGBT friends as being facilitative in the development of their sexual identities. Many of these friends introduced them to LGBT-specific neighborhoods, activities/events, and CBOs. Additionally, they provided participants with social support, either through explicitly giving advice or being positive role models. Some participants indicated that being in the vicinity of other LGBT-identified youth during a time when they were developing their own sexual identities was invaluable, helping to foster self-acceptance during their identity development. This finding supports theoretical perspectives on sexual identity development (Cass, 1979; Coleman, 1982; Troiden, 1989) that emphasize the value of positive interactions with supportive peers. The following quote from a 19-year-old Latino illustrates how one participant became a resource to other individuals who were struggling with their GBQ sexual identity:

> I was dating some guy and um, in school, so then I was just like, it was just about time where people were gonna start to [date], so then, and then um, I don't know, like we were sort of the first couple kind of, so then after that, like I guess it made it easier for everybody else, so then a lot of people came out after us. A lot of people. (chuckles) So it, it kind of felt good to sort of be the one to like free everybody else, in a way.

Participants also identified specific adults who helped facilitate comfort with their sexual identity. These adults were primarily service providers and included a therapist, a nurse, and a social worker. Participants indicated that these adults all took time to listen to the concerns of the youth and provided advice, affirmation, and acceptance. The following quote from an 18-year-old Latino illustrates how a nurse provided a supportive environment by opposing heterosexism in a school setting.

> She watched out for me a lot. This one time, there was this [gay] basher, and she practically like, I was in the nurse's office, there was this [gay] basher there who's been saying all these things, but he didn't, I guess he didn't know about me, because I was just sitting there. He was saying, oh, how he hates all these queers, get some guy like to hit on them or something. She just told him you know what it means to shut the fuck up? She literally snapped on him. And she kicked him out and, well, she didn't kick him out, she stepped outside with him. She had this huge conversation with him. And she calmed him down quite a bit.

The sexual orientation of these adults, however, did not affect the quality or the supportive effects of the interaction. Rather, participants found comfort in their acceptance and their abilities to listen to the participants' struggles and challenges in a nonjudgmental manner.

A number of participants also identified events within their GBQ communities as facilitating their sense of sexual identity. This connection was typically through the annual Pride parade, a festival celebrating the history and culture of the LGBT community. Some participants stated that they were involved in the actual parade itself, developing floats or marching in the parade. Others merely found connection through watching the parade and being instilled with a sense of pride through the positive and empowering images illustrating the diversity and solidarity of the LGBT community. Other participants spoke about dances for LGBT youth, organized by a local CBO. The following text from a 16-year-old Latino illustrates how he viewed the freedom and connection associated with this event:

> We're crazy, we're always joking about everything. Like when I'm at [event], all my friends are just like, oh, just go to the bathroom and ex-

plain all like that. It's funny because you're like, oh, this is, this is pretty interesting. We're always doing crazy things. And don't really see that with a lot of straight people.

Lessons Learned: How to Best Serve GBQ Male Youth of Color

The current study examined how youth developed their sexual and ethnic identities, while negotiating challenges to multiple-minority membership, such as racism and heterosexism. Overall, we found that youth were very creative and resourceful in the use of educational and informal contexts for the development of their identities. Youth found themselves and others like themselves by using supports within their immediate surroundings. Consequently, they were able to integrate multiple identities successfully into their larger holistic self-concept.

Given the pervasiveness of heteronormativity in school settings, which often serves to silence and pathologize GBQ youth (Quinlivan & Town, 1999), educators can use social constructivist and/or queer theories to create more accepting classroom environments for GBQ youth by guiding all students in a continual process of reconstructing inclusive notions of sexuality (Davidson, 2006; McCready, 2004). By focusing on *all* students, educators can act in a preventive fashion by attempting to shift negative heteronormative beliefs before they result in acts of violence and harassment directed at GBQ youth. In accordance with social constructivist and queer theories, this may be accomplished by creating activities and exercises that encourage students to explore and disrupt (hetero)normalizing social discourses about sexuality critically and to view sexuality as a fluid concept rather than a binary and fixed category.

Systems-level interventions are also needed to promote the healthy development of GBQ youth of color. School systems should confront cultural or institutionalized heterosexism by combating harassment of students who are perceived to be GBQ, by identifying potential role models who are GBQ, and by making the school curriculum more inclusive of the histories, lives, and experiences of GBQ individuals. By doing so, youth will be able to learn about their identities in a more public fashion without having to be labeled by others for seeking information and/or attending school-based groups. Additionally, heterosexism should be combated in all aspects of the school environment, which would involve all staff within the school setting. In addition to these classroom interventions, youth who identify as GBQ also need specific multidimensional support services and the creation of safe spaces for self-expression and reflection (Davidson, 2006; McCready, 2004).

Participants already referenced CBOs as being positive and inclusive of GBQ people of color, and many stated that CBOs were able to assist them in successfully navigating their multiple identities. Not all CBOs, however, are created equal. Participants noted that some GBQ-oriented CBOs are more inclusive of ethnic minority individuals than others. CBOs should, therefore, network with one another to assist in meeting the unique and multiple needs of gay youth of color.

In addition to existing institutions, it is important to acknowledge and create alternative resources and institutions to facilitate the overall development of GBQ male youth of color. For instance, by providing a range of developmentally appropriate materials either in physical (e.g., books and movies) or virtual (Web sites and Internet chat rooms) formats, educational institutions and other organizations could ensure that youth can have access to a variety of resources. It is equally important that youth have access to such materials and resources without fear of being "outed." This is especially important for GBQ youth who are dependent on their parents and still living at home, because parents may remove support if a child discloses his or her sexual orientation.

One of the most important resources, however, is the presence of supportive individuals during the process of identity development. Youth responded positively to role models who were either sexual or ethnic minorities, but especially favored those who reflected their same identities. From these individuals, youth would learn how to navigate their communities and identities successfully, especially as multiple-minority group members. Although individuals who best represented their own identities were ideal for role models and for support, other individuals perceived as being understanding were also quite beneficial. This was best evidenced through the youth's peer networks, which reflected a variety of sexualities and ethnic identities, but whose commonality was support for the youth. As a result, assisting youth in accessing helpful supports, regardless of sexuality or ethnicity, is also essential for successful identity development. Interventions that target the youth's already existing peer networks to be supportive of their sexual and ethnic identity would also be of great benefit to them. Additionally, because youth mentioned parents as being essential to the development of a positive identity, they would also benefit from interventions that involve helping families become supportive of their child's multiple minority, ethnic, and sexual identities.

Youth in our study were able to develop multiple sexual and ethnic identities simultaneously through the creative use of existing resources, drawing strength from affiliation with peers, CBOs, and supportive individuals. This required intricate negotiations with people and institutions in their immediate and extended communities. Consequently, existing resources and institutions must match their creativity in efforts to foster more inclusivity and breadth of services for GBQ youth of color. By becoming more inclusive, schools and communities can foster increased diversity, while assisting marginalized GBQ youth of color to develop well-integrated, positive identities.

APPENDIX

Ethnic/Racial Identity

Now we are going to talk a bit about your ethnic/racial identity. Some people may feel they belong to a particular ethnic/racial group but they may vary in terms of how they connect to that group. Remember, your answers will remain confidential. Let's begin.

Meaning

1. Earlier you mentioned that you identify as [EI] in terms of your racial/ethnic identity. What messages do you get about being [EI]?
2. Tell me some of the negative things about being [EI].
3. Tell me some of the positive things about being [EI].
4. What are the specific roles and responsibilities of [EI]?
   Probe:
   a. How should or does [EI] act?
   b. What should or does [EI] do?
   c. How should or does [EI] talk?

Self-Identification

5. You have just told me a little bit about what it means to be [EI]. How do you fit into this? What is that like for you?
   Probe: How do you see yourself compared to the things you told me?
6. *If they mention ways that they "fit," then ask,* In what ways don't you fit into what we have just talked about? What is that like for you?
   Probe: How are you different than the things you told me about being [EI]?
7. For some people, there is a time when they first realize that they are identified with a certain ethnic/racial community. Describe for me when you first realized that you were [EI]. That

is, when was the first time that you felt different because of your ethnicity?
Probe:
a. What were the circumstances around this?

Community

8. We've been focusing on you and how you think about and define your [EI]ness. For the next couple of questions, I would like for you to think about other people who may identify as [EI]. First, do you feel that there is an [EI] community [a group that shares some things in common]?
If "yes": Describe this community to me. How do you fit in to this?
If "no": Why? (*then, skip questions 9 and 10*)
9. In what ways are you connected with the [EI] community?
a. What's that like for you?
10. How did you develop this connection? Describe from as early as you can remember.
11. Are there other ethnic/racial communities that you feel a part of or connected to? [*If so,*] Tell me about them.

Facilitators/Supports

12. Now we are going to talk about the various things that have helped you see yourself as [EI]. People use resources, organizations, and other people all the time to help them in hard times or to help "learn the ropes" in terms of seeing themselves as [EI]. What has helped you in the process of seeing yourself as [EI]?
Probe:
a. Which people have helped you? [*Clarify the relationships of these people to the participant*]
b. What events have helped you?
c. Which institutions have helped you?
d. What resources have helped you?

SEXUAL IDENTITY

Now we are going to talk a bit about your sexual identity. Many of these questions may sound familiar, but I will be asking them with regard to your sexuality rather than to being a man or [EI]. Remember, your answers will remain confidential. Let's begin.

Meaning

13. Earlier you told me that you identify as [SI]. What messages do you get about being [SI[?
14. Tell me some of the negative things about being [SI].
15. Tell me some of the positive things about being [SI].
16. What are the specific roles and responsibilities of being [SI]?
    Probe:
    a. Are there certain things you have to do be [SI]?
    b. When do they happen or when do you have to do these things?
    c. How do they happen?
    d. How should [SI] act?
    e. What should [SI] do?
    f. How should [SI] walk?
    g. How should [SI] talk?

Self-Identification

17. You have just told me a little bit about what it means to be [SI]. How do you fit into this? What is that like for you?
    Probe: How do you see yourself compared to the things you told me?
18. *If they mention ways that they "fit," then ask:* In what ways don't you fit into what we have just talked about? What is that like for you?
    Probe: How are you different than the things you told me?
19. For some people, there is a time when they first realize that they are [SI]. Describe for me when you first realized that you were [SI].
    Probe:

What were the circumstances around this?

Community

20. We've been focusing on how you think about and define your [SI]ness. For the next couple of questions, I would like for you to think about other people who may identify as [SI]. First, do you feel that there is an [SI] community
If "yes": Describe this community to me. How do you fit in to this? Are there any other [SI] communities, such as an Internet [SI] community?
If "no": Why not?
If they say there is no community because there is no [SI] neighborhood or area, then say: A community can be any group that shares some things in common, even if they do not live close to each other, such as an Internet community. Do you think there are some of these other kinds of [SI] communities? *If they do not feel there is any kind of [SI] community, skip questions 21 and 22).*
21. In what ways are you connected with an [SI] community?
    a. What's that like for you?
22. How did you develop this connection? Describe how you came to develop this connection, starting as early as you can remember.
23. Are there other sexual communities that you feel a part of or connected to? [*If so,*] Tell me about them.

Facilitators/Supporters

24. Now we are going to talk about the various people, places, and things that have helped you see yourself as [SI]. People use other people, resources, organizations, and other things to help them in hard times or to help "learn the ropes" in terms of seeing themselves as [SI].
    a. When you first started to identify as [SI], who was helpful and supportive in this process?
25. We've just talked about people who have been helpful to you as you came to see yourself as [SI], now I'd like to talk to you about

those places and activities that may have also been helpful. That is, are there places, like a town, or events that have played a positive role as you started to identify as [SI]?
a. What events have helped you?
b. Which institutions have helped you?
c. What resources have helped you?

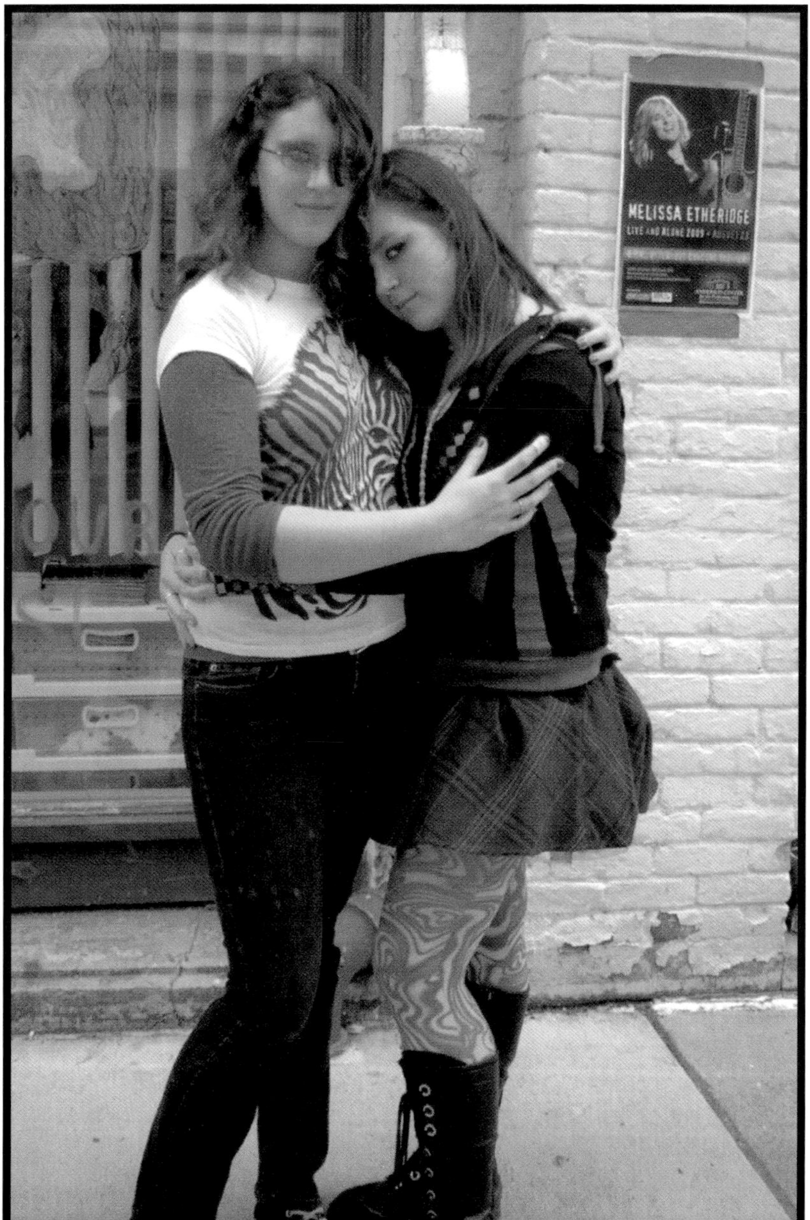
MELISSA ETHERIDGE

Chapter Eight

Strategies for Building a Learning Environment of Inclusion and Acceptance for LGBTIQ Students

Kim A. Case, Heather Kanenberg, and Stephen "Arch" Erich

DOCUMENTED FOR MORE than 20 years now, the hostile environment for lesbian, gay, bisexual, transgender, interesexed, queer, and questioning (LGBTIQ) individuals on college campuses was again confirmed by a national campus climate study conducted by the National Gay and Lesbian Task Force Policy Institute (Rankin, 2003). This survey of GLBT students, faculty, staff, and administrators at 14 universities included some of the most gay-friendly universities in the United States, many with established GLBT studies programs and resource centers. Within these seemingly accepting cultures, 30% of participants reported being harassed in the last year and 20% feared physical harm due to their GLBT identity (Rankin, 2003). Approximately half reported that, to avoid intimidation, they concealed their gender identity or sexual orientation (Rankin, 2003). With regard to overall campus environment, 43% described the climate as homophobic and 41% felt LGBTIQ concerns went unaddressed by the university (Rankin, 2003). On campuses across the country, students face bias in the classroom, anti-gay comments from peers and instructors, and often hide their identity for fear of retaliation. Faculty and staff face the possibility of harassment from peers on campus and may feel their jobs would be in jeopardy if they revealed their true identities. The consistent marginalization of one's group and threat of discrimination contribute to the heterosexist campus environment that LGBTIQ students, staff, and faculty navigate on a daily basis.

With an overwhelming amount of data concerning the hostile environment many LGBTIQ students (and faculty and staff) face on college campuses, researchers and advocates call for action to transform the campus climate. In the academic realm, faculty must centralize LGBTIQ issues by integrating and infusing such materials in all courses (Evans & Wall, 2000; Rankin, 2003; Taylor, 2002; Zavalkoff, 2002), a process we refer to as "queering across the curriculum." Although some diversity courses have incorporated course materials relevant to the LGBTIQ community, many neglect this population completely. Traditional classrooms of higher education systematically perpetuate power differences and marginalize LGBTIQ people by leaving out their contributions and perspectives (Connolly, 2000). Therefore, multicultural and humanities courses, as well as physics and engineering courses, offer opportunities for implementing this suggested curricular integration (Evans & Wall, 2000). Connolly (2000) urges faculty and administrators to examine anti-LGBTIQ bias in the classroom such as derogatory and stereotypical comments by instructors and students that go unaddressed. In addition, faculty must identify and address concerns for transgender students in the classroom such as appropriate pronoun usage (Lovaas, Baroudi, & Collins, 2002; Sausa, 2002).

To influence institutional culture, critical policy analyses and efforts to amend policies for LGBTIQ inclusion are needed (Broido, 2000; Carter, 2000; Evans & Wall, 2000; Rankin, 2003; Sausa, 2002). Rankin (2003) specifically suggests changing university nondiscrimination statements to include both sexual orientation and gender identity. Comprehensive analysis of policies throughout the university must include consideration of the impact on transgender campus members (Carter, 2000; Sausa, 2002). Carter (2000) also calls for elimination of gender segregation policies in settings such as sports teams, restrooms, and some student groups, which often result in discrimination against transgender students.

Faculty and student affairs staff may offer support to the LGBTIQ community on campus by advising student organizations (Broido, 2000), recruiting LGBTIQ staff and faculty as well as their allies (Evans & Wall, 2000; Rankin, 2003), and providing LGBTIQ diversity training and programming to employees (Broido, 2000; Connelly, 2000, Evans & Wall, 2000). Student services offices may also provide programming to raise awareness among students along with LGBTIQ resources, books, and films (Evans & Wall, 2000). Many campuses now house Safe Zone or Safe Space programs designed to create a network of visible allies and transform institutional culture (Draughn, Elkins, & Roy, 2002). A smaller number created LGBTIQ centers or offices devoted to programming, education, advocacy, and providing resources and support (Evans & Wall, 2000; Rankin, 2003).

Theoretical Background

The oppression of the LGBT communities within the context of college campuses can be understood through the theoretical lenses of feminist and queer theories. Feminist theory suggests that the oppression of disenfranchised groups such as women and the LGBT community manifests itself through the laws, policies, and cultural norms of a patriarchal society (Corey, Corey, & Callanan, 2007). In other words, institutional policies and cultural practices most benefit heterosexual males due to their positions within these privileged, culturally valued categories (Ore, 2006). Feminist theory also provides a framework for analysis of the social construction of sex and gender, as well as power differences and the impact of power on efforts toward social change.

Queer theory may be understood as an outgrowth of, specification of, or a corollary to feminist theory that advances our understanding of institutionalized oppression. It also stands on its own and more fully develops our understanding of sex, sexuality, gender, and gender identity and their roles in institutionalized oppression of the LGBT community (Burdge, 2007). Specifically, queer theory provides a framework for analyzing the social construction of sex and gender as strict binaries (Stein & Plummer, 1996). In other words, queer theory challenges the view that a person's sex must be either female or male and allows for more distinctions such as intersex categories. Essentially, queer theory argues that sex and gender represent fluid and dynamic aspects of identity rather than fixed and rigid concepts.

The University in Context

Our state university sits on the edge of the large and diverse metropolitan area of Houston, Texas. The university offers a variety of degrees in social sciences, humanities, sciences, computer engineering, education, and business. It serves approximately 7,500 graduate (46%) and upper-level undergraduate (54%) students. In spring 2007, 66% of the student body was female. The average student age was 32, with a racial makeup of 60% white, 16% Hispanic, 10.5% black, 7% international, 6% Asian, and 0.5% American Indian. Unfortunately, data regarding sexual orientation and gender identity are not available.

The university mission portrays the campus as an open and inclusive environment. Key administrators recently developed programs directing resources to increasing the diversity of the faculty, staff, and student populations. However, LGBTIQ campus members experience various levels of exclusion ranging from prejudiced comments by faculty, staff, and classmates to name calling, threats to those working for transgender inclusion, damage to LGBTIQ displays and student property, and active resistance to equal rights for members of the LGBTIQ communities.

Campus Efforts for Inclusion

Within the last 4 years, efforts to create a more inclusive campus for LGBTIQ students included challenges to exclusionary formal university policies and informal transformations in institutional culture. Two campus-wide partnerships among student leaders, faculty, and staff stand out as major contributions to a positive climate for LGBTIQ campus members: efforts to include gender identity in the nondiscrimination clause(s) and the development of a Safe Zone program. Within the formal policy structure of the institution, the nondiscrimination statement lists the following pro-

Inclusion and Acceptance

tected categories: race, color, religion, national origin, sex, age, disability, veteran status, and sexual orientation (defined as gay, lesbian, or bisexual). Notably, transgender communities remain invisible in this statement. Although the university added "sexual orientation" in the mid-1990s, the inclusion of transgender individuals did not occur at that time.

In 2003, a student leader in social work and a supportive faculty member initiated the lengthy process of advocating for adding a category called *gender identity and expression* to the institution's official nondiscrimination statement. In fact, this collaborative effort required approval of changes to two distinct nondiscrimination clauses. A successful addition to the student handbook policy addressed only the student code of conduct, but not faculty and staff. On the other hand, the university-wide nondiscrimination statement covers all campus members. After three years of working to raise awareness of transgender issues, build alliances, expand the advocacy team, untangle shared governance procedures, and articulate the need for this policy change, both policies successfully passed.

During the spring semester of 2006, students, staff from student services and student life, and faculty organized a committee to research, develop, and implement a Safe Zone program. Our Safe Zone program aims to cultivate a climate of acceptance that welcomes the LGBTIQ community. Campus allies may participate in Safe Zone orientation to become members and receive the ally manual full of resources and basic information such as terms and definitions. In addition, Safe Zone also collaborates with various organizations and offices within the university and the community to provide educational programming (e.g., speakers, films, and discussions).

Student Leadership Strategies

Student strategies for increasing LGBTIQ inclusion on campus included maintaining an active student organization; raising awareness through invited speakers, film discussions, and presentations in classroom and conference settings; increasing visibility on campus; working toward favorable university policy changes; and creating a Safe Zone program.

Although gay and lesbian pioneers on our campus formed a student organization more than 30 years ago, an active group with consistent leadership didn't emerge until the mid-1990s. This organization, UNITY, consists of LGBTIQ students as well as staff, faculty, and student allies. In the last 4 years, an amazing group of student leaders energized this organization and made significant contributions to the goal of LGBTIQ inclusion. Many UNITY officers became active in the student government association as advocates and educators. Transgender, lesbian, gay, bisexual, and heterosexual students spent countless hours raising awareness on campus through film screenings, discussions, expert panels, conference presentations, educational events, and field trips. Many students gave of their own time to visit classrooms as guest lecturers or as members of an LGBTIQ panel at the request of the instructor. At the annual conference for student leaders on campus, students organized panels to raise awareness of LGBTIQ issues and dispel stereotypes and myths. Students serving as officers in UNITY have collaborated with other student associations to sponsor viewings and facilitated discussions of films such as *TransAmerica* (Tucker, 2005) and the documentary *TransGeneration* (Simmons & Smothers, 2005).

Students also partnered with community members at the Holocaust Museum for a customized group tour highlighting Nazi persecution of homosexuals. In celebration of National Coming Out Day each October, students invite guest speakers to present lectures and lead interactive discussions of the coming-out process, heterosexual privilege, and anti-LGBTIQ discrimination. UNITY officers also organized the group's purchase of rainbow cords that members wear at each commencement ceremony. One of the officers described the rainbow cords as "a method of passively announcing to the school that we are real, we are proud, we are a part of the university's multicultural recipe." Another student believes "to express our pride (via rainbow cords), we are saying to our upcoming colleagues that being open on campus is possible and acceptable." Although relatively easy to accomplish, this formal public display at the university graduation makes a huge im-

Inclusion and Acceptance

pact by bringing visibility to the LGBTIQ community and contributing to an inclusive institutional culture.

Perhaps the most committed and passionate activist student leader, a transgender student, initiated a challenge to the university's nondiscrimination policies. While earning her bachelor's degree in social work, she conducted a policy analysis of the nondiscrimination statement as a course assignment. This policy analysis paper served as an educational tool for various committees involved in the decision to add *gender identity* to the university's list of protections. With the support of UNITY members, this student acted as a change agent, a representative from the transgender community, and a leader in campus transformation. This student felt it was important to update the policy

> For students to know they're coming to a campus where they can freely exchange ideas without fear of being negatively impacted, without fear of other students, other staff, other faculty retaliating in one form or another, either covertly or overtly. If a student knows this, a student comes on campus more relaxed, is able to be more productive, when they know they are in a safe environment they feel safer, more relaxed and more willing to engage and become better prepared through academia.

She not only made herself available to present the issue to various constituency groups on campus, she also managed to educate individuals serving on shared governance committees. Successful approval at each level, including from the president of the university, could not have occurred without this woman's unwavering commitment, energy, openness, and time.

UNITY officers, alumni, and other student allies joined with staff and faculty in the development and implementation of a long-overdue Safe Zone program on campus. The student presence on the Safe Zone founding committee provided an essential student voice during the process of creating a program appropriate for our campus needs. Several key UNITY officers and alumni joined the committee and took an active lead in recruitment of additional students to serve on the committee. In addition, they voiced their concerns that students participate fully in Safe Zone not only on the committee, but as members and facilitators of workshops. During the lengthy process of developing the Safe Zone mission goals, orientation materials, and ally manual, students offered creative ideas for marketing the program to students and keeping students involved long term.

Strategies among Faculty Allies

Faculty allies contributed with strategies such as infusing LGBTIQ content throughout the curriculum, modeling inclusive behaviors, rewarding and recognizing student ally behaviors, conducting research relevant to LGBTIQ populations, acting as advocates within the university shared-governance structure, and serving the LGBTIQ community as campus representatives. In these efforts, feminist and queer theories frame faculty teaching, research, and university service.

Queering across the Curriculum

Although a select few instructors develop consciously inclusive courses, the overwhelming majority of faculty members at our university neglect LGBTIQ content in the curriculum. As a result of the creation of a women's studies program in the 1970s, gender-focused courses provided the opportunity to discuss sexual orientation and gender identity. However, decisions about LGBTIQ inclusion rest solely with each individual instructor. Although not required to cover LGBTIQ content, some faculty members draw on feminist and queer theories to purposely and thoughtfully incorporate, for example, essays written by lesbian mothers, transexual women, and gays and lesbians of color. One faculty member assigned a paper offering students the opportunity to reflect critically on their own heterosexual privilege while linking it to discrimination against LGBTIQ people.

> As an instructor, I feel obligated to expose students to a variety of voices and perspectives. One of my major course goals is to illustrate that transgender issues are women's issues, heterosexism is a women's issue, racism is a women's issue, just as sexual harassment in the workplace is a women's issue. In my classes, students work toward developing their own feminist analysis skills so they continue asking the critical questions well beyond our semester together.

Inclusion and Acceptance

Instructors of diversity courses outside women's studies often contribute to an inclusive classroom environment for LGBTIQ students as well. As part of a course devoted to race and racism, the main textbook addresses not only racial prejudice, but also stereotypes, prejudice, and discrimination against LGBTIQ individuals. Given that the traditional structure of higher education marginalizes content relevant to oppressed groups into diversity courses, the goal of curricular integration (Evans & Wall, 2000) poses a challenge.

For any campus climate to be truly inclusive, teachers must begin "queering across the curriculum," with the goal of integrating LGBTIQ issues into all courses. Providing relevant LGBTIQ examples during lectures serves to decentralize heterosexuality and normalize LGBTIQ concerns. In addition, these simple actions on the part of the instructor create a classroom culture that challenges power and privilege while communicating acceptance. In his course on social movements, one sociology professor outlines the historical consolidation of various constituencies within the LGBTIQ community into an organized movement for social change. A professor of social psychology includes readings and lectures on gender socialization, gender identity, and transgender issues. In addition, she infuses LGBTIQ language into examples when the content appears unrelated. For example, when addressing the chapter on helping behavior, the lecture mentions two mothers that volunteer at their son's school. A professor of social work prompts students to consider policy implications for oppressed groups. During one particular class meeting, class discussion focuses on the impact of state and federal child welfare policies on LGBTIQ families and their access to resources. As part of her pedagogical approach, she believes that "incorporating this content provides students with the capacity to critically analyze future programs and policies as they work in social services to further combat oppression." Within her graduate education course on the family, another faculty member introduces future teachers to a video called *That's a Family* (Chasnoff, Ben-Dov, & Yacker, 2000) depicting diverse families, including those with same-sex parents. Her students then create their own activity designed to follow a classroom viewing of the film and write a reflection paper analyzing their own levels of comfort and discomfort associated with not only viewing the film in the graduate class, but also potentially showing it to their future students. These faculty members consciously infuse content toward goals of raising student awareness of oppression, privilege, and power differences with real-world consequences for disadvantaged groups.

Identification of "queering across the curriculum" within business, computer, science, and engineering courses proved more difficult, and many courses in education, social science, and the humanities continue neglecting LGBTIQ content. However, we submit that instructors could purposefully infuse LGBTIQ issues and materials into every single course on campus. For example, explanations of statistical correlations could include mention of a positive correlation between conservative Protestant religious beliefs and anti-gay attitudes (Newman, 2002). Business courses could incorporate discussions of workplace harassment of LGBTIQ individuals. An assignment in a computer science course might involve designing a website for an LGBTIQ bookstore or for a nonprofit that provides shelter to LGBTIQ runaway teens. Although rarely considered as potential sites for LGBTIQ inclusion, immense opportunities for implementing curricular integration (Evans & Wall, 2000) also exist in courses such as statistics, physics, chemistry, marketing, and accounting.

Teaching Inclusion beyond the Classroom

Faculty engagement with students at a teaching institution invariably extends beyond traditional classroom walls. Faculty facilitate student growth by

- Modeling advocacy and ally behaviors
- Supporting UNITY as faculty advisors and encouraging students to join
- Including students in the development of the Safe Zone program
- Incorporating LGBTIQ inclusion into formal program policies
- Presenting the program's social justice award to students working for LGBTIQ rights

- Teaching students as co-researchers in LGBTIQ research informed by critical, feminist, and queer theories
- Presenting posters and papers with students as co-presenters at regional and national conferences
- Co-authoring manuscripts published in peer-reviewed professional journals with students[2]

In the interest of creating another teaching venue, faculty conducting LGBTIQ research invite students into their research labs. Students in search of research experience gain exposure to hands-on research into prejudice against gays and lesbians, attitudes toward gay marriage, same-sex adoption, heterosexual privilege, social support for transgender individuals, and transgender experiences in the family. The presence of these labs promotes LGBTIQ visibility on campus, offers heterosexual students experience as allies through the academic research process, and provides LGBTIQ students the option of conducting research relevant to their own community. One psychology faculty member promotes student involvement in research to "introduce them to the vast literature addressing prejudice against lesbian and gay men and help them build a foundation for conducting their own LGBTIQ research." These collaborations sometimes culminate in independent student research projects, such as a master's thesis investigating effective techniques for reduction of prejudice against transexuals.

Faculty as Advocates and Visible Allies on Campus

Faculty research devoted to empirical investigations of LGBTIQ concerns not only benefits students, but also exposes the wider campus community to commonly marginalized topics. Active involvement in these research initiatives raises awareness among faculty peers, administrators, and staff. These research agendas also aid the establishment of a university culture that encourages academic dialogue regarding LGBTIQ issues.

---

[2] For example, three students and a faculty member in social work co-authored a paper on transgender individuals and the relationship between family support and life satisfaction (Erich, Tittsworth, Dykes, & Cabusas, 2008).

Faculty allies also contribute to the university's cultural transformation as advocates in meetings and informal discussions and as invited speakers at various campus events. When serving on search committees charged with hiring new faculty members, allies pay particular attention to each candidate's knowledge of diversity and LGBTIQ inclusion. Faculty allies offer presentations and facilitate discussions on campus for National Coming Out Day each year. One faculty member served on several panels on transgender issues with members of the transexual community. Student groups sponsoring educational film viewings on campus often host faculty as discussion leaders following films such as *Brokeback Mountain* (Lee, McMurtry, Ossana, & Proulx, 2005) and *TransAmerica* (Tucker, 2005). As faculty allies incorporate LGBTIQ concerns into hiring decisions and build campus dialogue through presentations and discussions, institutional norms begin to shift toward norms of genuine acceptance and inclusion.

Through participation in campus-wide initiatives such as the Safe Zone development committee and advocating for adding transgender protections to the nondiscrimination clause, faculty contributed to shifting institutional norms. By encouraging students to get involved in political activism for social change on campus and advocate for policy change, faculty modeled ally behavior for transforming organizational culture. As advocates for adding gender identity to the nondiscrimination statement, faculty attended countless meetings of student groups, staff associations, shared governance committees, and academic programs. Faculty deliberately supported student involvement and consulted with students as collaborative change agents. One particular faculty member worked with the transgender student leader who originally initiated the policy change for 3 full years leading up to the president's approval. The student expressed her views about the importance of her sense of team work with the most involved faculty member across power differences.

> We complement each other in this process. We are actually two professionals working together for a common goal and we've always approached it like that. . . . We recognize each other, when we're dealing with the issue, we recognize each other as equals, with each coming with a set of skills and knowledge that will complement each other.

That faculty member also commented on the collaborative strategies employed during the policy change process.

> It's been a really collaborative relationship from my position. . . . I really don't believe it's appropriate for me to dictate to [her] what she can do, can't do. I'm an outsider; doesn't matter that I'm a faculty. I ask for her permission to give her feedback and share my thoughts. In fact, I do it frequently and I clarify that. . . . I'm just sharing with you as a peer. And so I hope she feels that's been the case, but I think that's been a strategy.

By acknowledging power and collaborating to conduct ongoing power analysis of the policy change process, this student and faculty member strengthened their alliance. Faculty members not only advocated along with student leaders for amending the nondiscrimination statement, but also initiated a student/faculty collaborative research project documenting the change process. As founding members of Safe Zone, faculty worked with students and staff to turn vision into reality. Forming a subcommittee with a staff member, a faculty member conducted extensive research on established Safe Zone, Safe Space, and other ally programs, then customized a workshop designed to orient the campus community to our Safe Zone program. This research incorporated feminist and queer theories into the Safe Zone curriculum. Another faculty member managed the development of the program's mission and goals, facilitated meetings, and spent time solving miscommunication problems. In collaboration with another staff member, one faculty member helped create a resource manual for allies on campus.

Faculty as Campus Representatives

Along with on campus advocacy and ally behavior, faculty also act as university representatives by presenting research at conferences, publishing in professional journals, and providing service presentations within the local community. For example, a faculty member presented papers on effective strategies for anti-gay prejudice reduction, heterosexual privilege, and transgender curriculum inclusion at professional psychology conferences (Case, 2006; Case, Stewart, & Fisher, 2007). Public distribution of LGBTIQ research conducted by faculty from our institution sends the message of an affirming campus climate. Therefore, students and culty at regional and national professional conferences become aware of the presence of LGBTIQ allies at our university. In the community, faculty often facilitate discussions with LGBTIQ youth groups, local community college campuses, and social service agencies. A faculty member wellknown for his research on same-sex adoption recently appeared on a radio talk show to share the research findings. Through presentations to community groups, faculty members often recruit potential students and form community partnerships with academic programs.

Inclusion Strategies among Staff and Administrative Partners

Efforts to create a more inclusive and affirming environment within the university setting included campus offices as well as individual staff members and administrators. These offices and individuals engaged in efforts both large and small that contributed to climate change including financial support for LGBTIQ programming, providing LGBTIQ educational resources, advising students on steps toward policy change, and vocal advocacy for policy change within university committees. Informed by feminist praxis, campus change agents worked to develop collaborations across power differentials within the formal university structure in hopes of minimize the negative impact of power on the change process.

University Offices as Partners

The campus office responsible for intercultural and diversity programming and resources proved to be a great partner in efforts to advance the sense of inclusion within the university. The director of this campus resource was one of the founding members of UNITY, the LGBTIQ student organization, in the mid-1990s. This high-level administrator has consistently supported the group as an active member and advisor throughout the past 15 years. This office and its staff serve as major supporters of the Safe Zone efforts by serving as active members on the planning committee in addition to offering to provide financial and spatial support for the program. During 2004, the office developed a LGBTIQ library of resources for students, staff, and faculty to access. The library includes educational materials, pamphlets about organizations and support groups, as well as local and national resource materials.

The Dean of Students Office and Student Life Office both serve as active partners in supporting inclusion and promoting equity for LGBTIQ campus members. After reviewing the previously mentioned transgender student's policy analysis, the dean of students supported her advocacy efforts to amend the institution's nondiscrimination statements. This support included advisement on the appropriate steps within the university's decision-making process and assistance in identifying potential allies and opposition on campus. These two offices also support the development of the Safe Zone program by encouraging staff to serve on the planning committee and by attending the inaugural launch of the orientation for the full campus community. Such behavior provided powerful messages of support to other administrators and offices on campus. One high-level administrator also worked to ensure that committees followed appropriate procedures during the debate about adding gender identity to the nondiscrimination statement. Support of due process from such a prominent administrator established an expectation of fairness for committee discussions and voting procedures. Ultimately, allies that possessed institutional power proved to have an important role and function in helping to achieve goals of institutional inclusion.

Individual Staff Members as Partners

Individual administrators and staff members served as fantastic partners in the recent efforts to create a more affirming climate for LGBTIQ campus members and allies. When powerful leaders support a social justice initiative, those supporting change gain implicit permission to speak out more openly while those opposing the change may become less vocal and more careful about expressing their disagreement. For example, in a meeting of the Deans Council, one of the academic deans boldly proclaimed that transgender inclusion in the university's nondiscrimination statement simply supported the mission of the university to be an inclusive and affirming environment for all students. Soon after his statement, the council voted in unanimous support for the policy change. Additionally, the support of several staff members in the President's Office, the Provost's Office, and the Student Life Office allowed for the development of strengthened relationships and support for the nondiscrimination policy change and Safe Zone Program development. One faculty member commented on a key administrator:

> [She was] effective in her discussions on this committee because she has that hierarchy level that the others don't. [Another administrator] is right with the president, so she's really up there on hierarchy, right above the chair [of the committee], and so she has a lot of power.

In concert with faculty and students, having the support of individual staff and administrators as well as campus offices resulted in the capacity to create change at a reasonably rapid pace. Recognizing that there is still work to be done in creating an equitable, affirming, and inclusive environment within the university, there have been many successes and advances in this pursuit. It is clear that without participation and engagement from all levels within the university community, including passionate advocates at every level, these accomplishments would not have been possible.

Obstacles and Lessons Learned

Efforts to create an affirming climate for LGBTIQ students, staff, and faculty within the university community varied in levels of success and required resources and energy. Indeed, selected activities and experiences required less energy and involved very little risk. However, other attempts at creating change left those involved vulnerable and required a great deal of time and energy to accomplish even minimal progress. The obstacles and lessons learned are presented so that other change agents may prepare for such forces during their own campus efforts. This section certainly does not include answers to all questions or actions for removal of all barriers. Instead, we offer a selection of obstacles and lessons learned to consider when engaging in university, community, or organizational change.

Know Your Audience

When working within a relatively interconnected environment such as a university system, allies must understand the positions of campus members opposing inclusion efforts. When preparing for a presentation, consider whether the audience members support LGBTIQ equality. Identification of allies and their motivations proved an important exercise for those working to reform the university's nondiscrimination statements. This included consideration of the views of student groups, staff associations, and faculty groups, as well as influential individuals within the university community as a whole. During a shared-governance committee meeting, a student presented research evidence of the underlying causes of gender identity disorder without careful consideration of the background and academic expertise of each committee member. This issue was compounded by the student's relative inexperience in presenting research evidence and resulted in public criticism from a faculty member that may have served to undermine the student's credibility with other committee members present. The student leading this process advises others working for change to be prepared.

> You need to have a thorough understanding of the process. . . . You need to give them examples. You need to be prepared to educate and be accurate on what you say about education. I've seen transgender people . . . make blatant statement errors in their statements that I know were wrong because of the research I've done. . . . You're going to make those mistakes if you aren't prepared.

Therefore, public presentations necessitate careful consideration of one's own mastery of a particular topic along with reflection on the expertise of audience members.

Knowing the audience also requires knowledge of hot-button issues and political concerns of key decision makers whenever they can be identified. Awareness of important issues for decision makers and those opposing LGBTIQ inclusion allows those seeking change to address potential concerns in advance. For example, perhaps two campus offices with a history of conflict each have representatives serving on the Safe Zone committee. In this situation, awareness of previous problems and each committee member's perception of that conflict may allow for smoother, more effective communication. Students and faculty on the committee may keep watch for statements that indicate old business is impeding the committee's progress. If the historical conflict appears to influence the process, other committee members can take steps to acknowledge the concerns of the staff representatives from each office to bring everyone back to the purpose of creating a Safe Zone program. While not always possible, knowing the history of those in the audience and their political history on campus, as well as their views of LGBTIQ issues, may aid agenda development, identification of allies, and progress toward an inclusive campus.

Climate of Ignorance

Another obstacle, referred to here as a climate of ignorance, proved difficult for allies. The ignorance of campus community members with regard to the concerns of LGBTIQ students, staff, and faculty required allies to become effective educators for successful change. Statements within official meetings revealed that many campus members confused sexual orientation with transgender and transsexual, constructed transgender people as outsiders to the campus community, and believed gender identity was already covered by *sexual orientation* or *gender* in the nondiscrimination policy. In addition, based on questions fielded by allies presenting at Coming Out Day events and facilitating discussions of transgender issues, it was clear that many in the university community were completely uneducated on the topics, and in some cases, quite comfortable with their ignorance. Privileged status may have prevented dominant group members from cognitively engaging with arguments of oppression and calls for social justice.

In attempts to raise awareness and encourage paradigm shifts, we incorporated feminist theory and queer theory conceptions of critical analysis and terminology into educational materials. We found that providing resources and education to those previously unexposed to information and experiences with the LGBTIQ population helped create change. Of the materials provided by transgender allies working on the nondiscrimination policy, handouts with terms, definitions, and an overview of national trends in adding gender identity appeared to facilitate the most free-flowing open conversations and attitude change. A faculty member developed one handout for the committee members summarized the language being used by universities and colleges around the country as they updated their nondiscrimination policies.

> The handout reflected the use of "gender identity" and "gender identity and expression" as possible phrases for inclusion of transgender people. We passed out the handout at a February meeting and the committee voted unanimously that same day to add "gender identity" to the policy.

Ultimately, we realized that ignorance must be addressed repeatedly to create a shift in the general consciousness of the university. With every presentation, movie showing, student event, student government presentation, committee meeting, and individual conversation, we were educating the community and, therefore, creating a more affirming climate at our institution.

Entrenched Prejudice

The obstacle of entrenched prejudice surfaced in official committee meetings, informal discussions, and written expressions of anti-LGBTIQ bias. Individual prejudice surfaced at each level of attempted change. Most prejudiced comments reached allies through the grapevine from third parties, but biased opposition also occurred during formal meetings. Although most people refrained from making directly discriminatory comments on record during meetings, one faculty member told derogatory transgender jokes as a transgender student presented to the committee. In addition, the president of the Republican student organization wrote a letter to the editor that was printed in the campus student newspaper opposing adding gender identity and gender expression to the nondiscrimination statement. Littered with many prejudiced comments, erroneous assertions, as well as ignorant statements confusing sex, gender, gender identity, and sexual orientation, this letter accused one student advocate of a "personal crusade" and even labeled the shared-governance process a "fraud." Unfortunately, those working for LGBTIQ inclusion failed to submit a response and lost that particular opportunity to educate the campus. Whenever possible, allies countered prejudice with education and open communication. LGBTIQ events were promoted, issues discussed, detrimental policies identified and debated, and prejudicial comments challenged in an attempt to educate and expose perpetrators of discrimination to the experience of an affirming climate. Combating entrenched prejudice requires a critical mass of dedicated and skilled allies willing to counter hateful accusations and debunk myths at any given moment.

Subtle and Overt Threats

Unfortunately, opposing forces aimed several subtle and overt threats at students, staff, and faculty working for a more inclusive climate. During an official university committee meeting, one member threatened retaliation against anyone who labeled him a bigot. In addition, an unidentified person targeted a student working on the policy change by letting the air out of the tires on her scooter that was necessary for her mobility. Through a feminist lens, faculty also consciously considered the consequences of their actions in terms of administrative retaliation, promotion, and tenure as a result of their support, advocacy, and discussion of transgender inclusion. Given that those in power may possess biases with regard to transgender people, junior faculty often discussed the potential impact of their involvement on career advancement and "the risk involved with an assistant professor, first-year person, getting involved in something that's so charged for people." One faculty member reflected on how power might affect the process and his future employment.

> I'm still an assistant professor and so the power differentials within faculty are very present at our university. So as an untenured faculty person, I'm taken less seriously than I would be if I was a tenured faculty person . . . and nontenured and tenured faculty have real different senses of power.

When faculty infused LGBTIQ content into courses, they carefully considered the potential negative impact on their teaching evaluations by students unprepared or unwilling to discuss these topics. Although teaching evaluations directly affect merit increases and annual reviews, many faculty members continued "queering across the curriculum." These threats served to initiate a cautionary pause and reflection for those threatened as well as others involved in the change process. In most instances, planned actions continued despite having received direct or veiled threats. As a result of reflection on the circumstances, for example, a tenured faculty member often became the primary ally contact in order to protect students and untenured faculty. In light of these perceived and actual threats, allies consciously avoided attending meetings, presentations, and discussions alone.

Depletion of Time and Energy

Although many students, faculty, and staff were engaged in hosting events, promoting the addition of gender identity to the nondiscrimination statements, and developing the Safe Zone program, a core of faculty and students participated consistently in such efforts. This core group committed a great deal of time to brainstorming agendas, planning and attending events, coordinating allies, and educating others. This resulted in a sense of depleted energy and restricted time for other efforts and activities, including coursework and research. The relative time and energy required to create policy change, educate, and plan events resulted in both faculty and students feeling mentally and emotionally exhausted and needing a reprieve from the intensity of the activities. Many contextual factors may influence faculty activism, including institutional size, regional political climate, institutional research and teaching balance, and possibly religious affiliation of the university or college. Although teaching-focused institutions may encourage more faculty involvement with students, activist-oriented collaboration often requires additional time commitments beyond that of the typical workload. In addition, students may struggle with balancing work, studies, campus activities, and social activities, which limits the time they have available to commit to the change efforts. Students participated in many if not all activities, but their level of involvement was understandably restricted by their academic, employment, and family commitments. As a group of advocates working for an affirming and inclusive environment, we suggest acknowledgment of and reflection on the time and energy drain associated with social change efforts. A commitment to revisit this reality purposely throughout the action process may help individuals develop appropriate boundaries to ensure a balance between their advocacy work and other commitments.

Quality Communication

The impact of miscommunication became clear early in the efforts to transform campus culture. Open communication among team members is essential for progress. Given the different roles and capacities held by students, staff, and faculty, members of each constituency group must clearly communicate their strategies and planned actions to members of other constituency groups. As an example, while promoting transgender inclusion in the nondiscrimination statement at the university, students made decisions and took actions without consultation with the wider core of LGBTIQ advocates. In addition, the Safe Zone development committee almost dissolved because members of the 3 main constituencies (students, faculty, and staff) failed to communicate their feelings, concerns, and needs to the others involved. These group dynamics resulted in more time and energy to resolve miscommunication troubles. Admittedly, valuable time and energy for developing the program itself was instead invested in preventing the committee from disbanding.

Red Tape and Politics

Talcott Parsons's (1986) definition of power as "the capacity of persons or collectives 'to get things done' effectively, in particular when their goals are obstructed by some kind of human resistance or opposition" (94) clearly applied to our university setting. Entrenched in processes and systems in which power and politics play a central role, we quickly became entangled in red tape. For example, the efforts outlined above took place at one university within a 4-university system governed by a Board of Regents. Although the policy change to include gender identity in the nondiscrimination clause occurred at the individual university level, it ultimately required Board of Regents approval and implementation at all 4 universities. Although our campus passed the policy change, each individual university within the system had to approve the addition of gender identity. When meeting with allies from another university (from the same system), we learned that faculty and student allies refused to support the policy amendment because the change did not originate on their own campus. Sadly, this schism remains and the working relationships between allies and LGBTIQ individuals on the 2 campuses are strained. Another red-tape obstacle grew out of the existence of 2 different statements with 2 distinct paths to approval. This convoluted process resulted in confusion for allies and shared-governance committees. Due to this complicated structure, we studied in detail each specific procedure for altering the 2 separate university policies (student handbook policy and general university policy).

Conclusions

Building relationships and making allies of unexpected supporters, collaborating with the administration, and identifying members of the opposition aided our successes. Although the ignorance and prejudice perpetrated by individuals and groups within the campus community was often overwhelming and exhausting, we found repeated efforts to raise awareness proved effective in most situations. At any given time, allies may experience direct or indirect threats or pressure to alter their course of action in the classroom or on campus. Politics, power, and red tape influenced our collective capacity to develop an affirming and inclusive climate for LGBTIQ individuals. Allies and advocates on other campuses may encounter similar obstacles as they organize to transform campus culture. Advanced awareness of and preparation for these potential obstacles may minimize their impact on progress toward an environment completely open to LGBTIQ campus members.

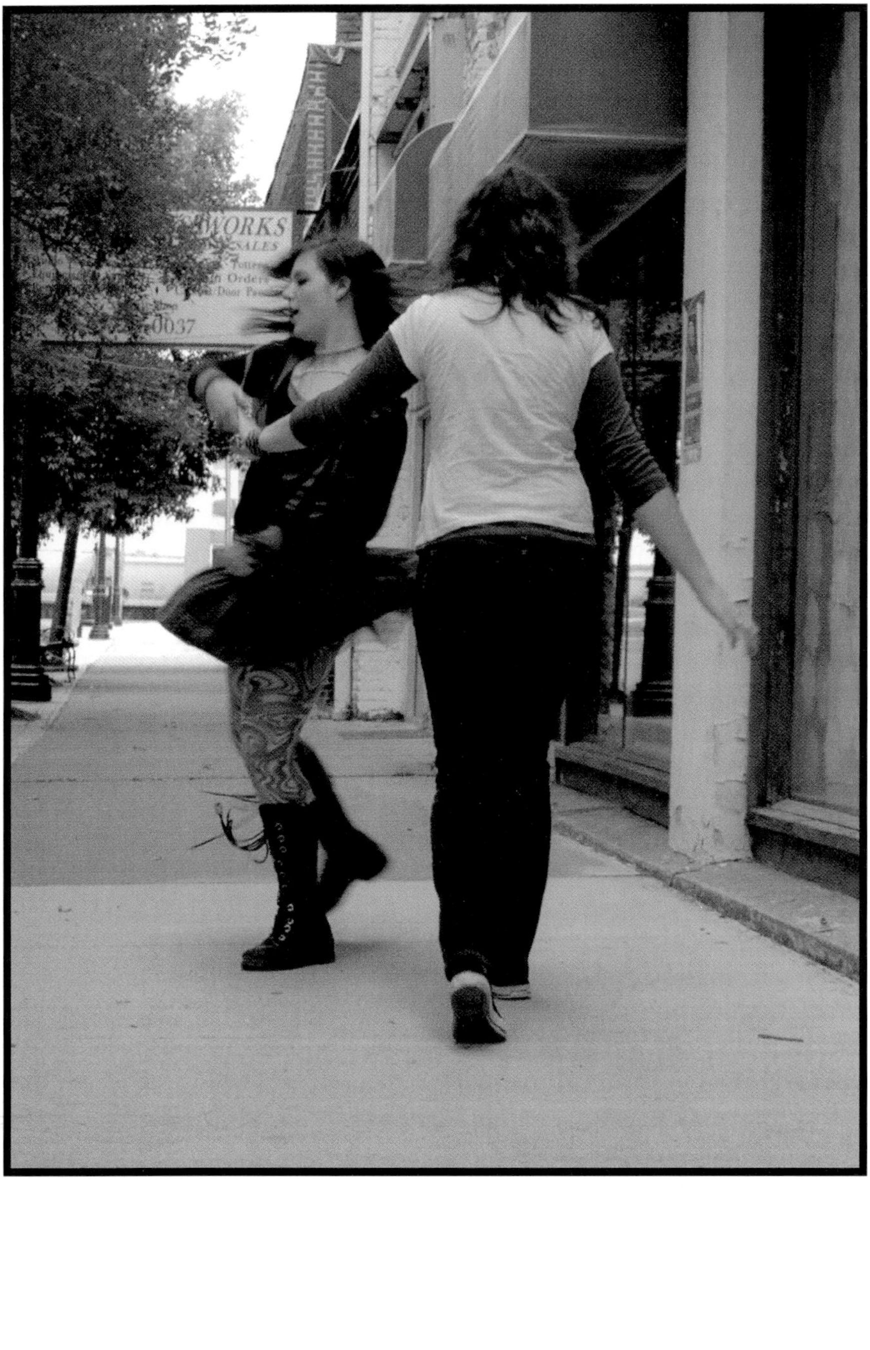
WORKS
SALES

Chapter Nine

Telling Stories Out of Class: Excavating LGBTQ Youth Knowledge from Liminal Spaces

Corrine C. Bertram

Examining Youth from a Queer Angle

SARAH CARNEY (2000) in her chapter *Body work on ice* discusses the relationship between adolescent girl ice skaters and the discourses about their bodies. During Carney's formal interviews, the ice skaters referred to eating disorders, weight, deprivation, and other concerns about body image. After the interviews, however, when the tape recorder was turned off and while the young women were skating, they stopped to tell Carney how wonderful it felt to use their bodies on ice. These liminal spaces, locations and moments betwixt, between and on the edges of interviews with youth, supplied Carney with new insights about girls, bodies, discourses, and methodologies. The data that emerged after Carney's formal interviews counter popular and psychological discourses on adolescent girls' bodies because they provide evidence of girls' positive embodiments.

This "discovery" pushes beyond the usual accounts discussed in research methods texts of immediate contexts producing biased interviewer effects. Rather, Carney's work demonstrates how the interview context may also produce and influence data because the participants are either fettered by discursive pressures or freed from them (and experience new ones?) to tell alternative stories to interviewers and field researchers. More importantly for my purposes, Carney's work suggests that the borders of youth space may provide insight into the limitations of not only methodologies but also youth programming designed to uncover and resist popular and psychological hegemonic discourses pertaining to marginalized youth, including same-gender-loving and gender-nonconforming youth. What might the edges of youth spaces reveal about youth programming and youth knowledge?

This liminality provides a methodological framework for the examination of my experience of mentoring a lesbian, gay, bisexual, transgender, queer, and questioning (LGBTQ) youth group. One might focus on the activities and everyday life of the group itself to analyze youth experience, but a focus on borders provides insight into the limits of community and group experience. As an example, moral community literature in psychology argues that all groups create an inside and an outside (Opotow, 1990). This includes organizations and groups whose expressed purpose is the creation of spaces that are inclusive. When conducting research and examining practice with youth, it is critical that methodologies examine the margins of youth space because youth may feel unable to voice their critical perspectives to adults within organizations and may seek passive, sideways, marginal, and queer forms of resistance to communicate their dissatisfaction on the margins.

Background

For about two and one-half years, I have been involved in a weekly after-school group for LGBTQ youth aged 14 to 21 who live in or near a small, deindustrialized city in the northeastern United States. A small number of LGBTQ adults co-created the space with youth to come out, talk about sexuality and gender expression, and simply have respite from the compulsory heterosexuality and gender policing of families, schools, locker rooms, homerooms, and city buses. We have successfully sustained this group despite the relative lack of volunteers and resources in small urban and rural settings of the United States and the difficult lives of the youth involved, many of whom are poor, working class, and/or have been in the foster-care system for some part of their lives.

During my involvement with the youth group, I have been intrigued by its edges—what happens in liminal space (Turner, 1967) before or after the group meets, on the bus on the way to group or to some other event, what is said over cigarettes outside the building, and what is shared with mentors when they are not in their formal roles. These moments on the margins, or after interviews in Carney's (2000) sense, occur whether or not a safe, nonjudgmental space has been established, and they stimulate speculation about the role of youth spaces organized around sexualities. Adolescents and adolescence may require activities and spaces outside of adult control and facilitation in order to develop and deepen. Put another way, to a certain degree, risk may be healthy for adolescents. Cullen (2005) describes such liminal spaces in her analysis of cotches, which are public, informal, hangout spaces for youth in the United Kingdom that serve developmental functions. Cotches are not free from all social and cultural constraints, but they are spaces that are free from adult surveillance where youth may rehearse independent selves that are still constrained by adult worlds. Drawing on field notes, e-mail communication, and experiences of mentoring, this chapter explores what liminal spaces and utterances teach about youth/adult engagement in queer communities. Social science and educational literature on the creation of youth space, critical youth studies, and scholarship that expands conceptions of healthy sexual development beyond avoiding harm, pregnancy, and sexually transmitted infections (STIs) provide the theoretical background.

Background Literature

There is a large body of literature within education and psychology that explores and outlines ways to create communities that are safe and that support members across many forms of difference (e.g., Bertram & Massey, 2007; Boyte & Evans, 1986; Fine, Weis, & Powell, 1997; Pratt, 1991). Variously called "free spaces," "contact zones," or "communities of difference," these spaces and the theorization of them complicate an easy understanding of the creation of simply "safe" spaces because they engage with privilege and conflict and do not conflate safety with comfort (Bertram & Crowley, under review; Bertram & Massey, 2007). This literature also examines how distributed discomfort may be a possible foundation for educational spaces rather than notions of safety since the meanings of safety are not universal (Bertram & Crowley, under review).

Although I did imagine that participatory research projects would emerge as I spent time in the youth group and the coalition, I did not enter these organizations primarily as a researcher, but as a lesbian-identified local resident who wanted to develop connections within the community and create opportunities for youth-adult engagement. My reflections then do not resemble systematic data analysis in its traditional form, but critical reflections on practice/mentoring/organizing with young people who may identify at many (moving) points along gender and sexual lines. My chapter emerges in a tradition of writing and reflection in the context of volunteer work in community settings (Bertram, 2008; Fine, 1989) where scenes of practice prompt critical reflection on the delivery and structure of social services, as well as the social worlds that influence and constrain the shape of those services. The practice of community spaces created for social justice purposes provides a touchstone with which to test theory and to generate new ideas to be pursued by social scientists, educators, and activists. This touchstone of practice tests the metal of social services as well as theory. Rather than simply generating ideas for better delivery and effectiveness of social services, it also challenges the very logic of social service delivery when contextualized within inequitable social relations.

Bridging theory and practice requires that researchers be cautious in our scholarly interpretations of youth spaces. As Best (2007) warns in her introduction to *Representing youth*

> ...a critical youth studies should involve the following as part of its methodological agenda . . . an acknowledgement of the connection between power and knowledge. Such an acknowledgement requires that we recognize that the accounts we provide shape and construct reality as much as they describe it. Youth researchers play a significant role in shaping

the social experiences of children and youth through the discursive constructions or accounts we provide. (1)

I take Best's cautions seriously as I analyze my two and one-half years of youth work in this local world. I attempt to make sense of the youth in their "being" youth rather than their "becoming" adults, trying not to impose my authorial voice on them as I maintain my authority as a feminist social scientist (Best, 2007; Caputo, 1995; Wulff, 1995). As scholarship in feminist social science suggests (Harding, 2004; Hill-Collins, 2000; Smith, 1987), the youths' social locations produce their knowledge, just as my social location created the knowledge to which I had access. As Wulff writes,

> because of the traditional socialization perspective, youth (and children) still tend to be viewed as incomplete adults, not real, full persons who have understood what life is actually about; that is mainly the responsibilities and hardship that come with adulthood. According to this view, they know less than adults, as opposed to knowing something else that has to do with their particular situation and surroundings. (11)

In my reflections on traveling, mentoring, chaperoning, collaborating, and, I confess, policing these youth, I attempt to illuminate that "something else" that LGBTQ youth in the early twenty-first century know. First, I begin with a discussion of the genesis and context of the group. Then, I turn to an analysis of three liminal scenes: the first happens on a bus ride home from a youth conference, the second occurs in e-mail messages, and the third is set at a high school graduation party. These scenes illustrate three themes of current LGBTQ youth knowledge and youth worker practice: sexual subjectivity, the interplay of intersecting identities, and sexual and gender fluidity.

History of the Group

In the late winter of 2005, a group of residents gathered in a library around a large conference table to discuss the challenges that LGBTQ youth faced locally. About one hundred people—social service providers, social workers, therapists, teachers, school administrators, students, professors, and clergy—were presented with an LGBTQ 101 that focused primarily on definitions of and relationships between sex, gender, and sexuality. A young woman who was then a graduate student spoke about her biography as a lesbian teen in the area and some of the challenges she had faced in local schools. After that meeting, some interested attendees formed a coalition composed of various committees. One of the committees created a local youth group for LGBTQ youth. The youth group began meeting regularly in the fall of 2005. At first, I provided transportation to and from the meetings and other events, but I could not attend the actual group times due to my college teaching schedule. After a schedule change and the loss of some mentors, I mentored by co-facilitating youth group sessions. When two of the co-facilitators left the area to attend graduate school, I took on an organizing and facilitation role as well as that of mentor.

LGBTQ youth and adults have relatively few outlets in this area. Three gay bars and several restaurants and businesses that are lesbian or gay owned and operated (although not always operated by lesbian and gay owners who are "out" in the community) comprise what might be called gay institutions locally. Although bars have been and continue to be key sites of identity development for lesbians and gay men (Wolfe, 1992), they have their shortcomings in communities where many lesbians and gay men are in recovery for substance abuse. These spaces are also limited in their ability to support sexual and gender identity development of youth as youth identify as LGBTQ at younger and younger ages, often quite below the legal drinking age of 21 (or 18 when youth can enter bars on "18 and over" nights). The area has several affirming churches, including a church denomination formed by and serving LGBTQ people and their allies, and three LGBTQ community groups: a lesbian and gay family building program that hosts educational meetings and home gatherings for LGBTQ adults who have children or are considering parenthood, a support and social group for transgender people and their allies, and a coalition of community members that organizes annual June Pride activities. The history of this area is marked by active lesbian and gay organizing spanning nearly 30 years. A women-only cultural space and bar was active for 20 years, another group was formed in response to the first cases of human immunodeficiency virus/acquired immune deficiency syndrome (HIV/AIDS) in the area, and a local gay pride group formed in the 1990s.

The following scenes of interaction at the edges of the youth group include mentor interactions with youth that were shared with me, e-mail correspondence with one of the group members, and my extra-group interactions with one youth. They provide an opportunity to offer some reflections about practice with queer youth in community settings. The scenes raise questions both about how spaces created for and by youth themselves may become spaces where youth voices are not heard and about the possible reasons behind the silencing, miscommunication, and miscues that youth and adults belonging to LGBTQ groups engage in.

Scene 1

Risky questions that desire answers and answer desires: Youth and "at-risk" sexuality

> We may be able to catch something like a sexuality from language, but sexuality does not always answer in the places where it is summoned. (Gilbert, 2004, p. 113)

> A group of youth has traveled to a conference on safer sex in a nearby town organized by a local HIV/AIDS advocacy nonprofit. After a long day of conference sessions, one of the mentors returns on the bus to our hometown with three youth between the ages of 17 and 19. These youth push each other to tell the mentor what they want for programming in a sort of, "You tell him. No, you tell him" way. Finally, one of them blurts out, "We want someone to come and discuss sm." The mentor discusses this conversation with me later and we are surprised that the youth did not bring this up within the regular group meeting. What made them think that we would not let someone present about this topic?

In the spring of 2006, the local HIV/AIDS nonprofit hosted a youth conference funded by a state assembly member. I served on the large conference planning committee, which also included many youth members. Youth from the LGBTQ youth group were represented on the committee as well and were excited to attend the conference, which contained programming addressing "risks" that youth face. The conference included panel topics "addressing preventing transmission of HIV and STDs; avoiding unintended pregnancy; fostering healthy relationships; building communication and negotiation skills; learning about the influence of personal body image on risk-taking behavior; hearing first-person accounts of life as an addict, and life as a transgendered individual; evaluating safety in piercing and tattooing practices; and understanding homophobia—the typical offerings at youth conferences hosted by social service agencies. The social service agency had surveyed approximately 200 local youth asking them what topics they would like to see addressed, so the conference session topics were youth generated. And yet youth did not feel comfortable bringing up bdsm[3] as a topic, even with supportive and lesbian, bisexual, transgender, and queer-identified adults. Given this, the bus conversation between the mentor and the trio of youth was all the more puzzling to us.

Some might argue that the youths' request for information about sm, however hesitant, was a marker of our successful creation of a "safe" space; they did eventually articulate their interest, even if it was after the conference. But this felt like a moment when youth desires had been temporarily tamed rather than empowered. Simple utterances like this one are easily subsumed under existing frameworks about deviant sexuality, safer sex discourse, or sexual terminology while youths' questions about desire, pain, and pleasure, essential to their sexual subjectivities, are often not discussed or addressed by youth programming and curricula (Fine, 1988; Fine & McClelland, 2006).

In our attempts to keep youth safe by creating a schedule of workshops addressing risks, we had also kept them silent within a discourse that defines them as "at risk" from HIV/AIDS, STDs, pregnancy, sexual assault, domestic violence, media images, anorexia and bulimia, drugs and alcohol, and suicide. The youths' suggestion for programming pushed the limits of where adults

---

[3]Bdsm describes a range of sexual practices not limited to same-gender relationships, but often understood as some of the many forms of queer sexualities including bd (bondage-domination), ds (domination-submission), and sm (sadomasochism). *Queer*, in the prior sentence, is used to mean nonheteronormative or transgressive sexual practices.

would or could go due to granting agency restraints and governmental sources of funding. Had the youth generated sm as a topic prior to the conference, I cannot imagine that it would have resulted in a panel of bdsm practitioners. Instead, imagine a room full of uncomfortable silence or laughter and well-meaning adults translating interest in sm into deviance or into a discussion of sm within a safer sex discourse at the conference.

> It seems to me that this is the crux of heteronormative discursive powers: they render ambiguous, indirect, and unstable ways of signifying desire invisible to the social analyst. What needs to be theorized are the very means through which the contested desires of youth become noticeable and meaningful to researchers. (Driver, 2007, p. 309)

With vigorous prevention protocols designed partly to provide proof of health outcomes to granting agencies, research, educational, and social service practices often diminish youth concerns, questions, and meanderings about bdsm and other sexual practices more linked to desire than health. In so doing, they make them seem irrelevant and unintelligible within youth spaces (Fine, 1988; Driver, 2007; Orenstein, 1994; Boyte & Evans, 1986).

A preliminary search for sources on bdsm and youth yielded few results, and those sources mostly dealt with its supposed connection to psychopathology and teen self-mutilation. Given the cultural reticence to discuss *heteronormative* sexuality in schools and with young people, this is not surprising. If teachers within classrooms are stifled by school policy regarding topics like masturbation, condoms, and same-gender sexuality, imagine how topics like bondage/domination/submission/sadomasochism could find a youth audience. But these topics are obviously of interest to youth and surround them in media accounts (e.g., Britney Spears's now somewhat-dated *I'm a Slave 4U* lyrics and video and Tila Tequila's donning of dominatrix attire and use of whips and paddles with her male suitors in *A Shot at Love* are but two semi-recent examples). Such topics also have the potential to open discussions of sexuality centered on pleasure and desire, making it difficult for adults to shift to a discourse of safety, safer sex, and sexual terminology rather than engage with youth questions, concerns, and curiosities.

Some readers might think that mentors of this group had behaved somehow inappropriately to elicit youth discussion of sm, that queer youth themselves are deviant in their mentioning this form of sexual practice, or that an abstinence-only curriculum seems all the more appealing if these are the topics that comprehensive sexual education will open up. Here, ironically, I agree with conservative critics of sexual education who argue that talk about sexuality is dangerous. Discussions of sexuality *are* dangerous in many contexts, perhaps particularly with youth, because one does not know where they will lead. Sexuality is not contained by discourses of repression, rather it is channeled, as Foucault argued and as current scholars contend, into new, deliciously perverse forms that both resist and reproduce discourses that seek to confine it (Foucault, 1990; Fine, 1988; Gilbert, 2004).

> ...no language, no matter how generous or explicit, can secure the meaning of sexuality. The pleasure, as well as the danger, of sexuality is made from the ways sexuality moves through language, refuses to stay in a proper place, and erupts in surprising and unlikely places, experiences, and languages. (Gilbert, 2004, p. 113)

Gilbert proposes that, rather than have our adult anxieties drive the sexual education of young people, we should let questions of language and desire inspire our connections with young people. She writes, "How do we use language to discover, obfuscate, and narrate what we want? What languages does sexuality speak? And how do we pose sexuality as a question? These ordinary questions, I suggest, might also become the questions of sex education and the grounds of our conversations with adolescents" (Gilbert, 2004, p. 118).

Although the youth group was not a sex education program per se because the organizing framework concerned sexual and gender identities, Gilbert's vision of youth/adult engagement in spaces where sexuality is under creation, construction, deconstruction, and reconsideration is useful. In such youth/adult engagement, questions of language might become fertile ground where youth teach us about new languages of desire accessible to them, where we suggest ways that this vocabulary might constrain them as much as our "old" language and concepts, and where we relearn or

Scene 2

Writing to/with Kit: Intersecting identities

> There are no idioms to describe the reality of coming from commonplace neighborhoods where people work too many jobs—if they can find them in the first place—going to those jobs every day regardless of how they feel. The lives of people who get paid too little and try to love each other enough to make it all worthwhile anyway, people who never become famous and never expect to. (Hollibaugh, 2000, p. 5)

> I just returned from a lunch with Kit celebrating her 21st birthday and her "aging out" of the group. She talks nonstop and has a bravado I recognize in working-class white women of her age. I remember it in myself. The tone of assurance and a tone of care that comes across as bossiness for many folks. At 21, she is worried that she is getting old. She is currently working the customer service lines for a cell phone company. It's a full-time job with fairly decent benefits, but she is not happy there. She is moved to a new cubicle each day, and as one call ends, another comes over her headset. Customers yell at her, people who have not paid their cell phone bills, much like Kit who told me she is behind on her cell phone bill even with her 25% discount. She explains cell phone charges to people all day with two 15-minute breaks and an hour-long lunch. When I asked her about school, she said, "I really liked the place. But I guess it wasn't meant to be." She's tried to enroll in local community colleges twice, and both times she has been withdrawn shortly after school started or before her first semester began. During lunch, we didn't talk about her sexuality at all. She mentioned another youth that she sees in her neighborhood sometimes. He has "straightened out" his ways. His long goth hair has been trimmed, and he is working as a salesman and alternately engaged and dating a woman. Kit seems like she has little time for her own romantic and sexual life. She is busy with work and then taking care of people around her—making sure her roommate leaves for work on time or hunts for new jobs, babysitting for her young nephew, worrying about her sister who is pregnant for the third time and on bed rest after miscarrying her second child.

Kit is a young woman with whom I have an e-mail correspondence[4]. She used to attend the youth group weekly in the first year but after that attended sporadically at best. When we first met, she lived in a less-populated rural community that was a 20-minute drive from the group's meeting location, and she needed a ride each week to and from her home to attend. These 20-minute car rides offered an opportunity for us to talk about school, exes, and families, both hers and mine. During one of the first car rides to her home, she mentioned that a few of the youth who attended the group thought my partner was "hot." She told me that she didn't think my partner was "all that." (I am drawn to people who speak their minds even when that might appear rude.)

I am somewhat ambivalent about my correspondence with Kit because some youth agencies have policies against contact between youth and mentors outside the group context. These policies are designed to protect youth from mentors with lascivious intentions and mentors from false accusations by youth. The no-contact policy thus creates a boundary where youth and adults are clear about their roles and relationships. However, these boundaries are blurred in places with small LGBTQ communities, because boundaries and dual relationships are nearly impossible to avoid if one does research and practice with LGBTQ populations and people of color in rural or small metropolitan, mainly white contexts (Schank & Skovholt, 1997; Sweitzer & King, 2004). Knowledge of these policies in other contexts did not prevent me from responding to Kit when she e-mailed me. I tried to encourage her to come to the group, asked her about how school was going, and how she was feeling.

Even after she moved closer to the group's location, Kit worked full time and could not attend most weeks. As her attendance at the group dropped off, she began an e-mail correspondence with me that has lasted about a year and a half. Her e-mails are upbeat for the most part. She has an optimism that is at odds with what I know about her childhood and early adolescence and some of her current struggles. Kit was in foster care during high school. She is

---

[4] I have chosen pseudonyms for youth group members.

a working-class young adult who has been employed in the last year as a babysitter for a family friend, at a fast-food restaurant, as a nurse's aid in a hospital, and (currently) as a full-time telemarketer. At times, some of the persistent difficulty in her life seeps into otherwise optimistic e-mails. My correspondence with Kit illustrates the simultaneous intersecting identities of youth that recede, emerge, and/or combine over time. These may take precedence over sexual and gender identities as youth explore the cusp of adulthood and attempt to carve out independent identities in worlds where that is increasingly difficult.[5]

Our correspondence began when Kit entered school at a community college. She e-mailed me excitedly on her first day of classes to let me know she would not be able to attend the youth group meeting with her new hectic schedule.

> Just to let you know I have decided to go full time at school and still have my Wednesdays open, but extra activities are going to be crazy hard.

Later that same day she wrote

> Today is actually my first day of classes . . . yeah, they are all pretty good except the math. It's like I am in eighth grade again, but they said it was b/c of the placement test. My Wednesdays are completely cleared. I have English at 8 in the morning and then that is it. Have A Great Day and remember to SMILE. ☺

A little over two weeks later, I heard from Kit again. She had been removed from her courses because she would be missing a month of classes due to a back injury. She wrote:

> Corrine, I have had a crazy week. My back has taken me out of school for a month and when I called the school, they took me out for the semester. I am . . . with my dad for the week and might stay longer. I haven't decided. I need to take some time to get my head back on my shoulders. Just tell everyone I said hi and to have a great week and remember to ☺ ☺ ☺ it confuses people.

I wrote back to her the same day.

---

[5] Kit has given me permission to use our correspondence in this book chapter.

> I hope you're not in a lot of pain. What's going on with your back? Is this an ongoing problem? I'm so sorry to hear that you won't be able to continue with school for the fall. Do your professors know? If I were you, I might e-mail them individually and let them know what has happened. That means a lot to professors and sometimes the registrar doesn't follow through with them. I hope staying with your dad . . . is a good thing. I haven't heard you talk about him much. Take some time to take care of yourself and get better. If you want to share your address, let me know. I'm sure people will want to send you [a] card or a letter.

As I reread my response to her, I cringed a bit. Although I use the phrase "if I were you," Kit had not asked for advice, but my professorial and mentor identity (probably incorrectly) moved in to do what I thought would be helpful: make nice with the institution so your options are not severed for next semester. However, I think my response is also marked by a straddling of working-class lives and middle-class educational institutions, imagining what is appropriate, how to play the game of the institution, how to navigate it so that one is not locked. She responded,

> Yes, I contacted my professors. It was hard but I did it. I don't think I want to go back to [community college] anyway. It wasn't my kinda school. I have three dislocated disks in my lower back and a pinched nerve in my right leg. I am in pain, but I am on some steroids that take the pain away and I'm okay other wise. I lay in bed all day and I'll tell you it sucks.

Kit e-mailed me in early March 2007 to tell me she was having more health problems. This time she had been diagnosed with a condition affecting her hormone levels. I asked her some questions about the condition in response and then asked whether she had been absent from the youth group at the last meeting because of her diagnosis. Her e-mail to me was the first sense I had about her feelings of self-doubt.

> ...that is part of it. But it's more of my own insecurity. I don't feel that I am important enough to come back after leaving. And work? Well, I have no idea. And I am looking for an apartment that allows little dogs because my landlord is a jerk and will not fix my oven. And to be honest, I live off microwave food and it's not healthy. But the good news [is] I have lost 15 lbs. in a week with a new med.

Kit sent an e-mail trying to figure out what she would do when she "aged out" of the group at 21.

> I haven't made it to group. I miss it, but I don't know if I can walk back in there and try to make my life as great as it used to be and all. And last time I went I felt really out of place and besides the fact I am going to age out in like 3 months. I'm [going to] be 21 so yeah I have no idea what to do.

She explained that she had been hired as a nurse's aide at a local hospital, but she would not be able to do much of the lifting of patients that was required because of her back injury. This e-mail had a different tone than her previous ones and so I replied within a half hour both attempting to problem solve for her as before and worrying in the text about what activities existed for local youth once they turned 21.

> Hi, Kit. Congratulations on the job and the apartment. Be careful about the weight limit. I worry that it will be easy to overexert yourself. I didn't realize you would be aging out so soon. It might be nice to come again and create some closure for yourself. You know to see where you have been and where you want to be. There really are an absence of things for young LGBTQ folks to do in this community unless they have kids...or are transgender...I think there might be a bowling night at [bowling alley]. There's [sic] always the bars, but that's not really my scene either. I think would be a good conversation for us to have in [group] sometime.

Kit responded, maybe speaking to my assumption that she needed me to brainstorm places for her to hang out as a young queer woman. Her "Yeah" in this passage also indicates that she thinks I would be judgmental for her "dating a guy."

> At this moment I have no idea what I identify as. I was dating a guy for three months. Yeah, not so great and I hated it. But I don't have to fit in a box and never plan on it and bars are not my scene since I'm not a big partier.

I ran into Kit a few days later at a bus stop. She hadn't been able to make it to group and we talked about how she was doing. She said she didn't feel like the group was for her because she wasn't sure she was a lesbian anymore. I found myself disappointed and angry that the group had not created a culture that served Kit—a fluidly sexual young working-class woman. Where would she find community?

This paper has provided me with the opportunity to reflect on the social, historical, and economic context of the youth within the group: although many embody the free spirit of the new gay teenager as described by Savin-Williams (2005), many also seem caught by the economic relations of a deindustrialized city, studying for the general educational development (GED) test, graduating from high school, going to the local community college, dropping out with health concerns, having parents who are absent with regard to or unsupportive of their educational goals, working part-time at fast-food restaurants, and imagining an escape to a larger city for a better job. In contrast, Savin-Williams describes youth apparently free of these economic realities with parents who are supportive both of their sexuality and their continuing education. These "new gay youth" (2005) seem to reside in almost entirely white and middle-class social contexts. Although Kit has the advantages of whiteness, her family has been on public assistance. She seems like someone who would easily fall between the cracks of educational and social service institutions.

As I reflect on my e-mail correspondence with Kit and consider Lisa Diamond's recently published work on the fluidity of women's sexual identities (2008), Kit's identifications, desires, and practices do not fit easily into either current master narrative of queer youth—victimized or affirmed—as outlined by Talburt (2007). Talburt argues that queer youth narrations by scholars, youth workers, youth advocates, and activists alike juxtapose a victimized and oppressed, suicidal and lonely gay youth with an affirmed, out, healthy, and happy gay youth. In these master narratives, youthful experience is universalized and connected to adult recollections of adolescent pain from which adulthood and outness offer freedom. Even positive gay youth narratives are potentially conservative when they presume a stable, fixed, sexual identity that assimilates into current institutions and becomes manageable as a subject in Foucault's sense (1990). In their eagerness to provide space for youth, schools and nonprofit agencies have segregated them by their sexuality and gender expression and then recapitulated a victim narrative to obtain funding for youth services. These narrations produce youth as subjects while they reveal ideological and institutional investments. LGBTQ youth concerns become isolated in school (e.g., in gay-straight alliances [GSAs]) and in organizational spaces, losing some of their radical potential to affect all youth lives within and out of school.

Kit is neither victimized and oppressed, nor affirmed and happy. She embodies both these positions simultaneously and complicatedly. Her correspondence describes difficult health conditions, job woes, and excitement at being able to attend the group and be involved in the various projects of the group. She also describes dating a guy for a few months and not liking it so much. In fact, Kit's biography marks her as inadequate in either narrative. In the antihomophobic narrative, she becomes evidence for the need for improved programming for queer youth. Her class position and her dislike for school do not fit with the affirmed and happy narrative either. They do not even enter into these discursive identity forms because, much like Diamond's subjects, her lack of a fixed identity makes her unintelligible to many.

LGBTQ youth programs in our area and throughout the country might use Kit as a case study with accompanying local statistics on homelessness among LGBTQ youth to establish justifications for granting agencies. "Certainly winning funding for services to queer youth, in the current American system of human services funding, demands a focus on the ways in which such funding might ameliorate issues of homelessness, substance abuse, suicide, or HIV infection in this population" (Rofes, 2004, p. 57). But reading Kit's correspondence simply as a victim narrative and martyr-target-victim (Talburt, 2004; Rofes, 2004) does not really capture the essence of her—even as that essence is constructed by her surroundings.

The extent to which the social sciences, specifically psychology and education, have decontextualized young queer bodies is troubling. For many of the youth who came to the meetings, their sexualities and gender expressions were not what I saw as their most pressing concerns. LGBTQ youth may be less tethered to categories of sexuality, but simultaneously marginalized by economic shifts that disadvantage them and a cultural individualism that convinces them they are "free" of these constraints. Many of the youth I met were stuck in a deindustrialized, northeastern city, trying to carve out lives with possibilities as factory jobs outside of the defense industry moved across the globe. I have seen youth leave the group and go to local community colleges and drop out after a semester or less. I have seen youth take jobs at fast-food restaurants and telemarketing firms with little chance at meaningful advancement and little chance of moving off the welfare rolls that their families were/are on.

Scene 3

Mercury and sexual fluidity

> ...there is no point at which sexuality completely finished developing, neatly tying off loose ends and therefore, ruling out the prospect of unexpected future transitions. (Diamond, 2008, p. 255)

> Mercury, a young gay man from the youth group, invites me to his high school graduation party in the backyard of his home. I am not looking forward to the party. No other youth or mentors that I know are going, and I imagine that I will be surrounded by parents, grandparents, aunts and uncles, family friends, and high school teachers. Family gatherings with my own extended family are difficult enough.

> I arrive at his parents' split-level ranch home with attached basement garage early in the day and talk to his mother briefly, telling her what a creative and kind-hearted son she has and that she should be proud of him. I pull Mercury aside and ask him how I should respond to questions about how I know him. He tells me that "everyone knows" about his participation in the LGBTQ youth group, but I'm still reticent as I talk to his aunts and uncles and just say that I am a mentor for an after school club. Am I closeting him or myself?

> As I'm standing next to the aboveground pool (I feel more comfortable with the younger cousins playing in the pool than I am with the adults eating potato salad under the rented canopy), Mercury says he wants me to meet someone. A petite dark-haired girl walks up to us from the driveway. Mercury introduces her as his girlfriend.

Mercury often confounded my expectations of him. When I met him, he was dating another young man from the group. They broke up shortly thereafter because Mercury had been having sex with someone else. This was in itself surprising because I had not imagined that Mercury was a "player." But in the short two and a half years I have known him, he has dated a young man his own age, an older man, a young woman from the group, the girlfriend I met at his graduation party, a steady girlfriend who became pregnant, and his current boyfriend. These are just the relationships that I know about and that Mercury has shared with me, although Mercury is not reserved in his disclosures, and I suspect his earnest nature and openness may be some of his draw as a partner.

Mercury's fluidity is also not confined to his sexual orientation. His gender expression and pursuits often change from one meeting to the next. At one point in the group, the youth proposed that when we introduced ourselves we could each decide what we wanted to be called during that meeting. That meant that we could choose names that had a shelf life of one group meeting. This was difficult for mentors who only attend a meeting once per month on average, but it did reflect the changing identifications of transgender youth who did not feel a connection to their given names and were experimenting with chosen names that matched their gender identity. Mercury used this as an opportunity to express his current (and fleeting) self. Sometimes asking to be referred to by a traditionally feminine name, he often claimed a name, as well as time and space, to discuss the history and worship of a new pagan deity about which he had been learning. Mercury also has been exploring his gender expression through drag performance.

At no time have I considered Mercury "confused." In fact, in each of his incarnations, he seems fully engaged and committed to his presentation. I do know, however, that communities both queer and straight may be less than supportive of his whimsical self-presentation and his nonexclusive (meaning not exclusively same-sex) sexual behavior. After-school programming, much like school-affiliated GSAs, may press youth to identify at younger ages, thereby truncating their sexual identity development when youth identify simply as gay or straight. As Crowley analyzes in another chapter in this volume, youth in places outside of adult constraints and surveillance, such as Internet chat rooms, may adopt new sexual and gender expressions that defy the labels of lesbian, gay, bisexual, and transgender. Mercury and many of the youth who participated in this local group demonstrated a sexual and gender fluidity not recognizable a generation ago in LGBTQ youth organizations. The most active members in the group were transmen who attended every meeting, dated young transmen, young women, or young men and challenged many of the assumptions of previous generations of LGB individuals through both their sexual fluidity and gender expression. This was not unusual in the group as many of the youth displayed a fluid sexuality, dating girls and boys within and out of the group. In my experience, this fluidity was not a source of gossip or consternation among group members, rather they took this in stride, shifting pronouns, chosen names, and interactions with ease. Adult mentors, however, had difficulty "keeping up" at times. This may be partly due to a nonweekly mentoring schedule, but may also indicate our lack of flexible gender and sexuality constructions reflecting our coming of age at a different time in LGBTQ social movements. The stability of gender and sexual identities reflects a particular era in civil rights organizing that required stability for legal recognition, a model still in operation within many social scientific, legal, and nonprofit social service settings.

Although social science research on sexuality since Kinsey has recognized the common incongruence between sexual orientation, identity, and behavior, much of current social science research presumes static sexual and gender categories or creates them by collapsing more fluid response sets into gay, lesbian, male, and female. Diamond's work (2008) documents women's fluid sexual and romantic connections, but research on men's sexual fluidity is not as prevalent. However, among the local male youth who participate in the youth group, I have witnessed a great degree of sexual fluidity that has challenged mentors' assumptions about youth and their sexualities.

A far more potentially radical stance for our educational and cultural contexts is a commitment to the knowledge that all of us—those who identify as gay, lesbian, bisexual, straight, and anything else; youth and adults; women (in particular), men (perhaps), and transfolk (whom we desperately need to include in social science research because transidentification in youth today seems quite different than that of a generation ago)—are engaged in a dynamic sexual process in which no one can be certain of how we will identify and with whom we will connect romantically and sexually. Diamond writes, "But to acknowledge that sexuality is fluid means to acknowledge that no matter how certain you feel about your sexuality at the moment, you might have an experience tomorrow or ten years from now that will place you squarely in sexual-minority territory" (2008, p. 255). This kind of acknowledgment destabilizes notions of static sexuality that prop up heterosexuality, causing presumably straight men and women to be unreflective desiring subjects who can separate themselves from homosexual subjects (Diamond, 2008). In schools, this may mean moving the work of GSAs into classrooms in the form of projects where students engage across what appear to be differences of sexuality and gender with (currently) heterosexual students, outlining the benefits of an inclusive understanding of sexuality.

Conclusion

Across these three scenes, I have illustrated how liminal experiences with youth highlight youth knowledge and lived experience that should give pause to youth advocates, social workers, youth development associates, educators, and mentors to reflect on the programming adults and youth create.

Sexuality programming for youth should move beyond both abstinence programming and risk reduction to encompass the full exploration and expression of youth curiosity with sexual subjectivities. This may include topics that public schools are not ready for and for which they will come under fire. For these reasons, community-based after-school programs may be better situated to engage with youth sexual subjectivity. If these topics are youth generated, adults can facilitate honest communication among and with youth that honors their interest in queer sexualities in their many forms.

Adults need to be prepared for the fluidity of sexual behavior and identities of all youth, perhaps young women in particular, whose sexualities seem to be marked by dynamic changes in whom they are attracted to, as well as how they choose to define themselves. As longitudinal research is conducted with young men and transidentified youth of all genders, scholars may discover that young people's narrations of their sexual identities are more dynamic than once thought. Programming that does not recognize the uncertainty of sexual identity risks alienating a new generation of young people who are demanding acceptance of their sexual lives and seeking safe(r) spaces in which to live their lives and develop into healthy, happy, and sexual adults.

Perhaps the key issue in the creation of spaces for and by young LGBTQ people is the recognition that sexuality is but one shifting identity category in a matrix of intersecting circumstances, situations, identities, and communities. Educational contexts from elementary schools to higher education institutions, after-school programs, nonprofit organizations, and LGBTQ-marked spaces, including bars, must recognize the diverse circumstances of young LGBTQ people. Although there are certainly LGBTQ youth who are organizing their communities and attending college on scholarship or funded by their families, there are also queer youth who are struggling within educational contexts. Acknowledgment of the constellation of identities that affect LGBTQ lives requires that researchers and educators not whitewash racial and ethnic, as well as class and gender diversity. When white middle-class samples are generalized to all LGBTQ youth, young men and women of color, working-class and poor youth, and transidentified youth wind up, yet again, labeled as immoral, illegal, and pathological. Rather than pathologize a new generation of LGBTQ youth, researchers should adopt methods, sampling procedures, and tools of analysis that underscore resiliency and marginalization, resistance and reproduction in diverse youth lives with their cooperation and participation in such projects. Imagine what researchers and participants, youth and adults might learn from such endeavors and each other.

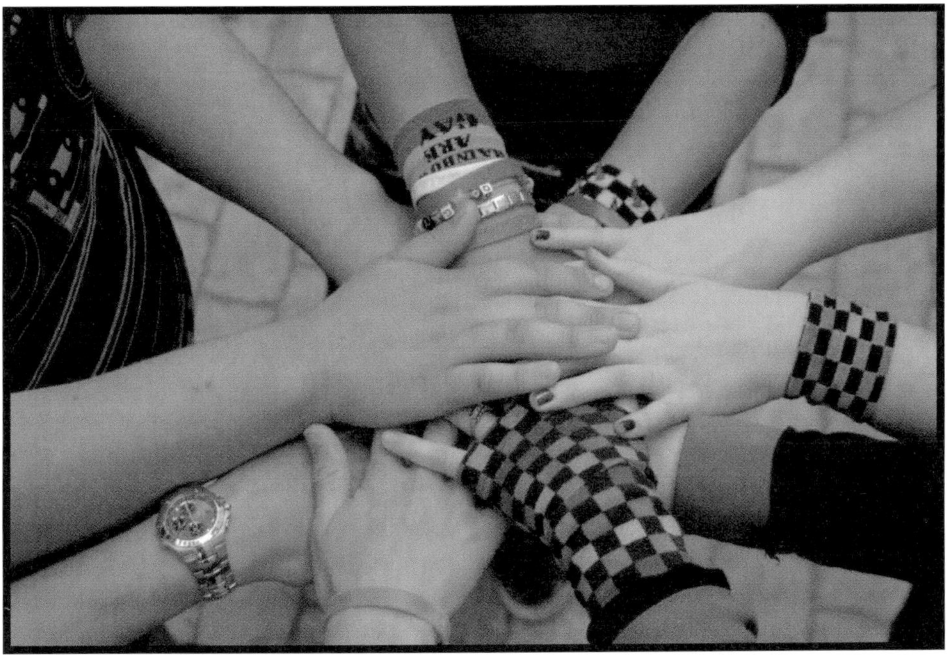

Chapter Ten

Defining Themselves: LGBQS Youth Online

M. Sue Crowley

WITHIN THE PAST 5 years, social networking sites have emerged as important virtual contexts within which teens and young adults interact to establish online identities and relationships. As Buckingham (2008) has noted, "A generation is growing up in an era where digital media are part of the taken-for-granted social and cultural fabric of learning, play, and social communication" (p. vii). Many of today's youth are digital natives (Prensky, 2006), having always been aware of various forms of technological communication. Lesbian, gay, bisexual, transgender, queer, and intersex (LGBTQI) youth are no exception. The Internet has been a consistent presence in their lives. Using digital media of all types, they seek out information on sexuality/attractionality, form trusting friendships, look for dates, and establish relatively independent communities. In contrast to their straight-identified peers for whom public awareness of their sexuality and identity exploration is seldom an issue, social networking sites serve as spaces where LGBTQI youth are relatively free to explore their identities in interaction with similarly inclined age-peers and allies.

Theory and Background

The relationship between communication technologies and social identity formation has been a subject of study among scholars in critical youth studies (Best, 2007) and social theory on identity (Buckingham & Willett, 2006; Renninger & Shumar, 2002; Turkle, 1997). Thus far, few studies have addressed these issues from the perspectives of marginalized youth (Everett, 2008), particularly young people who identify as LGBTQI (Driver, 2007). The research for this chapter was designed to add to that literature by exploring a particular, interactional subtype of social networking, namely, topic threads posted on Discussion Boards in MySpace and Facebook. These topic threads include virtual conversations on a range of issues relevant to the process of identity formation among LGBTQI youth.

Interdisciplinary theoretical perspectives guide the research for this project. From the standpoint of traditional psychology, Erikson's (1968) emphasis on the role of exploration and experimentation in interaction with peers and authorities remains relevant. This is particularly true insofar as it relates to the need to examine one's values, ideals, and goals in an effort to discover a positive social niche. From the standpoint of social constructionist and critical theories, the concept of identity is approached as a social, as well as psychological, process rather than a developmental achievement. The terms *adolescence* and *teenager* first appeared as labels for a period of time in the life span in the early twentieth century and reflect a shifting historical process of social definition rather than a fixed designation of age-based identity (Hine, 1999). For the purposes of this study, Eriksonian concepts of exploration and experimentation are situated within an understanding of identity as an ongoing, formative process that begins with the ability to distinguish one's self both *from* and *with* others in multiple domains of life across time (Jenkins, 2004). It is a process of framing and naming a variety of ways of being in the world that does not have an end point.

The changes that come with puberty and early adolescence shift the foundation on which the process of identity formation occurs. The visible emergence of secondary sexual characteristics combines with invisible cognitive advances in qualities of abstract thought, such as perspective-taking. For most, these physical and cognitive changes are linked to a period of social transition in school and family. The social and emotional challenges and opportunities presented by intimate friendships, cliques, groups, dating, and sexual exploration combine across adolescence, culminating in the need to establish significant relationships with others. In all these negotiations with the physiological, psychological, and social realities of adolescence, young people seek out others who can serve a mirrors, reflecting back to them a person they may be, may not want to be, or may not even recognize. It ought to be no surprise then, that adolescence can present LGBTQI youth with a genuine crisis of identity.

Whether in physical or virtual space, young people still need to interact with others to reflect on and share a variety of values, needs, and dreams for the future. These interactions include explorations of sexual, emotional, and social orientations that enable them to discover the ways in which they relate to others in the larger world. In a (post)modern world of multiple and mutable forms of identity, young people confront a complex set of expectations in the process of situating themselves in relation to others in ways that provide self-respect, community, and hope for the future. They still need to find where and with whom they belong.

Today, the social domains available for young people to seek out friendships, role models, sexual exploration, and alternative norms have expanded to include social networking sites on the World Wide Web. Understanding "how youth engage through social network sites today provides long-lasting insights into identity formation, status negotiation, and peer-to-peer sociality" (boyd, 2008, p. 119). The availability of such sites has special significance for LGBTQI youth who may need to keep their sexual orientation hidden from people in their families, schools, and other, local social contexts. When the "real" world fails to meet their needs for friendship and belonging, they can seek out a virtual one. When discussing the implications of such spaces for youth in general, boyd (2008) offers observations that may carry additional resonance for LGBTQI youth. She "examine(s) how teens are modeling identity through social network profiles so that they can write themselves and their community into being" (p. 120). In addition to the individual profiles boyd analyzes, MySpace and Facebook groups and Discussion Boards offer an interactional social domain in which questioning, queer, and LGBT youth may seek to establish a sense of identity and/or escape from one. This form of techno-communication may serve as a substitute for the social locales and contexts in which they do not belong; where the values, easy assumptions, and expectations of others neither reflect nor support their needs, interests, and ideals.

Methods

Two interrelated avenues of inquiry guide the study. It begins by examining what LGBTQI youth discover when they go to MySpace and Facebook seeking connections online. The study continues by exploring how these two social networking sites function as virtual educational contexts within which LGBTQI youth engage in a process of information sharing, discussion, disagreement, and self-definition that contributes to their identity formation.

Research Questions

The study is framed around by 4 research questions designed to guide the process of gathering information. The first avenue of inquiry noted above can be broken down into the following questions:

1. If you were a young LGBTQI person seeking connection, what would you find when first entering MySpace and Facebook?
2. And how might that guide your understanding of who you are and are not?

The second avenue of inquiry focuses on the processes and themes that emerge from narrative exchanges found on Discussion Boards in MySpace and Facebook. Discussion Boards are initiated by members of self-generating Groups. Groups offer opportunities for youth to join with others, either around a common interest (for example, dating tips, NASCAR, and video gaming) or identity (for example, race and ethnicity, nationality, and school). Group members may start or join Discussion Boards that include within them subtopic discussions. For the purpose of this study, these subtopic conversational narratives are defined as *topic threads*.

Questions guiding the second avenue of inquiry noted above include:

1. What terms or forms of language are used to identify self and/or others among LGBTQI youth?
2. How do these forms of language reflect self and other representations of LGBTQI youth in the larger society?

Procedures. To obtain information for the first two research questions above, MySpace and Facebook were explored to determine how LGBTQI groups are organized and used for self-other identification. The next two research questions were addressed by examining LGBTQI-oriented Discussion Boards for topic threads that specifically addressed issues of identity. No names or other identifying information is included from participants' comments. Individuals are sometimes described by age, state, and/or gender. Narratives drawn from these topic threads were used to provide a sample of the "social language" (Gee, 1999, pp. 12–13, 25) employed by youth when discussing self and other representations of LGBTQI identities. The narratives will be examined using "situated meanings as a tool of inquiry" (p. 53) and the process defined by Gee (1999) as "socioculturally-situated identity and relationship building" (pp. 85–86).

Results. To explore the first question ("What would they find there?") types and sizes of groups on MySpace and Facebook were examined. These two social networking sites appeared to provide different options and avenues of exploration for LGBTQI youth seeking community online. MySpace presented a much more intuitive and direct approach for people seeking to identify what LGBTQI groups were available and how to link up with them. Simply by clicking on Groups from the main menu, a new user is shown a list of various types including a specific category labeled "Gay, Lesbian, & Bi." Choosing this category resulted in the discovery of more than 40,000 separate Groups with 66 of those reporting memberships over 5,000 (as of January 2008).

Next, to provide information relevant to the second question ("How might these sites guide your understanding of identity?"), those 66 Groups were categorized into 9 subtypes (lesbian only; lesbian, bisexual, and questioning women; gay, lesbian, and bisexual people; gay men only; political advocacy; trans groups; gay, lesbian, bisexual, and straight inclusive; Lesbian and Bi-men couples only; and bi-women only) from largest to smallest, based on number of members.

Table 1

MySpace LGBTQI groups with more than 5,000 members each by category, number of groups, and total membership

Subtype	Number of Groups	Total Membership
Lesbian Only	5	261,495
Gay Men Only	20	244,561
Political Advocacy	5	204,849
Lesbian and Bi-women	5	105,190
Lesbian and Bi-couples	3	98,852
Transgender	12	96,144
Gay Men, Lesbian, and Bi	7	89,230
Inclusive: Gays and Allies	6	41,232
Bi-women Only	3	17,512

Total Groups = 66 Total Memberships = 1,159,065

In contrast, Facebook was organized primarily around general Areas of Interest. In an effort to identify specifically LGBTQI groups, keyword search terms, including variations on *gay, lesbian, bi, queer,* and/or *trans,* were entered. This search identified 304 groups. Of these, only one had a membership over 1,000. Using the search term *gay groups* resulted in a listing of over 500 sites, but again, only one had more than 1,000 members. Next, in an effort to identify larger communities of LGBTQI youth on Facebook, three Areas of Interest—Beliefs and causes, Dating and relationships, and Sexuality—were examined. They were chosen based on their potential to include specifically LGBTQI groups and/or Discussion Boards.

Within the Beliefs and causes category, only one group with a membership over 5,000 referenced LGBTQI issues. It was organized around an anti-gay/protect marriage theme. Within Dating and relationships, one small group (< 3,000 members) was labeled "The fastest way to a girl's heart is through her gay friend."

To find relatively large communities of people discussing LGBTQI issues on Facebook, it was necessary to search specifically within the Area of Interest labeled Sexuality. One Group named "I'm sexually inappropriate with my friends, but I'm actually not a lesbian" included an explicit WARNING printed in capital letters to discourage actual lesbians from joining or posting to their site. ("This group is for people who keep their lesbian encounters to JOKING. Please do not post skanky pictures.") A pro-gay group, "Cute, Gay, Single, and Available," made sure members knew they could separate their identities on Facebook to ensure their sexuality remained a secret on "your ordinary facebook profile." By far the largest Group in the Sexuality interest area, however, was called "Against Gay Marriage? Then Don't Get One and Shut the Fuck Up" (will subsequently be referred to simply as AGM?) with a membership of over 59,000 (as of February 2008).

The Language of Self-Identification

Research questions number 3 and 4 above were addressed by searching within Groups and Discussion Boards for topic threads focused specifically on identity issues. The Facebook group AGM? provided the largest number and longest topic threads for narrative analysis. One topic thread in particular, "Gay? Lesbian? Bi? "Fag hag"? ... STRAIGHT?" (henceforth, GLBFS?), directly addressed question 3 ("What terms and/or forms of language are used to identify self and/or others among LGBTQI youth?"). This topic thread was initiated by a woman using a college network and resulted in an extensive (942 posts by 628 people) series of comments, responses, explanations, disagreements, and personal stories over the course of several months. The following breakdown of identity categories is based on a subset of 210 entries contributed by 140 individuals that were randomly chosen across the length of this topic thread (as of January 2008). It provides some insight into the youths who were drawn to this discussion of language and labels.

The largest number of responses was contributed by people ($N = 54$; 38.6%) who self-identified as straight. The next largest category consisted of people describing their sexual preferences as bisexual ($N = 26$; 18.6%). Within this group, 14 appeared to be women (as determined by names and pronoun use), 4 men, and 2 people who were not identifiable by gender. Next were young people who identified as questioning ($N = 17$; 12.1%). This group was cross-referenced with other categories and examined for additional information. Eight of those who identified as questioning thought they might be straight, 6 bisexually identified women, 1 possible lesbian, 1 possible gay man, and 1 person who simply wrote "don't know."

Table 2

Categories and numbers of self-descriptions from discussion board thread, "Gay? Lesbian? Bi? "Fag hag" ...Straight?"

Category	Numbers	Uncertain/Questioning	Total
Straight	54	8	62
Bisexual	26		
Subtypes:			
Female	20	6	
Male	4		
Unknown	2		32
"Mehsexual"	16		16
Lesbian	15	1	16
Gay	10	1	11
Other:			
"Queer"	1		
"homosexual"	1		
"don't know"	1		3
Totals	124	16	140

The remaining two groups consisted of self-identified lesbians ($N = 15$; 10.7%) and people who explicitly refused to use the standard LGBTQI labels ($N = 16$; 11.4%). Some of these individuals incorporated bisexuality into this polymorphous category ($N = 6$). Self-described gays comprised the smallest group ($N = 10$; 7.1%). Two individuals described themselves separately as "queer," or simply "homosexual."

Three interrelated issues emerged from the narrative exchanges within this topic thread. They included (1) statements and explanatory comments describing *questioning in the process of exploration*, (2) *rejection of labels* dependent on sexuality, attraction, and/or gender, and (3) the creative *use of neologisms* (e.g., "mehsexual" and "pansexual") to avoid categories of sexuality based on gendered dichotomies of attraction. Given the degree of overlap among them, these three issues appeared to be integrated rather than discrete or separate themes. For instance, the processes (1) by which some people reported coming to choose a particular terminology might have resulted in frustration over gendered categories of sexual identity (2), leading to the adoption of a neologism (3). Finally, it should be noted that the issues of exploration, labeling, and questioning from this topic thread (GLBFS?), were echoed across other Groups, Discussion Boards, and topic threads on both Facebook and MySpace.

Processes of Exploration on High School and College Networks

Responses on GLBFS? ranged from specific declarations of identity to expressions of ongoing confusion. In an effort to determine if these variations might reflect changes across adolescence and young adulthood, comments by youth accessing Facebook from networks that specified high school (37 comments) or college (38 comments) were isolated for closer examination.

Among the high school students, two types of comments were most evident. One involved simple declarations of terms, such as one word responses, some featuring emoticons ("Straight," "bisexual," "Lesbian =]") or expressions with added emphasis ("100% lesbian," "straight, but not narrow," "im bi thanks XD," "Lesbian and loving it :P," "Fag hag and proud of it =]"). The other type of comment reflected varying degrees of confusion, processing emotions, and/or questioning. These responses tended to be slightly longer and sometimes referenced others' reactions to disclosure. One young man wrote, "Erm...pretty damn close to being gay." Another remarked, "How about, I think I'm straight, but still not sure."

Similarly, a young woman indicated, "straight or bi. not quite sure." Referencing others' reactions was seen in the questioning stance taken by this young woman.

> I'm sort of inbetween bi and gay. I haven't really sorted things out yet, and only one of my gay friends knows. noone else. Not even my best friends. soo i don't know.

Two others discussed fears and/or problems related to disclosure in their small towns and high schools ("im meh/bi but shhh . . . my town is VERY homophobic. so most don't say anything until after they graduate").

Among the college-age students, both similar and different patterns emerged. Similarities included short declarative self-statements, as well as questions and confusion ("Straight perhaps. I feel like I'm too young to determine something so . . . individual." "I'm probably kinda straight a little." "i think im straight! . . . i have had alot of boyfs but i don't know . . . anything can happen"). These entries reveal an active, questioning process of exploration in high school, across the transition to college, and perhaps later in life as well.

Another similarity between comments from high school and college networks included descriptions of sexual identity as an experiential and emotional process. Unlike the high school students, however, comments from college networks did not reference reactions by others. These young people were more internally, emotionally focused. Here is one young woman's account of her process.

> I used to think I was bisexual. Mostly because I decided I was gay, then fell in love with a man, which was very confusing. I then realized that I didn't want to have sex with guys at all.

Another young woman described different dimensions of attraction in an effort to name her sexual identity. "I'm bi. I think I'd be 80/20 guys to girls physically, 20/80 . . . emotionally . . . that's a sorta 50/50 :S."

Differences between comments on high school and college networks were also noted. College students displayed a greater tendency to employ neologisms for sexual identity ("omnisexual," "humansexual," "Pomosexual") and to include conceptual modifiers ("I'm sexual. I absolutely refuse to add a prefix to that." " gay . . . but i love the idea of mehsexual. i just love it." "Very liberal agnostic bisexual fag-hag"). The use of neologisms and modifiers may indicate a growing awareness of the multifaceted and intersectional relationships that exist between one's sexuality and other elements of one's identity.

Rejection of Categories

Another recurring issue was characterized by the rejection of sexual labels for self and others. These comments were focused on the extent to which the labels themselves were seen as divisive, inadequate, and increasingly unnecessary in the twenty-first century. For instance, two young women who identified reluctantly as bisexual, noted, "I don't really like categorizing myself" and "not a big fan of labels." Another person whose gender and sexuality were unclear went further, decrying the use of/need for any labels and challenged others to stop naming their sexual identities.

> HEY GANG what the fuck with all the labels? Why don't you all just have a good time and let the chips fall whee they fall. have safe sex with whoever and when u fall in love u will know . . . and it really doesn't matter it is 2007. labels r why gays have it so bad in the past . . . !

The next post to appear in the thread was by a self-identified young, straight man who agreed.

> RIGHT ON PAL! I don't quite understand the point of this thread. Does it matter what one's sexual orientation is? I don't think so . . . sexuality does not make one damn bit of difference to me. But anyway, I'm a guy and I get my kicks from women.

These entries were echoed by individuals who expressed confusion over their sexuality and/or did not see themselves represented adequately in the discussion because their sexual attractions were unbounded by gender ("I'm sexual. I absolutely refuse to add a prefix to that").

Creative Use of Neologisms

The rejection of sexual categories based on gender and sexuality was directly linked to the creation of new labels. In fact, the use of neologisms was evident within the first 20 responses on this thread (GLBFS?) when a young woman joined the discussion by describing herself as bisexual, then quickly modifying that response.

> Although I don't like that word, because "bi" means "two," and I certainly don't want to restrict myself to only the two "official" genders.

Two lines later she added, "I use the term 'mehsexual' as in 'meh, gender doesn't matter much to me.'" Later on, a female college student introduced the label "Pomosexual" this way.

> postmodern sexual, meaning no classification, only a sexual being with preferences . . . I think it was invented to get rid of prejudices. Cuz it doesn't really matter if your gay or straight, as long as ur happy.

The idea that the commonly used terms for LGBTQI people are inadequate or outdated resulted in an expansive list of terms. They included *omnisexual, pansexual, bi-permissive, pomosexual* (see above), and *nosexual.* Others were more expressive, "Drag Queen." "I'm GenderFuck or, a little more accurately, Gender-Queer." "...humansexual. Yep, I only do *people* (er, adult people)." Straight-identified people were also actively engaged in both enjoying old labels, such as "fag hag," and generating new ones ("str8"). One young man described himself as "probably kinda straight a little" and weighed in with the opinion that calling one's self a fag hag was "a goofy idea. Is there a male equivalent 'dyke Mike' or something goofy?" A presumably older woman weighed in with this comment, "I distinctly remember being straight, but now I'm Menopausal and Asexual. Thanks for asking LOL."

Self-Representations of LGBTQI Youth

The next step in the analysis was guided by question 4 ("How do these forms of language reflect various self and other representations of LGBTQI youth in the larger society?"). This question is two pronged. On the one hand, several topic threads on Facebook and MySpace revealed that young people who identify as LGBTQI think about and present their sexual identities in multiple, sometimes contradictory, ways. Therefore, representation is contested to some extent within their own virtual communities. On the other hand, they are also keenly aware of the ways in which they are represented by outsiders, particularly those who take various anti-LGBTQI positions in the larger society.

Issues of disagreement among LGBTQI youth were evident in the Facebook topic thread GLBFS? when it came to definitions of women's bisexuality. The label was introduced by a young man whose comment reflected a playful attitude toward negative representations. He wrote, "i feel like a homo for being the only bi so far." Four young women quickly reassured him that he was not alone, but did so in language suggesting ambiguity over the term ("No worries, you're not the only bisexual. Although I don't like the word." "I'm bisexual, but borderline lesbian." "bi, maybe? who knows." "I'm bisexual as well. Although I do like the concept of 'mehsexual"). Almost immediately another young woman weighed in with this criticism of bisexuality.

> Bisexuality is a bit crass from a gay point of view. Nothing like meeting a girl in a (gay) club and getting all the right signals, only to find her ten minutes later pulling a bloke. It gets tiring after a while.

The first bisexually identified young woman quoted above took issue with this point of view.

> I can't help but be a little offended by that. I've taken a lot of shit from a lot of "100% gay" men and women calling me "half closeted." I hope other bisexuals will join me in a hearty "fuck that."

Discussing their varied personal experiences, one woman noted that she has encountered others who "call themselves such [meaning bisexual] to get more attention from guys. go figure." The young woman who initiated the controversy over women's bisexuality weighed in to offer a political, as well as personal, perspective.

...a bisexual can pass for straight if they need to. . .while you are with your boyfriend you manage to avoid the discrimination we have no choice but face. You can marry a person you love and have children . . . , this isn't an option for us.

In a conciliatory tone she sought to clarify,

I'm not trying to say that it isn't possible to be bisexual, or that it is a bad thing, but there is a lot more going on behind the tendency of entirely homosexual people to dismiss bisexuals than you seem to take into account.

Another young woman who identified as bisexual concluded this exchange by saying, "Good talk ladies. Good talk."

That was not, however, the end of the discussion. In fact, it was a direct lead-in to the rejection of labels altogether, a theme examined above. In a follow-up post, another young woman declared,

...after some exploring . . . i realized, shit man, i don't have to be gay, straight, bisexual, asexual . . . i'm *Name* and sometimes i fall in love with People . . . and i like to fuck People. whatever you get the point.

On a different Facebook topic thread, "I'm not gay, but . . . ," the conversation explored the tendency of straights to begin their posts with the words, "I'm not gay, but. . . ." Speculation about their motivations included positive ("a way of introducing ourselves as supporters," "if they want to set the record 'straight' with us, that's cool") and negative ("afraid others will think they are gay," "give greater credence to what they have to say") assumptions. Eventually, the young woman who originated this topic thread introduced the issue of labeling one's sexuality.

Yeah I guess can see how it could be necessary for some people to mention it, I just don't. Probably just cuz I don't really care. I've kinda been labeled as one of those people that's not into labels. Haha, irony.

Again, this entry initiated a string of responses about the problems created by people assigning labels to their own and others' sexuality that was very similar to the comments found on the topic thread examined above (GLBFS?). With humor and self-deprecation, one high school senior explained the trouble she had with labels.

> I've never been into labels, but my god is it hard to stay away. Now I read them so fast, I've started making a timeline on . . . when kids in younger grades will become "drunk bisexuals" or "bi-curious fag hags" as if because I am an out and proud senior I just know these things.

Later, she added, "I almost miss the days when I didn't label myself...I'd just explain to people I didn't know yet, and I felt that I wouldn't until i was older." She concluded, "labels are an unnecessary evil."

Another area of disagreement among LGBTQI people involved the formation of Groups and topic threads that addressed the origins of homosexuality. One relatively small Group ($N = 3,126$) was called "I'm happy, I'm care free, I'm GAY, I was born this way!!!" This site featured a very long entry summarizing the findings in a research study on brain structure. In another Facebook Group, a topic thread was titled "Choice, genetics, and I-can't-help-it-ism." It began with the argument that assuming a biological basis for homosexuality is an inherently dangerous position because "you're inviting some crackpot geneticist to research 'cures' What's wrong with choice?" Soon, however, the issue of what constitutes choice emerged as a key factor. One man noted,

> Now at the age of 56, having tried marriage twice, and had three great kids, I have to say that if I chose to stay married, I would be under medical supervision. Hard to say why.

The line between biological determinism and free will was blurred.

Others' Representations of LGBTQI Youth

In addition to these internal disagreements, (mis)representation by others was an issue within many topic threads on both MySpace and Facebook. The largest LGBTQI Group on MySpace, "Support Same-Sex Marriage! (SSSM)" featured a discussion called "Why do people (straights) caRE!!!?" with 79 entries (as of March 2008). The topic originated with a negative comment to the effect that "straights like to talk a lot of S&#T!!!" One 17-year-old girl added, "Maybe they're afraid or it just makes them feel good to bash other people. Even my straight friends don't understand." This thought was echoed by an 18-year-old woman from Tennessee, who wrote, "they are just afraid basically and human instinct tells them to attack to scare us." A 21-year-old North Carolinian explained, "The main reason why straight people hate gay people is mostly religion." Combining these two explanations, a 16-year-old boy from Nevada added, "...it seems many people are afraid of what they do not know. So between ignorance and religion you have a nasty mix."

Others, however, were quick to point out the importance of straight allies. "There are straight people that support us though so . . . not all straight people are bigoted, elephant trunk hurling, bible thumping assholes." A 23-year-old man from Alabama added, "It was hot and I wouldn't have made it through my teenage years in the closet without my 'straight' friends."

In another MySpace Group, "Support Gay Rights (SGR)," a humorous topic thread listed "15 Reasons to Choose to Become Gay." Each of these described a negative consequence (e.g., "rejected by society," "multiple religious groups against me," "losing family and friends," "target for rude jokes," "degraded by others," "lose myself because I'm hiding from everyone else"). This list elicited many humorous responses and examples, but it was clear that social representations of LGBTQI as outcasts were a common and ongoing experience for many young people.

An 18-year-old young man from southern California described an experience he'd had while walking down the street.

> Just yesterday...one of the guys in the car sticks his head out and yells "You're a fuckin' faggot!" I kept walking and ignored the comment...

This prompted a response from a 22-year-old man, also from southern California, who shared a similar experience, ending with "I ignore...I'm used to it."

One institution that appeared to be a breeding ground for ugly, antigay stereotypes and, therefore, particularly problematic for

LGBTQI youth was school. A 15-year-old girl from North Carolina described this experience with homophobia.

> ...people just don't like to accept new things...this girl at Skewl came and asked if I was ok cause i was upset then her friend came up and said no she can't be shes gay it made me angry

An 18-year-old from Nashville, Tennessee, described his experiences with homophobia from both school authorities and peers.

> i attend a christian school an i got caught with my boyfriend my secret boyfriend so now im out and i came all the way out because i got so mad about how everyone making fun of me its so weird the way people are responding to the real me. I hate highschool i need someone to rescue me!!!! i really need some real friends.

College students also were not immune from homophobia in the classroom. For one young woman, the issue involved the certainty with which her straight peers assumed that homosexuality was a choice. "I was so surprised how many people in my class said Gay people chose to be gay." Noting that "none of them were gay," she went on to ask the rhetorical question,

> How can someone who knows nothing about it decide they know who people are? I lost my voice trying to get my point across to those narrow minded assholes.

One Facebook Group was called "Against Homophobics or anyone who dislikes Bi's, Gay's, Or Lesbian's," featured a topic thread on the theme, "First gay experience." The young man who initiated this thread appeared to be a college student, identifying his location as "Loyola Chicago." It began with a relatively long entry about walking through a park one evening and coming upon two men having sex in the bushes. He describes approaching them slowly from behind,

> That's when I brought the cinder block down on his head, hard. He collapsed on top of his faggot friend and I quickly finished them both off.

He ended the post with, "That was only my first of many such gay encounters."

This is an example of "trolls" and "trolling," defined as people or comments, respectively, that deliberately disrupt, anger, and/or threaten others in a Group. In this instance, the troll was attracted to the Group because it was called "Against Homophobics." When challenged, he justified his continuing threats and insults on this topic thread by invoking the language of reverse discrimination. "This is nothing more than a backlash that is well deserved." He added, "Expressing myself against a bigot group is a right...especially when such bigotry is everywhere."

Analysis and Discussion

What do LGBTQI youth find on MySpace and Facebook? And how does that guide their understanding of who they are and are not?

The two major social networking sites, MySpace and Facebook, offer both opportunities and challenges for LGBTQI youth. For instance, MySpace makes it easier to identify specifically LGBTQI Groups and Discussion Boards, enabling users to avoid some of the negative, antigay content that is easy to encounter on this and other Web sites. Facebook requires users to search under broadly defined Areas of Interest to find large-scale LGBTQI communities. Also, these communities are mostly limited to the category of "Sexuality," even though much of the content within those virtual communities reflected broader issues and needs. Underlying this way of organizing LGBTQI Groups is the unspoken, but widespread heternormative assumption that LGBTQI identities are determined by sexual behavior alone. Although narratives on the topic threads contrasted sharply with such prejudicial assumptions, LGBTQI youth may have internalized those assumptions when choosing which Area of Interest to inhabit.

Other negative messages were also conveyed when exploring Areas of Interest on Facebook. For instance, searching under categories defined by "Beliefs and causes" located only one group focused on LGBTQI issues. It was an antigay/protect marriage Group. Even within the "Sexuality category, mixed messages about LGBTQI identities were conveyed. One Group named "I'm sexually inappropriate with my friends, but I'm actually not a lesbian" included an explicit WARNING in capital letters to discourage actual lesbians from joining or posting to their site ("This group is for people who keep their lesbian encounters to JOKING. Please do not post skanky pictures..."). Another Group, "Cute, Gay, Single, and Available," made sure members knew they could separate their identities on Facebook to ensure their sexuality remained a secret on "...your ordinary facebook profile..." By conveying the need to be careful while searching for safety in community online, an implicitly negative message was clearly communicated.

Narrative Analyses: What terms or forms of language are used to identify self and/or others among LGBTQI youth?

The quotes from Discussion Boards presented above are examined using discourse analyses based on Gee's (1999) concept of "discourse, with a little 'd,' to mean language-in-use or stretches of language (like conversations or stories)" (p. 17). The language used on topic threads is defined as "grammar two" (p. 29), meaning informal communications that do not rely on traditional grammatical structures. The specific method of analysis is based on the use of "situated meanings as a tool of inquiry" (p. 53) and the ways in which identities are socially positioned in terms relative to dominant norms and assumptions. This involves asking specific questions about the discourse based on comparing the perspectives of the writer, the reader, and the interpreter. The researcher/author serves as the interpreter who brings knowledge from other sources (e.g., research literature and prior experience) to the process of interpretation (see addendum).

Perhaps the most obvious aspect of the language used by LGBTQI youth in this study was the *reliance on patterns of brief, almost staccato, exchanges of words and symbols* meant to communicate "situated identities and specific activities" (Gee, p. 29). These young people sought to express ideas and emotions in as few words as possible, often substituting single letters and emoticons for words (e.g., :P; :-(; :S ; : D, or =]). Short statements were interspersed with longer entries when someone wanted to clarify a position, tell a story, or present a contrary point of view, for example.

This form of writing conveys the assumption that the reader shares an understanding of these abridged forms of expression. Underlying these verbal shortcuts is an apparently agreed upon, informal protocol suspending the ordinary rules of spelling, punctuation, and grammar. This protocol enables writers to convey as much meaning as possible with as few characters, symbols, and words as possible. These assumptions of shared meaning are evident across formats for text messaging that have been pioneered by youth who have come of age using new communication technologies (Buckingham, 2008). The use of these forms of language by LGBTQI youth implies "situated meanings" (Gee, p. 53) and "socially situated identities and activities" (p. 29) that place them within a historical and generational context with similar age peers. To some extent, it also may mark generational distinctions within LGBTQI communities, wherein older members are less likely to appreciate, use, or understand these communication protocols.

Next, a notable aspect of the discourse employed by LGBTQI youth involved the *rejection of standard signifiers* for sexual, gender, and/or attractional identities, leading to the *creation of neologisms* designed to mix meanings across these elements of identity. The six letters most commonly employed to designate the already varied types of sexual and gender minorities (lesbian, gay, bisexual, transexual, questioning, and intersex) were viewed as confining, exclusionary, and inadequate. Standard labels failed to capture either the complexity of their process of exploration and/or changing levels of personal awareness. This was demonstrated by statements such as "I'm sort of *inbetween* bi and gay," "80/20 guys to girls physically, 20/80 . . . emotionally . . . that's *sorta 50/50* :S," "don't want to restrict myself to *only the two* 'official' genders" (italics added).

Many LGBTQI (for lack of a better vocabulary) youth in this study were seeking and creating a new language to capture (1) how they are situated in relation to their emergent sexualities, (2) the interplay of their sexual and emotional attractions, and (3) their dissatisfaction with binary notions of gender. In a fundamental sense, they are only able to approximate a shared, situated meaning through the use of neologisms designed to disrupt distinctions across sexuality/gender/attraction. The social networking sites offer a context within which they may build a discourse for sharing frustrations, playing with language, and generating new ways of thinking about their identities with readers. Readers serve the purpose of reflecting back the language used, modifying terms, offering additional neologisms, disagreeing, but ultimately confirming a shared sense of frustration. The most popular neologism appeared to be the term 'mehsexual' as in 'meh, gender doesn't matter much to me." These comments are reminiscent of Butler's (1990) argument that identities based on gender invite essentialist assumptions that are simultaneously confining and inadequate to capture the complexity, multiplicity, and fluidity of identity.

A related element of the social networking discourse involved expressions of *label-blaming* that sought to establish the existence of signifiers for one's sexual, attractional, and/or gender identity as the source of discrimination against sexual/gender minorities. Label-blaming was paired with expressions connoting the lack of significance of the terms used to signify one's sexual-gender-attractional orientation ("unnecessary evil"). Simultaneously, however, the process of sharing new terms and playing ("I feel like a homo for being the only bi so far") with the language of identity appeared to be quite important. These comments suggest some degree of internal contradiction insofar as LGBTQI youth want to claim their own unique identities in relationship with others, both "str8" and "gay," while situating the social problem of discrimination both "in the past" and as resulting from previous designations of identity (e.g., gay, lesbian, and homosexual).

Resolution of this contradiction between simultaneously seeking a language of identity unbounded by sexuality-gender-attraction and blaming currently established signifiers for discrimination was achieved through an appeal to affective individualism (e.g., valuing individual, emotional, and experiential ways of knowing) (Hutter, 1981).

The language used in statements rejecting and blaming LGBTQI labels tended to be constructed in such a way as to privilege individual, personal, and emotional perspectives. This was captured most forcefully by the comment, "what the fuck with all the labels? . . . and *it really doesn't matter . . . labels r why gays have it so bad in the past.*" Followed immediately by a comment from a straight identified man, "sexuality does not make one damn bit of difference *to me*." Another comment described the term pomosexual, noting, "I think it was invented to get rid of prejudices. Cuz *it doesn't really matter* if your gay or straight, *as long as ur happy.*" A high school senior declared, "labels are an *unnecessary evil*" (italics added).

The situated identities and meanings drawn from such comments suggest that these youth not only want to live in a social reality where sexuality, gender, and attractional orientations are all mutually and equally acceptable ("it is 2007"), but believe that eliminating designations of difference may achieve that goal ("Cuz it *doesn't really matter,*" "just cuz *I don't really care,*" "*labels r why gays have it so bad in the past*"). Embedded within these comments is the unspoken, unquestioned belief in the power of individual viewpoints and emotional experiences to define or refuse to define sexual, gendered, and/or attractional identities ("does not make on damn bit of difference *to me*" "*as long as ur happy*").

There appeared to be considerable agreement on these viewpoints between writers and readers in the conversational strings that were sampled. No comments critical of the assumptions underlying these statements were evident in the excerpts from the topic threads used in this analysis. From the standpoint of the interpreter/researcher (and author), however, the rejection of past labels/language as inadequate and blaming those labels for discrimination ("in the past") highlights difficulties that are unique to LGBTQI youth as a group, rather than as individuals, precisely because their explorations and experimentations in identity formation are framed within heternormative social structures that confine their sexual-gender-attractional relationships to the margins.

The Groups and Discussion Boards on MySpace and Facebook offer LGBTQI youth opportunities to form virtual communities within which to openly discuss their struggles in identity formation for the first time, not only in their lives, but arguably in human history. As social spaces (virtual and otherwise), one function of communities is to mark spaces for negotiating situated, shifting ways of being with others wherein it is possible to understand who belongs, who does not, and how we move within and across the boundaries of our communities. Therefore, communities require various forms of designation. Whether in language rejection, language play (creative neologisms), or language blaming, these young people appeared to be working to find a vocabulary of identity and meaning that allowed them the same freedom to explore that their "str8" peers enjoy, as well as recognition of their personal, if sometimes confusing, desires. From the perspective of this interpreter, what emerges is a playful, earnest, sometimes painful, occasionally angry rejection/blaming of the language associated with an older generation of gays and lesbians. Through an unquestioned appeal to affective individualism, these young people effectively negate any sociopolitical frame of reference that would require engagement with broader social dimensions and meanings of identity.

Narrative Analysis: How do these forms of language reflect self and other representations of LGBTQI youth in the larger society?

Disagreements about the origins of homosexuality on the topic threads hint at the social significance of identity issues insofar as they tend to reference and even rely on the primary form of knowledge production in modern society: science. The appeal to science suggests legitimacy that lends credence to individual, experiential frameworks of meaning. Comments on these threads were often framed in the binary language of biology-or-choice, which did not capture the complexity of the issue for some. From the standpoint of this interpreter/author, the most compelling and complex comments about the origins of homosexuality were written by a 56-year-old man who chose to be straight for most of his life, having married twice and fathered "three great kids." For him, heterosexuality was a choice that he could only continue making at the expense of his sanity "if I *chose* to stay married, I would be under medical supervision." He ended with the humble statement, "Hard to say why." This contrasted sharply with the opinions expressed by others, particularly men, on these sites. There was a strong commitment to genetic and biologically driven explanations of homosexuality that was linked to an apparent belief in the power of science to put the question to rest. It was also interesting to note that these topic threads appeared to be initiated by men and the comments they drew were also predominantly, though not exclusively, from men.

Bisexuality was a trigger point for controversy among young women. The expressions used, however, often conveyed confusion rather than scientific certainty. "Straight *perhaps.*" "I'm *probably kinda straight a little.*" "i *think* im straight! . . . i have had alot of boyfs *but i don't know* . . . anything can happen." "*borderline* lesbian." "bi, *maybe? who knows.*" And finally, "is there such a thing as *halfway* bi?" These young women were not as interested in the potential origins of homosexuality as they were with sorting through emotions and attractions that did not fit within the binaries of sexual and emotional attraction.

Contentious language was related to a contrast between the value placed on personal freedom ("I'm bi, and I'm proud of it! . . .anyone should *love/fuck anyone they choose.*") and recognition of how women's bisexuality can be used to attract men ("I hate when girls are like ';] *I'm bi look at me boys* isn't it sexy?'") and confuse lesbians ("Problem is the vast majority of bi girls *end up choosing men*"). The anger and suspicion expressed by young women who identified as lesbians was sometimes met with anger in return by those who were questioning and/or confused, "...after some exploring . . . I realized shit man, *i don't have to be gay straight, bisexual, . . . or duck,* i'm *Name* and sometimes i fall in love with People . . . and i like to fuck People." This woman concluded with the comment, "*Labels are dumb* and they *limit you*, think outside the box."

Again, the language is couched in terms that privilege individuality, emotionality, and personal choice. The young, college-aged lesbian who initiated one contentious exchange attempted to place the issue in a more sociopolitical frame of reference,

> *You know* (italics added) you are bisexual, but while you are with your boyfriend you manage to avoid the discrimination we have no choice but face.

In this comment, she reframes the issue of personal choice in political terms, suggesting that personal knowledge ("*You know* you are . . .") of the freedom to explore one's sexuality is a choice framed by external realities of gender and sexual discrimination. She approached the sociopolitical argument indirectly, however, suggesting only that "*there is a lot more going on* behind the tendency of entirely homosexual people to dismiss bisexuals than you seem to take into account." The "*a lot more"* remained unexplored.

How LGBTQI minorities are represented by others, the heterosexual majority, revealed a bit about the "a lot more" mentioned above. Language describing experiences with personal support, encounters with prejudice, and threats of violence from trolls suggested awareness of social problems, but continued the focus on individual responses. One topic thread in particular addressed prejudice and discrimination with a list of "15 Reasons to Choose to Become Gay." Co-opting the language of choice, the comments on this thread explored how LGBTQI youth are socially positioned as outcasts, as well as the types of experiences they are subjected to when identified by others as LGBTQI. Although many of the comments posted on this thread employed humor, the pain caused by hetero-identified people's representations of sexual minorities was evident. Comments incorporated the language of loss ("*losing* friends and family"), degradation ("*degraded* by others," "target of rude jokes"), and fear ("lose myself because I'm *hiding*"). An account of verbal assault by an 18 year old ("yells, 'You're a fucking faggot!"), elicited advice from a 22 year old, "*ignore* . . . used to it." High school student accounts were especially poignant, recounting ways in which their emotions and experiences are denied meaning ("no she can't be [upset] shes gay"). Or ways in which they are abandoned to the verbal harassment of peers ("*everyone making fun* of me").

At the same time that many LGBTQI youth are seeking new ways of identifying themselves that signify a long-term, evolving process, the language used by opposition groups and individuals reflects fixed terms of reference (e.g., "gay" and "faggot"). Although aware of these terms and epithets, the most consistent comments on the topic threads sampled for this study emphasized individual coping mechanisms and emotional responses, such as retaliatory anger and/or appreciation of allies. Their own rejection of established labels such as gay, lesbian, and homosexual, as self-referents or signifiers may constitute an attempt to spurn the prejudices associated with them in heteronormative representations and "real" social domains.

Summary and Conclusion

The language of self-identification found within LGBTQI communities on MySpace and Facebook reflected both the list of signifiers used for this research project, namely LGBTQI, and rejection of those signifiers as outmoded and limiting labels. Examining 210 separate comments on a topic thread focused specifically on how members identified themselves (Gay? Lesbian? Bi? "Fag hag?"...STRAIGHT?), 5 forms of self-identification were noted. Each of those 5 categories included within it young people who were actively questioning whether they actually belonged within that designation. (See Table 1.) These young people were given a subgroup designation as *Questioning*. Other young people wondered why they needed to choose any designation at all, challenging the usefulness of labels that failed to convey the complex mixtures of sexual, emotional, and gendered dynamics they were experiencing. Some of them appeared to be engaged in ongoing explorations of identity through either serial or simultaneous relationships. Others remained in a state of confusion, processing emotions and just beginning to explore their emotional and sexual needs in relationships with others.

In many ways, the young people who were continuing to explore their sexual, attractional, and gender orientations reflect the dominant psychological model of identity development based on Erikson's theory (Marcia, 1980). From Marcia's (1980) perspective, some of the young people might be described as in a state of moratorium, which is considered normal for adolescents. Others might be viewed as in a state of diffusion whereby they are unable to establish an integrated sense of identity. In either case, the terminology of moratorium and diffusion does not adequately capture the complexity of the task for young people whose identities occupy a marginalized position within dominant, heteronormative social domains.

At the same time that these young people were claiming, questioning, debating, and continuing to explore designations for their own sexual identities, they were encountering other representations of LGBTQI youth online, in pop culture, and in person. Their efforts to understand prejudice involved name calling that paralleled the insults used to describe them ("bigoted . . . bible thumping assholes"). Explanations focused in fear ("maybe they're afraid"), ignorance, and traditional religion ("between ignorance and religion you have a nasty mix.") appeared to predominate. A college student made a connection between ignorance and arrogance, asking, "How can someone who knows nothing about it decide they know who people are." Counterpoints noted personal experiences with supportive straight people, noting "not all . . . are bigoted, . . . bible thumping assholes." Overall, however, when LGBTQI discussed prejudice and discrimination, it was mostly through the personal lens of experience.

The use of discourse analysis designed to explicate situated meanings and activities revealed language focused primarily on individual and emotional meanings. Disagreements in discussions of both the origins of homosexuality and women's bisexuality carried implicit allusions to heteronormative assumptions about sexual identities, but these were not framed by any language reminiscent of a politics of identity. The comments emphasized deeply personal emotions and individual experiences in an effort to determine the situated meanings emerging from their own lives in relationship to like-minded peers.

This chapter has explored the ways in which LGBTQI youth use social networking sites as virtual communities and contexts for learning about themselves and others. This is viewed as part of a larger process of personal and social identity formation. Many online resources exist for young people whose understanding of what it means to be LGBTQI today is constantly evolving in relation to both self and other representations of their identities. Their interactions on social networking sites suggest many opportunities to share experiences and opinions in community with young people who are negotiating similar challenges to their identity formation.

They also find places to discuss differences and debate the meaning of their experiences with other LGBTQI and/or other ("pomosexual," "mehsexual," "omnisexual," "sorta," "kinda," "maybe," "halfway") young people. At the same time, they are targets of trolls who seek out their Groups and topic threads to harass and threaten them.

In his introduction to *Youth, Identity, and Digital Media*, Buckingham (2008) noted that "online chat provides young people with a safe arena for rehearsing and exploring aspects of identity and personal relationships not available elsewhere" through "participation in a community of users." He went on to say, "They are likely to experience a strong sense of their own autonomy, and of their right to make their own choices and follow their own paths—however illusory this may ultimately be." The language of affective individualism employed by LGBTQI youth to reject and blame established signifiers of sexual/gender/attractional identities may reflect a claim to autonomy apart from negative social realities, even as they grapple with trolls and nondigital insults to the complex sexuality, gender, and attractions that do not reflect the simple, dominant dualities of heteronormativity.

LGBTQI youth are situated historically as members of their techno-communicative generation. Yet, within these virtual communities, they seldom referenced the social structures that frame their identities on the margins of heteronormative social domains. Separated from that dominant gaze, many express the need for a new language of identity, blurring boundaries and binary distinctions between female/male and gay/straight. It is a language of "*inbetween*" and the "*borderline*" where identities may be multiple and mutable, remaining formative rather than fixed, committed to the personal freedom to "*love/fuck anyone they choose.*" Labels, categories, various designations "*limit*" you. Yet, "*there is a lot more going on*" beyond their personal explorations and the practice of individual freedoms.

Addendum

One form of validity in qualitative research that draws on critical and social constructionist theories involves *situating the research-*

er in relationship to the issues under investigation and the people about/from whom information is obtained. The researcher is not objectively outside the process of inquiry, but inherently connected to both the issues and the people about whom she or he seeks a more informed understanding. In the interests seeking this type of critical constructionist validity, background information on the researcher(s) is not only legitimate, but necessary.

As a late middle-aged, white lesbian, my experience with the Web has been largely academic and career based. Therefore, I come to these research questions with a set of assumptions guided not only by the literature, but also by the limitations of my generational (1960s and 1970s) and racial experiences.

Given this experiential perspective, it seems that young people encounter the online world quite differently. It is a familiar place to them. The students in my classes have been raised on the Web's many possibilities for gaming, music, and social connection. It is the at-your-finger-tips encyclopedia of all things virtual. What better place to explore the boundaries of one's emerging sexual identity, especially if that identity appears to run counter to the expectations of parents, teachers, and even friends?

Of course, another question arises when an older adult, a feminist no less, considers the Internet and its potential influence on curious, questioning, maybe queer, youth. Adults often worry about the influences and dangers that exist for young people who wander the information highway unsupervised. Will it be the storehouse, funhouse, whorehouse, house of mirrors, etc., that many adults fear when they think of online predators, wild teen sex, and wasted hours of violent gaming? Or is it something else, neither more nor less, all or perhaps none of the above?

These concerns and assumptions exist within the mind of this researcher/author and, no doubt, played some role in several aspects of the study. These may include the choice of language (gay, lesbian, bi, queer) used in search terms, the discussion topics identified for analysis, and the process of analysis itself. These acknowledgments of subjectivity, however, do not render the work meaningless. In fact, beginning with an awareness of one's assumptions is an important starting point for any research endeavor, qualitative or quantitative.

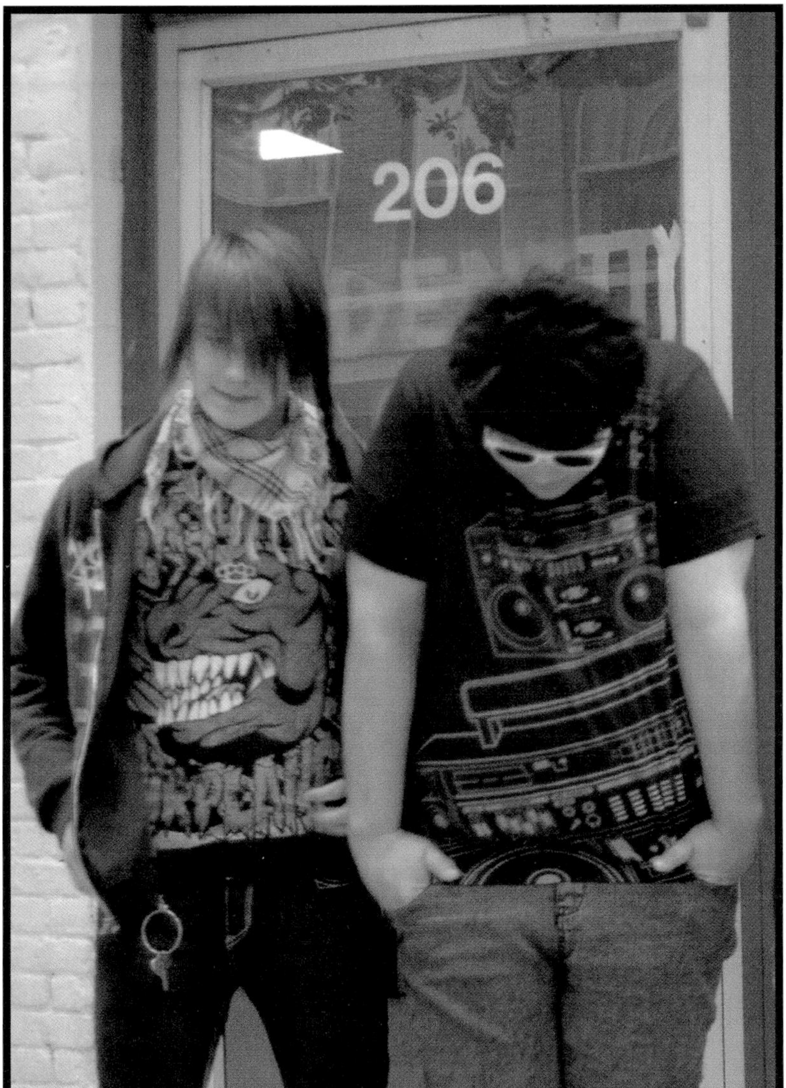
206

Chapter Eleven

Runners-Up: How Lesbian and Gay Sidekicks in Mainstream U.S. Cinema Can Influence Lesbian and Gay Youth and Those Who Work with Them

Diane R. Wiener and Christine M. Smith

WE BELIEVE THAT it is important for social service practitioners, educators, viewers, critics, and others who are concerned about lesbian and gay images in the mainstream U.S. media to advocate for media companies and producers to offer representations that depict lesbian and gay characters in ways that increasing numbers of lesbian and gay viewers themselves may actually find to be "more realistic." The term *more realistic*, as used herein, suggests that images might be able to represent a wider array of lesbian and gay experiences than is typically the case today. Although it has long been argued that mainstream television and film images do not come close to approximating the "real" experiences of many lesbian and gay people, and that it is consequently desirable to address this concern, the main argument in this essay is that mainstream representations and their attendant limitations are not going away any time soon. Therefore, rather than merely advocating for more "adequate" representations (a valid enterprise in its own right, as noted above), it is our position that it is perhaps even more crucial for social service practitioners, educators, and other viewers to become familiarized with the extant film images that many lesbian and gay youth are likely to continue to encounter, day to day. In this way, people who work with lesbian and gay youth may be better prepared to foster critical conversational opportunities, respond to concerns, and welcome questions that might arise.

Media and Economic Contexts

In *Up from Invisibility: Lesbians, Gay Men, and the Media in America* (2001), Larry Gross makes the argument that things have come a long way in terms of representations of gay and lesbian characters on-screen. In *The Celluloid Closet* (1981), Vito Russo argued famously that mainstream audiences ought to be concerned about the rampant negative stereotyping of lesbian and gay characters in mainstream films. While it used to be the case (and in many ways continues to be true) that gay and lesbian media characters were (and are) typically depicted as individuals to be laughed at and about whom viewers were (and are) meant to feel fear, contempt, and/or pity, viewers are more likely now to find laudable or otherwise welcoming images of gays and lesbians. Nevertheless, these representations, per Gross, may come at a "cost." According to Gross (2001),

> In the last decade of the twentieth century gay people were no longer invisible—as a group; but many, if not most, lesbians and gay men remain at least partially closeted. The public stages of media and politics became open to lesbian and gay people to an extent that would have been inconceivable [fifty years ago]. But as always, the price of access to the corridors of power is firmly exacted: play by our rules if you want to stay in the game. (p. 262)

Therefore, although it is true that youth are now likely to grow up familiarized with images of gay and lesbian people in mainstream television and film, they are also likely to be presented with images that are limited and that do not speak to the experiences of "fringe" or "non-normative" identities. The gay and lesbian characters depicted in mainstream media are most often middle class, intellectually sophisticated, witty, thin, and, usually, white.

An important issue to consider when discussing the structural or "macro" contexts for mainstream U.S. film representations is the niche marketing of lesbian and gay people. Amy Gluckman and Betsy Reed (1997), Alexandra Chasin (2000), and others have argued that lesbians and gay men have become an increasingly important "target market" in late U.S. capitalism. As Chasin (2000) points out, "...the capitalist market makes possible, but also constrains, social movements whose central objective is the expansion of individual political rights" (p. xvii). Chasin's claims echo Gross's observations in at least two ways. First, acknowledging the very existence of gays and lesbians comes at a price. Second, lesbians and gay men are expected to operate (both on- and off-screen) within a set of frameworks that they typically did not design.

Even when lesbians and gay men are featured in mainstream films, they often are not the main characters. Frequently, they are what we will refer to henceforth as "sidekicks" or "runners-up." In *Playing in the Dark* (1993), Toni Morrison argues that many white male authors use black characters to forward the plots of their novels and to aid the white characters in developing insight into their own lives. She remarks, "Black people ignite critical moments of discovery or change or emphasis in literature not written by them" (p. viii). Similarly, the particular purpose of lesbian and gay characters in mainstream U.S. films is often to act as comic relief, to support the primary "straight" characters in finding themselves in one way or another (e.g. in their identity formation), and otherwise to forward the cinematic plot. Our argument is in no way intended to create a systematic division between race and sexual orientation or sexuality, nor is it meant to elide the many ways in which these categories are interconnected and serve to constitute one another. Instead, we find Morrison's argument to be extremely relevant in considering the ways in which "unmarked," privileged characters (on-screen, in novels, and in "real life") exploit, utilize, or otherwise benefit from the presence of their disenfranchised, "othered" peers.

Heroes and Sidekicks

In the discussion that follows, we present an interpretation of the film *Under the Tuscan Sun* (2003) to address how images of lesbian and gay adult "sidekicks" in mainstream U.S. films have the potential to influence lesbian and gay youth in conversation, both inside and outside school settings. We are interested in exploring how teachers and social service practitioners might use media representations such as *Under the Tuscan Sun* to open a dialogue between youth, educators, and social service practitioners. We are aware that there are often overlaps between these various groups. Our use of these categories is a kind of shorthand that allows us to discuss the themes below as candidly as possible.

What are a sidekick's functions? According to *The Rough Guide to Superheroes* (2004), "In addition to assisting a hero, a sidekick has a specific and important role to fulfill. With the exception of a common heroic goal, the two are often very different in personality or skills . . . The sidekick can also provide comic relief and ask important plot questions" (p. 90). As the *Rough Guide* highlights, sidekicks, as they appear in comic book discourse, were preceded by their presence in novels. Similarly, superheroes and their less-powerful counterparts appear in mainstream films. Sometimes, everyday heroes and their sidekicks are depicted as having even more power or, perhaps, a different kind of power than their superhero and sidekick counterparts.

The hero in *Under the Tuscan Sun* is Frances (Diane Lane), and her sidekick is Patti (Sandra Oh). Frances, a middle-class, Caucasian American straight woman in despair in the aftermath of a devastating breakup with her husband, is seeking to put her life back together again. Patti, a middle-class, Asian American lesbian, is Frances's best friend. Without Patti's ample assistance, Frances would not be able to pursue her dreams. Patti and her lesbian partner are about to have a baby (Patti is pregnant), and Patti insists that Frances take her tickets to Tuscany and have a holiday from her troubles, because Patti is unable to fly due to her circumstances. Frances grudgingly accepts her friend's generosity and goes to Italy with the initial intention of taking a ten-day trip. Instead, she winds up buying a villa and becoming a central figure in the regional community. The packaging on the DVD released in 2004 suggests uncritically that Frances becomes enamored with "local color" and notes that she "finds herself immersed in a life-changing adventure filled with enough unexpected surprises, laughter, friendship and romance to restore her new home—and her belief in second chances."

Implications for Lesbian and Gay Youth and Those Working with Them

Although arguably an example of mainstream U.S. cinema, *Under the Tuscan Sun* may not be a film with which many U.S. youth (including, but not limited to, gay and lesbian youth) might be familiar. However, if youth are introduced to this film, conversations surrounding or fostered by this cinematic text could take place. In many ways, *Under the Tuscan Sun* reflects the ages-old trajectory of what Joseph Campbell (2008) and others refer to as the myth of the heroic return. While gay and lesbian youth certainly come from a wide variety of backgrounds, the myth of the heroic return may be relevant to youth who are negotiating their transition to adulthood in different ways. According to most versions of the mythical narrative, a hero must leave *his* place of origin and travel far away in order to learn important life lessons; only once a set of life-risking tasks are completed is *he* able to return to *his* home, a changed *man*. Youth of various genders and sexual orientations may identify with Frances, Patti, or others in the film's plot who are themselves navigating and perhaps growing from the changes they face in their daily lives.

In Frances's case, she stays in Italy, and the country becomes her new home. Still pregnant, Patti comes to live with Frances after she and her partner have broken up. Patti asks Frances to help her learn how to live with the pain that accompanies Patti's breakup. Although in this way the film seems to suggest that these women are able to be helpers to one another, the majority of the film's representations of Patti involve her being "there" to help Frances become a better version of herself. Frances's self-actualization in part involves her rediscovering men (and sex) in her life, but her changes are not limited to themes of sexuality. It is interesting that her lesbian comrade is the main reason why she is able to explore her own heteronormative lifestyle. Frances cannot realize her potential in the absence of her dependence on Patti.

The class politics of the film are centrally important. Clearly, Frances and Patti are deeply privileged from a socioeconomic standpoint. Frances has the privilege to have self-actualization in large part because of her wealth and Patti's wealth and access to cultural resources. Frances's white privilege gives her access to a life in Tuscany that would not have been the same had she been from another kind of background or come from a different set of experiences than her own. Her insights and transformations are contingent on money and the support of a lesbian woman who also has significant financial means. The film therefore has very little to say about how deprivileged and oppressed individuals might come to develop self-actualization, and/or what if anything non-wealthy persons might be able to do to feel better about themselves in the aftermath of a breakup, regardless of their sexual orientations. Frances has to learn from her experiences, from time spent away from her own past, literally and figuratively. However, she has the resources to spend time anew and spend it, she does, indeed.

What might lesbian and gay youth watching Patti and Frances's relationship on-screen come to think about this set of representations? According to reception theory, the meaning of these representations may vary greatly from viewer to viewer. Some gay and lesbian youth might be happy just to see someone even a little bit "like them" (by virtue of the similarity in sexual orientation between them and Patti's character). As the DVD package suggests, others might be intrigued by the fantasy offered by the film's scenery and "local color," and see the film as an opportunity for escape and an experience of so-called "eye candy."

The "local color" for other viewers might be interpreted as quite offensive, given that Frances hires a group of working-class Polish immigrants (who speak neither English nor Italian) to repair and renovate her villa. The Polish men are figured largely in this idea of "local color" in the film as it is summarized in the DVD packaging. In turn, the Polish men become like members of a new extended family to Frances, and she becomes like a new family member to each of them. Frances cooks them meals and welcomes them into her home as they repair it for her. One of the men develops an unrequited affection for her. She even goes so far as to advocate for the right of the youngest of the men to marry a young, local Italian woman. Frances's efforts counter the protests of the young woman's parents, who object to the young man because he is poor, and not Italian, and therefore not "good enough" for her in terms of class and ethnic heritage. Frances, the sophisticated, worldly American, is indexed as being so important in this film that she changes the minds of the young woman's traditional parents. Moreover, she creates opportunities (both wittingly and unwittingly) for the youth that they otherwise would not have had. Without her knowledge, Frances's villa is used by the two youths as an arena for exploring their intimacy and sexuality. Lesbian and gay youth interested in these facets of the film might appreciate the ways in which young adults are able to express themselves, although the youths' freedoms are necessarily conscripted (the youth in the film, it seems, have to be straight and they are in need of adult intervention, so their rights are delimited, as such).

Patti's figuration as the sole "out" lesbian character in the film (there is no "out" gay character in the film, although it is possible that some characters might be read in this way) is intriguing as well as problematic in a variety of ways. Social service practitioners and educators working with youth might screen this film as part of a series of movies that feature gay and lesbian heroes and sidekicks and ask the youth about their initial impressions of Patti. Youth might also be asked to discuss how they feel about how Patti looks, acts, is treated, and treats others, including but not limited to her important and caring alliance with Frances, her best friend. The importance of friendship in the development of gay and lesbian (and allied) youths' lives is a theme that could easily be picked up in a discussion of the film.

The film's explanation (or lack thereof) of class politics and U.S. heteronormativity might be useful arenas to explore with youth. Consequently, youth might be introduced to the idea of gay and lesbian niche marketing and the role of the film industry in forwarding as well as limiting certain sets of representations. Along these lines, the film can be further interpreted by youth in terms of their awareness of what values and beliefs the film wants to sell. As Timothy Corrigan (2004) notes,

> In critical writing attuned to ideology, any cultural product or creation carries, implicitly or explicitly, ideas about how the world is or should be seen and how men and women should see each other in it: the clothes you wear express social values just as the films you watch communicate social values. Whether we agree or disagree with the values expressed in a particular movie, the ideological critic maintains that these movies are never innocent visions of the world and that the social and personal values that seem so natural in them need to be analyzed. (p. 89)

What are the implicit and explicit messages, per Corrigan, that are forwarded by the film? How might lesbian and gay youth imagine themselves as cultural critics, and what unique analytical contributions do they have to make about *Under the Tuscan Sun* and other films about "men and women" and other gendered persons? Put differently, lesbian and gay youth might be encouraged by educators and social service practitioners to become "Queer Theorists," in their own right.

Whether *Under the Tuscan Sun* is screened as part of a series of gay- and lesbian-themed films or it is screened on its own, it assuredly has a lot of promise as a text for discussion purposes. Youth might be asked to comment on what they believe the film says about life for gay and lesbian individuals as well as what it leaves out. We feel in general that a set of discussions including, but not limited to, the sorts that we have just described would best be accomplished with youth at the high school level as well as in college settings.

Under the Tuscan Sun could be rewritten by lesbian and gay youth through a variety of conversations with educators and social service practitioners. In these and other ways, youth could be asked to join educators and social service practitioners in developing and raising a host of questions in order to examine hero and sidekick issues in the film. Youth could be encouraged to ask each other their own questions about how the film helps or does not help them to think critically about representations of gay men and lesbians in mainstream U.S. media. Youth might be asked by educators and social service providers how the film could have been written differently, for example. What could have occurred if the two primary characters' roles were switched? Specifically, what might have happened if Patti had been the main character and

Frances the sidekick? Would such a switch even work with the existing plot structure? Why or why not? What would the plot become if the switch could really work?

Youth could also be encouraged by educators and social service practitioners to consider what Adrienne Rich (1985) famously termed a politics of location. What would it be like to imagine the film in differently gendered, sexed, raced, geographic, and socioeconomic locations, among others? When *Romeo and Juliet* was transformed into *West Side Story*, its audience was not only broadened, but changed. Many individuals (especially youth) who found the original text to be removed from and irrelevant to their own experiences came to find it familiar and meaningful.

Following bell hooks's work, youth could be encouraged to critique the DVD packaging, as well as the film itself, in terms of the intersections between various categories of identity and difference. In her 1994 book *Outlaw Culture: Resisting Representations*, hooks describes a variety of films as being particularly "concerned with exploring the boundaries of race, gender, and nationality" as well as "boundaries of race and class" (p. 55). She asserts, "At a time when critical theory and cultural criticism calls [sic] us to interrogate politics of locations, and issues of race, nationality, and gender, [certain] films usurp this crucial challenge with the message that desire, and not the realm of politics, is the location of reconciliation and redemption" (p. 55). Youth might be asked to comment on their understandings of reconciliation and redemption in conversations with educators and social service practitioners, as well as in interactions with one another. Just as race is far more integral to the film plots described by hooks than some viewers may be led to believe, Patti's race is perhaps more important to *Under the Tuscan Sun*'s narrative (and, therefore, to Frances's self-discovery) than is explicit in the ways that the film is marketed. It could be argued, as well, that Frances's racial identity and attendant white privilege, as noted above, are important to the film's "successes" and "failures."

Concluding Remarks

We hope that our discussion of *Under the Tuscan Sun* provides educators and social service practitioners with some preliminary guidelines for talking with lesbian and gay youth about the power of representations to affect all of our lives. Each individual who enters into conversations about representational implications, and thereby establishes a kind of "contract" for the interactions, needs to take into account the ways in which the conversational participants and partners may or may not be familiar with, and/or have access to, film images. Discussing a lack of exposure to presumably mainstream and thus familiar images is a worthwhile activity in its own right.

There are many practical applications to the conversations that we seek to foster, including encouraging gay and lesbian youth to feel increasingly empowered to address their self-perceptions and self-esteem on individualized levels as well as to advocate for systemic change at both group and societal levels. Research into the most effective ways to work with gay and lesbian youth might be enhanced by using empowering approaches to film analysis. Including youth centrally in critical conversations and questioning, rather than talking to, youth about their own experiences make for a far richer and more equitable exchange, without denying the power dynamics that necessarily exist between youth and adult practitioners and educators. Moreover, educational, social service, and other public policy changes might be possible with the input that could be provided by such research. The connections between theory (including empowerment theory), research, policy, and daily practice on the part of educators and social service practitioners may be further strengthened with the use of these conversational approaches.

As we have mentioned, the mere existence of lesbian and gay characters in mainstream U.S. cinema (while a move in the right direction) is not enough, because these representations, due to their limitations, are problematic. Until the mainstream U.S. film industry offers a much broader array of depictions of lesbian and gay lives and lifestyles, we need to deconstruct and explore those images that are currently available for view on the big screen.

Working together with lesbian and gay youth on such exploratory projects, educators and social service practitioners, as the editors of this volume suggest, can help these youth and those who care about them to think critically about their lives in dynamic relation to their surroundings.

Bibliography

Abberley, P. (1987). The concept of oppression and the development of a social theory of disability. *Disability, Handicap, and Society, 2,* 5–20.

Advocates for Children of New York. (2005). *In harm's way: A survey of lesbian, gay, bisexual, and transgender students who speak about harassment and discrimination in New York City schools.* New York: Author.

Alquijay, M. A. (1997). The relationships among self-esteem, acculturation, and lesbian identity formation in Latina lesbians. In B. Greene (Ed.), *Ethnic and cultural diversity among lesbians and gay men* (pp. 249–265). Thousand Oaks, CA: Sage.

Americans with Disabilities Act of 1990, PL 101-336, 42 U.S.C. at 12101 et seq.

Anderson, A. L. (1998). Strengths of gay male youth: An untold story. *Child and Adolescent Social Work Journal, 15*(1), 55–71.

Anzaldua, G. (1999). *Borderlands/La Frontera: The new Mestiza* (2nd ed.). San Francisco: Spinsters/Aunt Lute.

Appleby, J., Hunt, L., & Jacob, M. (1994). *Telling the truth about history.* New York: W. W. Norton.

Atkinson, D., Morten, G., & Sue, D. (1979). *Counseling American minorities: A cross-cultural perspective.* Dubuque, IA: William C. Brown.

Barnes, M., & Massey, S. (2001, June 3). Voices of gay Austin. *Austin American-Statesman,* pp. A1, A18–19, K1, and K10–11.

Berger, K. (2000). *The developing person through the life span.* New York: Worth.

Berkley, B. (2004). Making Gay Straight Alliance student groups curriculum-related: A new tactic for schools trying to avoid the Equal Access Act. *Washington and Lee Law Review, 61*(4), 1847–1901.

Bertram, C. C. (2008). Narrating neighborhood: Denying young women's public voices about violence. *Urban Review, 40*(5), 454–471.

Bertram, C. C., & Massey, S. G. (2007). Queering dialogue: Safety and discomfort in a lesbian, gay, bisexual, and transgender psychology course. *Lesbian and Gay Psychology Review, 8*(2), 127–140.

Best, A. L. (Ed.). (2007). *Representing youth: Methodological issues in critical youth studies.* New York: New York University Press.

Blanchett, W. (2002).Voices from a TASH forum on meeting the needs of gay, lesbian, and bisexual adolescents and adults with severe disabilities. *Journal of the Association for Persons with Severe Handicaps (JASH), 27*(1), 82–86.

Blumenfeld, W. J. (1994). "Gay/Straight" Alliances: Transforming pain to pride. *The High School Journal, 77*(1/2), 113–121.

Blustein, D. L., Chaves, A. P., Diemer, M. A., Gallagher, L. A., Marshall, K. G., Sirin, S., & Bhati, K. S. (2002). Voices of the forgotten half: The role of social class in the school-to-work transition. *Journal of Counseling Psychology, 49,* 311–323.

Blustein, D. L., McWhirter, E. H., & Perry, J. C. (2005). An emancipatory communitarian approach to vocational development theory, research, and practice. *Counseling Psychologist, 33*(2), 141–179.

Bochenek, M., & Brown, A. W. (2001). *Hatred in the hallways: Violence and discrimination against lesbian, gay, bisexual, and transgender students in U.S. schools*. New York: Human Rights Watch.

Bohan, J. S. (1996). Heterosexuality, gender, and heterosexism/homophobia. In G. Unks (Ed.), *The gay teen* (pp. 31–59). New York: Routledge.

Bornstein, K. (1994). *Gender outlaw: On men, women, and the rest of us*. New York: Vintage.

boyd, d. (2008). Why youth ♥ social networking sites: The role of networked publics in teenage social life. In D. Buckingham (Ed.), *Youth, identity, and digital media* (pp. 119–142). Cambridge, MA: MIT Press.

Boyte, H. C., & Evans, S. M. (1986). *Free spaces: The sources of democratic change in America*. New York: Harper & Row.

Brent, D. A. (1995). Risk factors for adolescent suicide and suicidal behavior: Mental and substance abuse disorders, family environmental factors, and life stresses. *Suicide & Life-Threatening Behavior, 25*, 52–63.

Broido, E. M. (2000). Ways of being an ally to lesbian, gay, and bisexual students. In V. A. Wall & N. J. Evans (Eds.), *Toward acceptance: Sexual orientation issues on campus* (pp. 345–369). Lanham, MD: University Press of America.

Brown, S. (2003). *Movie stars and sensuous scars: Essays on the journey from disability shame to disability pride*. Brookline, MA: iUniverse.

Brown, S. D., & Krane, N. R. (2000). Four (or five) sessions and a cloud of dust: Old assumptions and new observations about career counseling. In S. B. Brown & R. W. Lent (Eds.), *Handbook of counseling psychology* (3rd ed.) (pp. 740–766). New York: John Wiley.

Buckingham, D. (Ed.). (2008). *Youth, identity, and digital media*. Cambridge, MA: MIT Press.

Buckingham, D., & Willett, R. (Eds.). (2006). *Digital generations: Children, young people, and new media*. Mahwah, NJ: Erlbaum.

Burdge, B. (2007). Bending gender, ending gender: Theoretical foundations for social work practice with the transgender community. *Social Work, 52*(3), 243–250.

Burn, S. M. (2000). Heterosexuals' use of "fag" and "queer" to deride one another: A contributor to heterosexism and stigma. *Journal of Homosexuality, 40*(2), 1–11.

Buston, K., & Hart, G. (2001). Heterosexism and homophobia in Scottish school sex education: Exploring the nature of the problem. *Journal of Adolescence, 24*(1), 95–109.

Butler, J. (1990). *Gender trouble: Feminism and the subversion of identity*. New York: Routledge.

Byrne, D. N. (2008). The future of (the) "race": Identity, discourse, and the rise of computer mediated public spheres. In A. Everett (Ed.), *Learning race and ethnicity: Youth and digital media* (pp. 15–38). Cambridge, MA: MIT Press.

Campbell, J. (2008). *The hero with a thousand faces* (3rd ed.) Novato, CA: New World Library.
Cannella, G. S. (1997). *Deconstructing early childhood education: Social justice and revolution.* New York: Peter Lang.
Caputo, V. (1995). Anthropology's silent "others": A consideration of some conceptual and methodological issues for the study of youth and children's cultures. In V. Amit-Talai & H. Wulff (Eds.), *Youth cultures: A cross-cultural perspective* (pp. 19–42). London: Routledge.
Carney, S. (2000) Body work on ice: The ironies of femininity. In L. Weis & M. Fine (Eds.), *Construction sites: Excavating race, class, & gender among urban youth* (pp. 121–139). New York: Teachers College Press.
Carroll, L., & Gilroy, P. J. (2002). Transgender issues in counselor preparation. *Counselor Education & Supervision, 41*(3), 233–242.
Carter, K. A. (2000). Transgenderism and college students: Issues of gender identity and its role on our campuses. In V. A. Wall & N. J. Evans (Eds.), *Toward acceptance: Sexual orientation issues on campus* (pp. 261–282). Lanham, MD: University Press of America.
Carter, M. (1998). Strategies to strengthen our anti-bias practices. *Childcare Information Exchange, 121,* 85–87.
Case, K. A. (2006, October). *Decreasing anti-gay bias and raising heterosexual privilege awareness in students.* Paper presented at the 5th Annual Conference on Best Practices in Teaching Diversity & International Perspectives across the Psychology Curriculum, Atlanta, GA.
Case, K. A., Stewart, A. B., & Fisher, C. (2007, November). *Transgender across the curriculum: A psychology for inclusion.* Paper presented at the Southwest Teachers of Psychology Conference, Houston, TX.
Casper, V., Cuffaro, H., Schultz, S., Silin, J., & Wickens, E. (1996). Toward a most thorough understanding of the world: Sexual orientation and early childhood education. *Harvard Educational Review, 66*(2), 271–293.
Casper, V., Schultz, S., & Wickens, E. (1992). Breaking the silences: Lesbian and gay parents and the schools. *Teachers College Record, 94,* 109–137.
Cass, V. C. (1979). Homosexual identity formation: A theoretical model. *Journal of Homosexuality, 4*(3), 219–235.
Center for Information and Research on Civic Learning and Engagement (Circle). (2005). *Attitudes of young people toward diversity.* Retrieved February 22, 2006, from http://www.civicyouth.org/research/products/national_youth_ survey2004.htm.
Chamberlain, K. (1999). Using grounded theory in health psychology. In M. Murray & K. Chamberlain's (Eds.), *Qualitative health psychology* (pp. 183–201). London: Sage.
Chasin, A. (2000). *Selling out: The gay and lesbian movement goes to market.* New York: Macmillan.
Chasnoff, D. (Director/Producer), Ben-Dov, A., & Yacker, F. (Producers). (2000). *That's a family* [Motion picture]. (Available from Women's Educational Media, 2180 Bryant Street, Suite 203, San Francisco, CA 94110).

Chesir-Teran, D. (2003). Conceptualizing and assessing heterosexism in high schools: A setting-level approach. *American Journal of Community Psychology, 31*(3). 267–279.

Chesney-Lind, M., & Irwin, K. (2004). From badness to meanness: Popular constructions of contemporary girlhood. In A. Harris (Ed.), *All about the girl: Culture, power, and identity* (pp. 45–56). New York: Routledge.

Chung, Y. B. (1996). Career decision making of lesbian, gay, and bisexual individuals. *The Career Development Quarterly, 44,* 178–190.

—— (2001). Work discrimination and coping strategies: Conceptual frameworks for counseling lesbian, gay, and bisexual clients. *The Career Development Quarterly, 50,* 33–50.

—— (2003). Career counseling with lesbian, gay, bisexual and transgendered persons: The next decade. *The Career Development Quarterly, 52,* 78–86.

Chung, Y. B., & Katayama, M. (1998). Ethnic and sexual identity development of Asian American lesbian and gay adolescents. *Professional School Counseling, 1,* 21–25.

Cohen, K. M., & Savin-Williams, R. C. (1996). Developmental perspectives on coming out to self and others. In R. C. Savin-Williams & K. M. Cohen (Eds.), *The lives of lesbians, gays, and bisexuals: Children to adults* (pp. 113–151). Fort Worth, TX: Harcourt Brace.

Coleman, E. (1982). Developmental stages of the coming out process. *Journal of Homosexuality, 9,* 105–126.

Connolly. M. (2000). Issues for lesbian, gay, and bisexual students in traditional classrooms. In V. A. Wall & N. J. Evans (Eds.), *Toward acceptance: Sexual orientation issues on campus* (pp. 109–130). Lanham, MD: University Press of America.

Consolacion, T. B., Russell, S. T., & Sue, S. (2004). Sex, race/ethnicity, and romantic attractions: Multiple minority status adolescents and mental health. *Cultural Diversity and Ethnic Minority Psychology, 10*(3), 200–214.

Corbett, S. (1993). A complicated bias. *Young Children, 48*(3), 29–31.

Corey, G., Corey, M. S., & Callanan, P. (2007). *Issues and ethics in the helping professions* (7th ed.). Pacific Groves, CA: Brooks/Cole.

Correl, S. J. (1999). Lesbian and gay Americans. In A. G. Dworkin & R. J. Dworkin (Eds.), *The minority report: An introduction to racial, ethnic and gender relations* (pp. 436–456). New York: Harcourt Brace.

Corrigan, T. (2004). *A short guide to writing about film.* (5th ed.). New York: Pearson.

Council for Exceptional Children. (2003). *What every special educator must know: Ethics, standards, and guidelines for special education* (5th ed.). Upper Saddle River, NJ: Prentice Hall.

Creswell, J. W. (1998). *Qualitative inquiry and research design: Choosing among five traditions.* Thousand Oaks, CA: Sage.

Cross, W., Jr. (1978). The Thomas and Cross models of psychological negrescence: A literature review. *Journal of Black Psychology, 4,* 13–31.

Croteau, J. M., Anderson, M. Z., Distefano, T. M., & Kampa-Kokesch, S. (2000). Lesbian, gay, and bisexual vocational psychology: Reviewing foundations and planning construction. In R. M. Perez, K. A. DeBord, & K. J. Bieschke, *Handbook of counseling and psychotherapy with lesbian, gay, and bisexual clients* (pp. 383–408). Washington, DC: American Psychological Association.

Cullen, F. (2005). *Cotching in the cotch: Young women, embodied geographies and transition.* Paper presented at the Gender and Education 5th International Conference, Cardiff, Wales.

D'Augelli, A. R. (1994). Identity development and sexual orientation: Toward a model of lesbian, gay, and bisexual development. In E. J. Trickett & R. J. Watts (Eds.), *Human diversity: Perspectives on people in context* (pp. 312-333). San Francisco, CA: Jossey-Bass.

—— (1998). Developmental implications of victimization of lesbian, gay and bisexual youth. In G. Herek (Ed.), *Stigma and sexual orientation: Understanding prejudice against lesbians, gay men and bisexuals* (pp. 187–210). Thousand Oaks, CA: Sage.

D'Augelli, A. R., Hershberger, S. L., & Pilkington, N. W. (2001). Suicidality patterns and sexual orientation-related factors among lesbian, gay, and bisexual youths. *Suicide and Life-Threatening Behavior, 31*, 250–264.

Davidson, S. M. (2006). Exploring sociocultural borderlands: Journeying, navigating, and embodying a queer identity. *The Journal of Men's Studies, 14*(1), 13–26.

Denny, D. (1994). You're strange and we're wonderful: The gay and lesbian transgender communities. In J. Sears (Ed.), *Bound by diversity* (pp. 47–53). Columbia, SC: Sebastian Press.

Diamond, L. M. (1998). Development of sexual orientation among adolescent and young adult women. *Developmental Psychology, 34*, 1085–1095.

—— (2002). Sex and gender are different: Sexual identity and gender identity are different. *Clinical Child Psychology and Psychiatry, 7*(3), 320–334.

—— (2003). New paradigms for research on heterosexual and sexual-minority development. *Journal of Clinical Child and Adolescent Psychology, 32*(4), 490–498.

—— (2008). *Sexual fluidity: Understanding women's love and desire.* Cambridge, MA: Harvard University Press.

Diaz, R. (1998) *Latino gay men and HIV: Culture, sexuality, and risk behavior.* New York: Routledge.

Donnay, D., Morris, M., Schaubhut, N., & Thompson, R. (2005). *Strong Interest Inventory manual* (rev. ed.). Mountain View, CA: CPP.

Draughn, T., Elkins, B., & Roy, R. (2002). Allies in the struggle: Eradicating homophobia and heterosexism on campus. In E. P. Cramer (Ed.), *Addressing homophobia and heterosexism on college campuses* (pp. 9–20). New York: Harrington Park Press.

Driver, S. (2007). Beyond "straight" interpretations: Researching queer youth digital video. In A. Best (Ed.), *Representing youth: Methodological issues in critical youth studies* (pp. 304–324). New York: New York University Press.

Dube, E., & Savin-Williams, R. C. (1999) Sexual identity development among ethnic sexual-minority male youths. *Developmental Psychology, 35,* 1389–1398.

Duke, T. S. (2004). Problematizing collaboration: A critical review of the empirical research on teaching teams. *Teacher Education and Special Education, 27*(3), 307–317.

—— (2007). Hidden, invisible, marginalized, ignored: A critical review of the professional and empirical literature (or lack thereof) on gay and lesbian teachers in the United States. *Journal of Gay and Lesbian Issues in Education, 4*, 19–38.

Dunbar, J., Brown, M., & Amoroso, D. M. (1973). Some correlates of attitudes toward homosexuality. *The Journal of Social Psychology, 89*, 271–279.

Dunkle, J. H. (1996). Toward an integration of gay and lesbian identity development and Super's life-span approach. *Journal of Vocational Behavior, 48*, 149–159.

Elliot, M., & Kilpatrick, J. (1994). How to stop bullying. A Kidscape guide to training. London: Kidscape.

Erich, S., Tittsworth, J., Dykes, J., & Cabuses, C. (2008). Family relationships and their correlations with transsexual well-being. *Journal of GLBT Family Studies, 4*(4),419-432.

Erikson, E. (1968). *Youth: Identity and crisis.* New York: Norton.

—— (1980). *Identity and the life cycle.* New York: Norton.

Ettner, R. (1999). *Gender loving care: A guide to gender-variant counseling.* New York: W. W. Norton.

Evans, N. J., & Wall, V. A. (2000). Parting thoughts: An agenda for addressing sexual orientation issues on campus. In V. A. Wall & N. J. Evans (Eds.), *Toward acceptance: Sexual orientation issues on campus* (pp. 389–402). Lanham, MD: University Press of America.

Everett, A. (Ed.). (2008). *Learning race and ethnicity: Youth and digital media.* Cambridge, MA: MIT Press.

Fassinger, R. E. (1996). Notes from the margin: Integrating lesbian experience into the vocational psychology of women. *Journal of Vocational Behavior, 48*, 160–175.

—— (2000). Gender and sexuality in human development: Implications for prevention and advocacy in counseling psychology. In S. D. Brown & R. W. Lent (Eds.), *The handbook of counseling psychology* (3rd ed.) (pp. 346–378). New York: John Wiley.

Faulkner, A. H., & Cranston, K. (1998). Correlates of same-sex sexual behavior in a random sample of Massachusetts high school students. *American Journal of Public Health, 88*, 262–265.

Fergusson, D. M., Horwood, L. J., & Beautrais, A. L. (1999). Is sexual orientation related to mental health problems and suicidality in young people? *Archives of General Psychiatry, 56*, 876–880.

Fine, M. (1988). Sexuality, schooling, and adolescent females: The missing discourse of desire. *Harvard Educational Review, 58*(1), 29–53.

—— (1989). Coping with rape: Critical perspectives on consciousness. In R. Unger (Ed.), *Representations: Social constructions of gender* (pp. 186–200). Amityville, NY: Bagwood Press.

—— (1994). Working the hyphens: Reinventing self and other in qualitative research. In N. K. Denzin & Y. S. Lincoln (Eds.), *Handbook of qualitative research* (pp. 70–82). Thousand Oaks, CA: Sage.

Fine, M., & McClelland, S. I. (2006). Sexuality education and desire: Still missing after all these years. *Harvard Educational Review, 76*(3), 297–338.

Fine, M., Weis, L., & Powell, L. C. (1997). Communities of difference: A critical look at desegregated spaces created for and by youth. *Harvard Educational Review, 67*(2), 247–284.

Fishbein, H. (2002). *Peer prejudice and discrimination: The origins of prejudice.* Mahwah, NJ: Erlbaum.

Flick, U. (1998). *An introduction to qualitative research.* Thousand Oaks, CA: Sage.

Fontaine, J. H. (1998). Evidencing a need: School counselors' experiences with gay and lesbian students. *Professional School Counseling, 1,* 8–14.

Foucault, M. (1973a). *The birth of the clinic: An archaeology of medical perception.* New York: Pantheon Books.

—— (1973b). *The order of things: An archaeology of the human sciences.* New York: Vintage Books.

—— (1977). *Discipline and punish: The birth of the prison.* New York: Pantheon Books.

—— (1978). *The history of sexuality: An introduction.* New York: Random House.

—— (1980). *Power/knowledge: Selected interviews and other writings 1972–1977.* New York: Pantheon.

—— (1981/1997a). The ethics of the concern for the self as a practice of freedom. In P. Rabinow (Ed.), *Ethics: Subjectivity and truth* (pp. 281–301). New York: New Press.

—— (1981/1997b). Friendship as a way of life. In P. Rabinow (Ed.), *Ethics: Subjectivity and Truth* (pp. 135–140). New York: New Press.

—— (1986). *The care of the self.* New York: Vintage.

—— (1990). *The history of sexuality: An introduction.* New York: Vintage.

Foucault, M., & Miskowiec, J. (1986). Of other spaces. *Diacritics, 16*(1), 22–27.

Fox, R. K. (2007). One of the hidden diversities in schools: Families with parents who are lesbian or gay. *Childhood Education, 83*(5), 277–281.

Freire, P. (1970). *Pedagogy of the oppressed.* M. B. Ramos (Trans.). New York: Seabury Press.

—— (1974). *Education for critical consciousness.* M. B. Ramos (Trans.). New York: Seabury Press.

Friend, R. A. (1992). Listening to silenced voices: Strategies for undoing homophobia in schools. *Independent School, 51,* 33–37.

—— (1993). Choices, not closets: Heterosexism and homophobia in schools. In M. Fine & L. Weis (Eds.), *Beyond silenced voices: Class, race and gender in United States schools* (pp. 209–223). Albany: State University of New York Press.

—— (1998). Heterosexism, homophobia, and the culture of schooling. In S. Books (Ed.), *Invisible children in the society and its schools* (pp. 137–165). Mahwah, NJ: Erlbaum.

Fullman, M. (1985). Change processes and strategies at the local level. *The Elementary School Journal, 85*(3), 390–421.

Garofalo, R., Wolf, R. C., Wissow, L. S., Woods, E. R., & Goodman, E. (1999). Sexual orientation and risk of suicide attempts among a representative sample of youth. *Arch Pediatric Adolescent Medicine, 153,* 487–493.

Gay, Lesbian and Straight Education Network (GLSEN). (2000). *Gay-Straight Alliance handbook.* Retrieved January 20, 2005, www.glsen.org.

—— (2005). *From teasing to torment: School climate in America, a survey of students and teachers.* Retrieved December 20, 2005, from http://www.glsen.org/cgi-bin/iowa/all/news/record/1859.htm.

—— (n.d.). *About GLSEN.* Retrieved July 6, 2008, from http://www.glsen.org/cgi-bin/iowa/all/about/index.html.

Gee, J. P. (1999). *An introduction to discourse analysis: Theory and method.* London: Routledge.

Gibson, P. (1989). Gay male and lesbian youth suicide. In *Report of the Secretary's Task Force on Youth Suicide,* vol. 3. Washington, DC: U.S. Department of Health and Human Services.

Gilbert, J. (2004). Between sexuality and narrative: On the language of sex education. In M. L. Rasmussen, E. Rofes, & S. Talburt (Eds.), *Youth and sexualities: Pleasure, subversion, and insubordination* (pp. 110–126). New York: Palgrave Macmillan.

Glaser, B. G. (1992). *Basics of grounded theory analysis: Emergence vs. forcing.* Mill Valley, CA: Sociology Press.

Glaser, B. G., & Straus, A. L. (1967). *The discovery of grounded theory: Strategies for qualitative research.* Chicago: Aldine.

Gluckman, A., & Reed, B. (1997). The gay marketing moment. In A. Gluckman & B. Reed (Eds.), *Homo economics: Capitalism, community, and lesbian and gay life* (pp. 3–10). New York: Routledge.

Gonsiorek, J. C. (1995). Gay male identities: Concepts and issues. In A. R. D'Augelli & C. J. Patterson (Eds.), *Lesbian, gay, and bisexual identities over the lifespan* (pp. 24–47). Oxford: Oxford University Press.

Graber, J. A., & Archibald, A. B. (2001). Psychological change at puberty and beyond: Understanding adolescent sexuality and sexual orientation. In A. R. D'Augelli and C. J. Patterson (Eds.), *Lesbian, gay, and bisexual identities and youth* (3-26). New York: Oxford University Press.

Grange, P., Tewksbury, R., & McGaughey, D. (1997). Coming out and crossing over: Identity formation and proclamation. *Gender & Society, 11,* 478–508.

Greene, B. (1997). Ethnic minority lesbians and gay men: Mental health and treatment issues. In B. Greene (Ed.), *Ethnic and cultural diversity among lesbians and gay men* (pp. 216–239). Thousand Oaks, CA: Sage.

Griffin, P., Lee, C., Waugh, J., & Beyer, C. (2004). Describing roles that Gay-Straight Alliances play in schools: From individual support to school change. *Journal of Gay & Lesbian Issues in Education, 1*(3), 7–22.

Gross, L. (2001). *Up from invisibility: Lesbians, gay men, and the media in America.* New York: Columbia University Press.

Grossman A., & Kerner, M. (1998). Self-esteem and supportiveness as predictors of emotional distress in gay male and lesbian youth. *Journal of Homosexuality, 35*, 25–37.

Gustavsson, N. S., & MacEachron, A. E. (1998). Violence and lesbian and gay youth. *Journal of Gay & Lesbian Social Services, 8*(3), 41–50.

Harbeck, K. (Ed.). (1992). *Coming out of the classroom closet: Gay and lesbian students, teachers, curricula.* Binghamton, NY: Haworth Press.

Harding, S. G. (2004). *The feminist standpoint theory reader: Intellectual and political controversies.* New York: Routledge.

Harley, D. A., Nowak, T. M., Gassaway, L. J., & Savage, T. A. (2002). Lesbian, gay, bisexual, and transgender college students with disabilities: A look at multiple cultural minorities. *Psychology in the Schools, 39*(5), 525–538.

Harper, G. W. (2007). Sex isn't that simple: Culture and context in HIV prevention interventions for gay and bisexual male adolescents. *American Psychologist, 62*(8), 803–819.

Harper, G. W., Jernwall, N., & Zea, M. C. (2004). Giving voice to emerging science and theory for lesbian, gay, and bisexual people of color. *Cultural Diversity and Ethnic Minority Psychology, 10*, 187–199.

Hegarty, P., & Massey, S. (2006). Anti-homosexual prejudice . . . as opposed to what?: Queer theory and the social psychology of anti-homosexual prejudice. *Journal of Homosexuality, Special Issue: The Contested Terrain of LGBT Studies and Queer Theory, 52*(1/2), 47–71.

Helms, J. E. (1990). *Black and White racial identity: Theory, research, and practice.* Westport, CT: Greenwood Press.

Herek, G. M. (1984). Attitudes toward lesbians and gay men: A factor analytic study. *Journal of Homosexuality, 10*(1–2), 39–51.

— (1986). The instrumentality of attitudes: Toward a neofunctional theory. *Journal of Social Issues, 42*(2), 99–114.

— (1987a). Can functions be measured? A new perspective on the functional approach to attitudes. *Social Psychology Quarterly, 50*(4), 285–303.

— (1987b). On heterosexual masculinity: Some psychical consequences of the social construction of gender and sexuality. In M. S. Kimmel (Ed.), *Changing men: New directions in research on men and masculinity* (pp. 68–82). Thousand Oaks, CA: Sage.

— (1988). Heterosexuals' attitudes toward lesbians and gay men: Correlates and gender differences. *The Journal of Sex Research, 25*(4), 451–477.

— (1990). Homophobia. In W. Dynes (Ed.), *Encyclopedia of homosexuality* (pp. 552–555). New York: Garland.

— (1993). On heterosexual masculinity: Some psychical consequences of the social construction of gender and sexuality. In L. Garnets & D. Kimmel (Eds.), *Psychological perspectives on lesbian and gay male experiences* (pp. 316–330). New York: Columbia University Press.

— (1994). Assessing heterosexuals' attitude toward lesbians and gay men: A review of empirical research with the ATLG scale. In B. Green and G. M. Herek (Eds.), *Lesbian and gay psychology: Theory, research, and clinical applications, Vol. 1.* Thousand Oaks, CA: Sage.

—— (1995). Psychological heterosexism in the United States. In A. R. D'Augelli & C. J. Patterson (Eds.), *Lesbian, gay, and bisexual identities over the lifespan* (pp. 321–346). New York: Oxford University Press.

—— (2000). The psychology of sexual prejudice. *Current Directions in Psychological Science, 9*(1), 19–22.

—— (2003). *Do public opinion polls show signs of an anti-gay backlash?* Retrieved March 30, 2009, from http://psychology.ucdavis.edu/rainbow/html/prej_Recent_Polling_ Data.html.

Herek, G. M., & Capitanio, J. P. (1996). "Some of my best friends": Intergroup contact, concealable stigma, and heterosexuals' attitudes toward gay men and lesbians. *Personality and Social Psychology Bulletin, 22*(4), 412–424.

—— (1999). Sex differences in how heterosexuals think about lesbians and gay men: Evidence from survey context effects. *Journal of Sex Research, 36*(4), 348–360.

Herek, G. M., & Glunt, E. K. (1993). Interpersonal contact and heterosexuals' attitudes toward gay men: Results from a national survey. *Journal of Sex Research, 30*(3), 239–244.

Herr, K. (1997). Learning lessons from school: Homophobia, heterosexism, and the construction of failure. *Journal of Gay & Lesbian Social Services, 7*(4), 51–64.

Hetherington, C. (1991). Life planning and career counseling with gay and lesbian students. In N. J. Evans & V. A. Walls (Eds.), *Beyond tolerance: Gays, lesbians, and bisexuals on campus* (pp. 131–145). Alexandria, VA: American College Personnel Association.

Hill Collins, P. (2000). *Black feminist thought: Knowledge, consciousness, and the politics of empowerment.* New York: Routledge.

Hine, T. (1999). *The rise and fall of the American teenager.* New York: Bard.

Hollibaugh, A. (2000). *My dangerous desires: A queer girl dreaming her way home.* Durham, NC: Duke University Press.

hooks, b. (1994). *Outlaw culture: Resisting representations.* New York: Routledge.

—— (2003). *Teaching community: A pedagogy of hope.* New York: Routledge.

Horn, S. S. (2006). Heterosexual adolescents' and young adults' beliefs and attitudes about homosexuality and gay and lesbian peers. *Cognitive Development, 21*, 420–440.

Human Rights Campaign Foundation (2004). *Transgender issues in the workplace: A tool for managers.* Washington, DC: Author.

—— (n.d.). *Transgender Americans: A handbook for understanding.* Retrieved June 13, 2006, from http://www.hrc.org/Content/ContentGroups/Publications1/TransgenderAmericans.pdf.

Human Rights Watch. (2001). *Hatred in the hallways: Violence and discrimination against lesbian, gay, bisexual, and transgender students in U. S. schools.* New York: Author.

Hunter, J., Rosario, M., & Rotheram-Borus, M. (1993, June). Sexual and substance abuse acts that place adolescents lesbians at risk for HIV. Poster presented at the 9th International Conference on AIDS/HIV STD World gress, Berlin, Germany.

Hutchins, L., & Kaahumanu, L. (Eds.). (1991). *Bi any other name*. Boston: Alyson.

Hutter, M. (1981). *The changing family: Comparative perspectives*. New York: Wiley.

Individuals with Disabilities Education Act of 1990, PL 101-476, 20 U.S.C. at 1400 et seq.

Individuals with Disabilities Education Act Amendments of 1997, PL 105-17, 20 U.S.C. at 1400 et seq.

Jackson, R. L., & Hendrix, K. G. (2003). Racial, cultural, and gendered identities in educational contexts: Communication perspectives on identity negotiation. *Communication Education, 52*(3/4), 177–317.

Jordan, K. M., & Deluty, R. H. (1998). Coming out for lesbian women: Its relation to anxiety, positive affectivity, self-esteem, and social support. *Journal of Homosexuality, 35,* 41–63.

Jordan, K. M., Vaughan, J. S., & Woodworth, K. J. (1997). I will survive: Lesbian, gay and bisexual youths' experience of high school. *Journal of Gay & Lesbian Social Services, 7*(4), 17–33.

Jenkins, R. (2004). *Social Identity*. London: Routledge.

Katz, D. (1960). The functional approach to the study of attitudes. *Public Opinion Quarterly, 24,* 163–204.

Kerlin, B. A. (2002). Chapter 6: Coding Strategies. In *NUD.IST4 Classic Guide*. Retrieved January 4, 2005, from http://kerlins.net/bobbi/research/nudist/coding/strategies.html.

Kim, J. (1981). *The process of Asian American identity development: A study of Japanese American women's perceptions of their struggle to achieve positive identities*. Unpublished doctoral dissertation, University of Massachusetts, Amherst.

Kincheloe, J. (2003). *Teachers as researchers: Qualitative paths to empowerment* (2nd ed.). New York: Routledge.

Kite, M. E. (1994). When perceptions meet reality: Individual differences in reactions to lesbians and gay men. In B. Greene and G. Herek (Eds.), *Psychological perspectives on lesbian and gay issues, Vol. 1* (pp. 25–53). Thousand Oaks, CA: Sage.

Kite, M. E., & Deaux, K. (1986). Attitudes toward homosexuality: Assessment and behavioral consequences. *Basic and Applied Social Psychology, 7*(2), 137–162.

Kivel, B. D., & Kleiber, D. A. (2000). Leisure in the identity formation of lesbian/gay youth: Personal, but not social. *Leisure Sciences, 22,* 215–232.

Kosciw, J. G. (2003). *The GLSEN 2003 National School Climate Survey. The school-related experiences of our nations lesbian, gay, bisexual, and transgender youth*. Washington, DC: Office for Public Policy of the Gay, Lesbian, and Straight Education Network.

Kosciw, J. G., & Cullen, M. (2001). *The GLSEN 2001 National School Climate Survey: The school-related experiences of our nation's lesbian, gay, bisexual, and transgender youth*. Washington, DC: Office for Public Policy of the Gay,

Lesbian, and Straight Education Network.

Kunc, N. (1992). The need to belong: Rediscovering Maslow's hierarchy of needs. In R. Villa, J. Stainback, & S. Stainback (Eds.), *Restructuring for caring and effective education* (pp. 28–39). Baltimore: Brookes.

Lamme, L. L., & Lamme, L. A. (2002). Welcoming children from gay families into our schools. *Educational Leadership, 59,* 65–69.

Lasser, J., & Tharinger, D. (2003). Visibility management in school and beyond: A qualitative study of gay, lesbian, bisexual youth. *Journal of Adolescence, 26,* 233–244.

Lather, P. (1986). Research as praxis. *Harvard Educational Review, 56*(3), 257–277.

—— (1991). *Getting smart: Feminist research and pedagogy with/in the postmodern.* New York: Routledge.

Lather, P., & Smithies, C. (1997). *Troubling the angels: Women living with HIV/AIDS.* Boulder, CO: Westview Press.

Lawrence v. Texas, 539 U.S. 558 (2003).

Leck, G. M. (2000). Heterosexual or homosexual? Reconsidering binary narratives on sexual identities in urban schools. *Education and Urban Society, 32*(3), 324–348.

Lee, C. (2002). The impact of belonging to a high school gay/straight alliance. *The High School Journal, 85*(3), 13–27.

Lee, A. (Director), McMurtry, L. (Writer), Ossana, D. (Writer), & Proulx, A. (Writer). (2005). *Brokeback mountain* [Motion picture]. United States: Universal Pictures.

Leland, J. (2000, March 20). Shades of gay. *Newsweek,* 46–49.

Lent, R. W., Brown, S. D., & Hackett, G. (1994). Toward a unifying social cognitive theory of career and academic interests, choice, and performance. *Journal of Vocational Behavior, 45,* 79–122.

—— (2000). Contextual supports and barriers to career choice: A social cognitive analysis. *Journal of Counseling Psychology, 47,* 36–49.

Lincoln, Y., & Guba, E. (1985). *Naturalistic inquiry.* Beverly Hills, CA: Sage.

Linville, D. (2008). Queer theory and teen sexuality: Unclear lines. In J. Anyon (Ed.), *Theory and educational research: Toward critical social explanation* (pp. 153–174). New York: Routledge.

Linville, D., & Carlson, D. L. (2007). *Fashioning sexual selves: Examining the care of the self in urban adolescent sexuality and gender discourses.* Unpublished manuscript.

Lipkin, A. (2004). Gay-straight alliances: Introduction. *Journal of Gay & Lesbian Issues in Education, 1*(3), 3–5.

Little, J. N. (2001). Embracing gay, lesbian, and transgendered youth in school-based settings. *Child & Youth Care Forum, 30*(2), 99–110.

Lovaas, K. E., Baroudi, L., & Collins, S. M. (2002). Transcending heteronormativity in the classroom: Using queer and critical pedagogies to alleviate trans-anxieties. In E. P. Cramer (Ed.), *Addressing homophobia and heterosexism on college campuses* (pp. 177–189). New York: Harrington Park Press.

MacGillivray, I. (2000). Educational equity for gay, lesbian, bisexual, transgendered, and queer/questioning students: The demands of democracy and social justice for America's schools. *Education and Urban Society, 32*(3), 303–323.

Malinsky, K. P. (1997). Learning to be invisible: Female sexual minority students in America's public high schools. *Journal of Gay & Lesbian Social Services, 7*(4), 35–40.

Mallon, G. P. (1997). When schools are not safe places: Reconnecting gay and lesbian young people to schools. *Reaching Today's Youth, 2,* 41–45.

Mallon, G. P., & DeCrescenzo, T. (2006). Transgender children and youth: A child welfare perspective. *Child Welfare, 85,* 215–241.

Marcia, J. E. (1966). Development and validation of ego-identity status. *Journal of Personality and Social Psychology, 3,* 551–558.

—— (1980). Identity in adolescence. In J. Adelson (Ed.), *Handbook of adolescent psychology* (pp. 159–187). New York: Wiley.

Marinoble, R. M. (1998). Homosexuality: A blind spot in the school mirror. *Professional School Counseling, 1,* 4–7.

Martin, A. D., & Hetrick, E. S. (1988). The stigmatization of the gay and lesbian adolescent. *Journal of Homosexuality, 15,* 163–183.

Martinez, D. G., & Sullivan, S. C. (1998). African American gay men and lesbians: Examining the complexity of gay identity development. *Journal of Human Behavior in the Social Environment, 1,* 243–264.

Maslow, A. (1970). *Motivation and personality.* New York: Harper & Row.

Mason, A., & Palmer, A. (1996). *Queer bashing. A national survey of hate crimes against lesbians and gay men.* London: Stonewall.

Massachusetts Governor's Commission on Gay and Lesbian Youth. (1995). *Breaking the silence in schools and in families.* Boston: Pub. 17296-60-500-2193-CK.

Massey, S. G. (under review). Illumination and obfuscation: The paradoxical role of journalism in the conversation between social science and social change. *Journal of Social Issues.*

—— (2002, March 3). Laramie: Could it happen here? Bowie High students, volunteers respond to play about the killing of Matthew Shepard in 1998. *Austin American-Statesman,* section K1.

—— (2009). Polymorphous prejudice: Liberating the measurement of heterosexuals' attitudes toward lesbians and gay men. *Journal of Homosexuality, 56,* 147–172.

Masten, A. S., & Coatsworth, J. D. (1998). The development of competence in favorable and unfavorable environments: Lessons from research on successful children. *American Psychologist, 53*(2), 205–220.

McCready, L. T. (2004). Understanding the marginalization of gay and gender non-conforming black male students. *Theory Into Practice, 43*(2), 136–143.

McDonald, G. (1982). Individual differences in the coming out process for gay men: Implications for theoretical models. *Journal of Homosexuality, 8,* 47–60.

McFarland, W. P. (2001). The legal duty to protect gay and lesbian students from violence in school. *Professional School Counseling, 4*(3), 171–179.

McIntosh, P. (1992). White privilege and male privilege: A personal account of coming to see correspondence through work in Women's Studies. In M. Anderson & P. H. Collins (Eds.), *Race, class and gender* (76-87). Belmont, CA: Wadsworth. Originally published as working paper #189 (Wellesley, MA: Wellesley College Center for Research on Women, 1988).

—— (1997). Privilege. In C. A. Grant & G. Ladson-Billings (Eds.), *Dictionary of multicultural education* (pp. 219–222). Phoenix, AZ: Oryx.

Merrick, E. (1999). An exploration of quality in qualitative research: Are "reliability" and "validity" relevant? In M. Kopala & L. Suzuki (Eds.), *Using qualitative methods in psychology* (pp. 25–36). Thousand Oaks, CA: Sage.

Meyer, I. H. (1995). Minority stress and mental health in gay men. *Journal of Health and Social Behavior, 36*, 38–56.

—— (2003). Prejudice, social stress, and mental health in lesbian, gay, and bisexual populations: Conceptual issues and research evidence. *Psychological Bulletin, 129*, 674–697.

Miceli, M. (2005). *Standing out, standing together: The social and political impact of gay-straight alliances.* New York: Routledge.

Miles, M. B., & Huberman, A. M. (1994). *An expanded sourcebook: Qualitative data analysis* (2nd ed.). Thousand Oaks, CA: Sage.

Mohr, J., & Fassinger, R. E. (2000). Measuring dimensions of lesbian and gay male experience. *Measurement and Evaluation in Counseling and Development, 33*, 66–90.

Monteiro, K. P., & Fuqua, V. (1994). African-American gay youth: One form of manhood. *The High School Journal, 77*, 20–36.

—— (1995). African-American gay youth: One form of manhood. In G. Unks (Ed.), *The gay teen* (pp. 159–188). New York: Routledge.

Morrison, T. (1993). *Playing in the dark: Whiteness and the literary imagination.* New York: Vintage Books.

Morrow, R., & Brown, D. (1994). *Critical theory and methodology.* Thousand Oaks, CA: Sage.

Morrow, S. L., Gore, P. A., & Campbell, B. W. (1996). The application of a sociocognitive framework to the career development of lesbian women and gay men. *Journal of Vocational Behavior, 48*, 136–148.

Moustakas, C. (1994). *Phenomenological research methods.* Thousand Oaks, CA: Sage.

Munoz-Plaza, C., Quinn, S. C., & Rounds, K. A. (2002). Lesbian, gay, bisexual and transgender students: Perceived social support in the high school environment. *The High School Journal, 85*(4), 52–63.

Nairn, K., & Smith, A. B. (2003). Taking students seriously: Their rights to be safe at school. *Gender & Education, 15*(2), 133–149.

National Gay & Lesbian Task Force (NGLTF). (1984). *Anti-gay/lesbian violence: A study by the National Gay & Lesbian Task Force in cooperation with lesbian organizations in eight U.S. cities.* Washington, DC: Author.

—— (1994). *Anti-gay/lesbian violence, victimization and defamation in 1994.* Washington, DC: Author.

National Mental Health Association (NMHA). (2002). *National survey of teens shows anti-gay bullying common in schools.* Retrieved June 26, 2003, from http://www.nmha.org/ newsroom/system/news.vw.cfm?do=vw&rid=474.

Nauta, M. N., Saucier, A. M., & Woodard, L. E. (2001). Interpersonal influences on students' academic and career decisions: The impact of sexual orientation. *The Career Development Quarterly, 49,* 352–362.

Newman, B. S. (2002). Lesbians, gays, and religion: Strategies for challenging belief systems. In E. P. Cramer (Ed.), *Addressing homophobia and heterosexism on college campuses* (pp. 87–98). New York: Harrington Park Press.

Nichols, S. (1999). Gay, lesbian, and bisexual youth: Understanding diversity and promoting tolerance in schools. *The Elementary School Journal, 99,* 505–519.

Noddings, N. (1992). *The challenge to care in schools: An alternative approach to education.* New York: Teachers College Press.

O'Neil, M. E., McWhirter, E. H., & Cerezo, A. (2008). Transgender identities and gender variance in vocational psychology: Recommendations for practice, social advocacy, and research. *Journal of Career Development, 34,* 263–285.

Opotow, S. (1990). Moral exclusion and injustice: An introduction. *Journal of Social Issues, 46*(1), 1–20.

Ore, T. (2006). *The social construction of difference and inequality: Race, class, gender, and sexuality* (3rd ed.). New York: McGraw-Hill.

Orenstein, P. (1994). *Schoolgirls: Young women, self-esteem, and the confidence gap.* New York: Doubleday.

Otis, M. D., & Skinner, W. F. (1996). The prevalence of victimization and its effects on mental well-being among lesbian and gay people. *Journal of Homosexuality, 30,* 93–121.

Parents, Families, and Friends of Lesbians and Gays (n.d.). *About PFLAG.* Retrieved July 6, 2008, from http://community.pflag.org/NETCOMMUNITY/Page.aspx?pid=191&srcid=194.

Parks, C. W. (2001). African American same-gender-loving youths and families in urban schools. *Journal of Gay & Lesbian Social Services, 13*(3), 41–56.

Parsons, T. (1986). Power and the social system. In S. Lukes (Ed.), *Power* (pp. 94–143). New York: New York University Press.

Patterson, C. J. (1995a). Lesbian mothers, gay fathers, and their children. In A. R. D'Augelli & C. J. Patterson (Eds.), *Lesbian, gay, and bisexual identities over the lifespan* (pp. 262–290). New York: Oxford University Press.

—— (1995b). Sexual orientation and human development: An overview. *Developmental Psychology, 31,* 3–11.

Patton, M. Q. (1987). *How to use qualitative methods in evaluation.* London: Sage.

—— (2002). *Qualitative research & evaluation methods* (3rd ed.). Thousand Oaks, CA: Sage.

Peters, A. J. (2003). Isolation or inclusion: Creating safe spaces for lesbian and gay youth. *Families in Society: The Journal of Contemporary Human Services, 84*(3), 331–337.

Peterson, N., & Gonzalez, R. C. (2005). *The role of work in people's lives: Applied career counseling and vocational psychology.* Belmont, CA: Wadsworth/Thomson Learning.

Peyser, M., & Lorch, D. (2000, March 20). High school controversial. *Newsweek,* 55–56.

Pharr, S. (1998). *Homophobia: A weapon of sexism* (2nd ed.). Little Rock, AR: Chardon Press.

Phillips, L. M. (2000). *Flirting with danger: Young women's reflections on sexuality and domination.* New York: New York University Press.

Phinney, J. S. (1989). Stages of ethnic development in minority group adolescents. *Journal of Early Adolescence, 9,* 34–49.

Powell, M. (2003). Homophobia: Hate's last refuge? *Montessori Life, 15,* 14–16.

Pratt, M. L. (1991). Arts of the contact zone. *Profession '91,* 33–40.

Prensky, M. (2006). *Don't bother me, mom—I'm learning!* St. Paul, MN: Paragon House.

Price, J. H., & Telljohann, S. K. (1991). School counselors' perceptions of adolescent homosexuals. *Journal of School Health, 61,* 433–438.

Quinlivan, K., & Town, S. (1999). Queer pedagogy, educational practice, and lesbian and gay youth. *International Journal of Qualitative Studies in Education, 12*(5), 509–524.

Rankin, S. R. (2003). *Campus climate for gay, lesbian, bisexual, and transgender people: A national perspective.* New York: The National Gay and Lesbian task Force Policy Institute.

Rasmussen, M. L. (2004a). Safety and subversion: The production of sexualities and genders in youth spaces. In M. L. Rasmussen, E. Rofes, & S. Talburt (Eds.), *Youth and sexualities: Pleasure, subversion, and insubordination in and out of schools* (pp. 131–152). New York: Palgrave Macmillan.

—— (2004b). "That's so gay!" A study of the deployment of signifiers of sexual and gender identity in secondary school settings in Australia and the United States. *Social Semiotics, 14*(3), 289–308.

—— (2006). *Becoming subjects: Sexualities and secondary schooling.* New York: Routledge.

Rasmussen, M. L., Rofes, E., & Talburt, S. (Eds.). (2004). *Youth and sexualities: Pleasure subversion, and insubordination in and out of schools.* New York: Palgrave Macmillan.

Reitzug, U. C., & Burrello, L. C. (1995). How principals can build self-renewing schools. *Educational Leadership, 52*(7), 48–51.

Remafedi, G. (1987). Adolescent homosexuality: Psychosocial and medical implications. *Pediatrics, 79,* 331–337.

—— (Ed.). (1994). *Death by denial: Stories of suicide in gay and lesbian teenagers.* Boston: Alyson.

Remafedi, G., Farrow, J., & Deisher, R. (1991). Risk factors for attempted suicide in gay and bisexual youth. *Pediatrics, 87*(6), 869–876.

Remafedi, G., French, S., Story, M., Resnick, M., & Blum, R. (1998). The relationship between suicide risk and sexual orientation: Results of a population-based study. *American Journal of Public Health, 88,* 57–60.

Renninger, K. A., & Shumar, W. (Eds.). (2002). *Building virtual communities: Learning and change in cyberspace.* New York: Cambridge University Press.

Rhodes, J., Ebert, L., & Fischer, K. (1992). Natural mentors: An overlooked resource in the social networks of young, African American mothers. *American Journal of Community Psychology, 20*(4), 445–461.

Rich, A. (1985). Notes toward a politics of location. In M. Díaz-Diocaretz & I. M. Zavala (Eds.), *Women, feminist identity, and society in the 1980's* (pp. 7–22). Amsterdam: John Benjamins.

Rivers, I. (2000). Social exclusion, absenteeism and sexual minority youth. *Support for Learning, 15*(1), 13–18.

Robinson, K. E. (1994). Addressing the needs of gay and lesbian students: The school counselor's role. *The School Counselor, 41,* 326–332.

Rofes, E. (1989). Opening up the classroom closet: Responding to the educational needs of gay and lesbian youth. *Harvard Educational Review, 49,* 444–453.

—— (1995). Making our schools safe for sissies. In G. Unks (Ed.), *The gay teen* (pp. 79–84). New York: Routledge.

—— (2004). Martyr-target-victim: Interrogating narratives of persecution and suffering among queer youth. In M. L. Rasmussen, E. Rofes, & S. Talburt (Eds.), *Youth and sexualities: Pleasure, subversion, and insubordination* (pp. 41–62). New York: Palgrave Macmillan.

Rotheram-Borus, M. J., & Langabeer, K. A. (2001). Developmental trajectories of gay, lesbian, and bisexual youths. In A. R. D'Augelli and C. J. Patterson (Eds.), *Lesbian, gay, and bisexual identities and youth* (97-128). New York: Oxford University Press.

Rotheram-Borus, M. J., Rosario, M., VanRossem, R., Reid, H., & Gill, R. (1995). Prevalence, course, and predictors of multiple problem behaviors among gay and bisexual male adolescents. *Developmental Psychology, 31*(1), 75–85.

Russell, S. T., & Truong, N. L. (2001). Adolescent sexual orientation, race and ethnicity, and school environments: A national study of sexual minority youth of color. In K. K. Kumashiro (Ed.), *Troubling intersections of race and sexuality: Queer students of color and anti-oppressive education* (pp. 113–130). Lanham, MD: Rowman & Littlefield.

Russo, V. (1981). *The celluloid closet.* New York: Harper & Row.

Ryan, G. W., & Bernard, H. R. (2000). Data management and analysis methods. In N. K. Denzin & Y. S. Lincoln (Eds.), *The landscape of qualitative research* (pp. 769–802). London: Sage.

Ryan, C., & Futterman, D. (2001). Social and developmental challenges for lesbian, gay, and bisexual youth. *SIECUS Report, 29*(4), 5–18.

Ryan, D., & Martin, A. (2000). Lesbian, gay, bisexual, and transgender parents in the school systems. *School Psychology Review, 29*(2), 207–216.

Saad, L. (2007, May 29). *Tolerance for gay rights at high-water mark. Public evenly divided over whether homosexuality is morally acceptable or wrong.* Retrieved August 19, 2007, from http://www.gallup.com/poll/27694/Tolerance-Gay-Rights-HighWater-Mark.aspx.

Sadowski, M. (2001). Sexual minority students benefit from school-based support—where it exists. *Harvard Educational Letter, 17*(5), 1–5.

Sausa, L. A. (2002). Updating college and university campus policies: Meeting the needs of trans students. In E. P. Cramer (Ed.), *Addressing homophobia and heterosexism on college campuses* (pp. 43–55). New York: Harrington Park Press.

Savin-Williams, R. C. (1994). Verbal and physical abuse as stressors in the lives of lesbian, gay male, and bisexual youths: Associations with school problems, running away, substance abuse, prostitution, and suicide. *Journal of Consulting and Clinical Psychology, 62*(2), 261–269.

—— (1995). Lesbian, gay male, and bisexual adolescents. In A. R. D'Augelli & C. J. Patterson (Eds.), *Lesbian, gay, and bisexual identities over the life span: Psychological perspectives* (pp. 165–189). New York: Oxford University Press.

—— (1998). The disclosure to families of same-sex attractions by lesbian, gay, and bisexual youths. *Journal of Research on Adolescence, 8,* 49–68.

—— (2001). A critique of research on sexual minority youth. *Journal of Adolescence, 24*(1), 5–13.

—— (2005). *The new gay teenager.* Cambridge, MA: Harvard University Press.

Sawicki, J. (1991). *Disciplining Foucault: Feminism, power, and the body.* New York: Routledge.

Scales, P., & Gibbons, J. (1996). Extended family members and unrelated adults in the lives of young adolescents: A research agenda. *Journal of Early Adolescence, 16*(4), 365–389.

Schank, J. A., & Skovholt, T. M. (1997). Dual-relationship dilemmas of rural and small-community psychologists. *Professional Psychology: Research and Practice, 28*(1), 44–49.

Schmidt, C. K., & Nilsson, J. E. (2006). The effects of simultaneous developmental processes: Factors relating to the career development of lesbian, gay, and bisexual youth. *The Career Development Quarterly, 55,* 22–37.

Schutz, A. (1970). *On phenomenology and social relations.* Evanston, IL: Northwestern University Press.

Sears, J. T. (1987). Peering into the well of loneliness: The responsibility of educators to gay and lesbian youth. In A. Molnar (Ed.), *Social issues and education: Challenge and responsibility* (pp. 79–100). Alexandria, VA: Association for Supervision and Curriculum Development.

—— (1991). *Growing up gay in the South: Race, gender, and journeys of the spirit.* New York: Haworth.

—— (1992). Educators, homosexuality, and homosexual students: Are personal feelings related to professional beliefs? In K. Harbeck (Ed.), *Coming out of the classroom closet: Gay and lesbian students, teachers, and curricula.* New York: Haworth.

—— (1996). Thinking critically/intervening effectively about homophobia and heterosexism: A twenty-five year retrospective. In J. Sears & W. Williams (Eds.), *Combating heterosexism and homophobia* (pp. 13–48). New York: Columbia University Press.

—— (2003). *Fifteen years later: A report on the state of the field of lesbian, gay, bisexual, and transgender issues in K-16 and professional education, a re-*

search review (1987–2001). Paper presented at the American Education Research Association Annual Meeting, Chicago.

Shakespeare, W. (1975). Romeo and Juliet. In *The complete works of William Shakespeare* (pp. 1011–1044). New York: Avenel Books.

Shilts, R. (1982). *The Mayor of Castro Street: The life and times of Harvey Milk.* New York: St. Martin's Press.

Shulman, I. (1990). *West side story.* New York: Pocket Books.

Simmons, J. (Director), & Smothers, T. (Producer). (2005). *TransGeneration* [Motion picture]. (Available from New Video, 902 Broadway, 9th Floor, New York, NY 10010)

Simpson, P., Rodiss, H., & Bushell, M. (2004). *The rough guide to superheroes.* London: Haymarket Customer Publishing for Rough Guides Ltd.

Skrtic, T. M. (1995a). Deconstructing/reconstructing public education: Social reconstruction in the postmodern era. In T. Skrtic (Ed.), *Disability and democracy: Restructuring (special) education for postmodernity* (pp. 233–273). New York: Teachers College Press.

—— (1995b). The functionalist view of special education and disability: Deconstructing the conventional knowledge tradition. In T. Skrtic (Ed.), *Disability and democracy: Restructuring (special) education for postmodernity* (pp. 65–103). New York: Teachers College Press.

—— (1995c). Power/knowledge and pragmatism: A postmodern view of the professions. In T. Skrtic (Ed.), *Disability and democracy: Restructuring (special) education for postmodernity* (pp. 25–62). New York: Teachers College Press.

—— (1995d). Special education and disability as organizational pathologies: Toward a metatheory of school organization and change. In T. Skrtic (Ed.), *Disability and democracy: Restructuring (special) education for postmodernity* (pp. 190–232). New York: Teachers College Press.

—— (1995e). Theory/practice and objectivism: The modern view of the professions. In T. Skrtic (Ed.), *Disability and democracy: Restructuring (special) education for postmodernity* (pp. 3–24). New York: Teachers College Press.

—— (2005). A political economy of learning disabilities. *Learning Disability Quarterly, 28,* 149–155.

Smith, B. (1999). *The truth that never hurts: Writings on race, gender, and freedom.* New Brunswick, NJ: Rutgers University Press.

Smith, D. E. (1987). *The everyday world as problematic: A feminist sociology.* Boston: Northeastern University Press.

Smith, E. J. (1991). Ethnic identity development: Toward the development of a theory within the context of majority/minority status. *Journal of Counseling and Development, 70,* 181–188.

Smith, G. W. (1998). The ideology of "fag": The school experience of gay students. *The Sociological Quarterly, 39*(2), 309–335.

—— (2005). The ideology of "fag": The school experience of gay students. In L. Weis & M. Fine (Eds.), *Beyond silenced voices: Class, race and gender in United States schools* (rev. ed.) (pp. 95–113). Albany: State University of New York Press.

Stacey, J., & Bilbarz, T. (2001). How does the sexual orientation of the parent matter? *American Sociological Review, 66*(2), 159–183.

Stein, A., & Plummer, K. (1996). "I can't even think straight": "Queer" theory and the missing sexual revolution in sociology. In S. Seidman (Ed.), *Queer theory/sociology* (pp. 129–144). Cambridge, MA: Blackwell.

Strauss, A. (1987). *Qualitative analysis for social scientists.* New York: Cambridge University Press.

Super, D. E. (1980). A lifespan/lifespace approach to career development. *Journal of Vocational Behavior, 16,* 282–298.

—— (1990). A lifespan/lifespace approach to career development. In D. Brown & L. Brooks (Eds.), *Career choice and development: Applying contemporary theories to practice* (2nd ed.) (pp. 197–261). San Francisco: Jossey-Bass.

Swartz, P. C. (2003). Bridging multicultural education: Bringing sexual orientation into children's and young adult literature classrooms. *Radical Teacher, 66,* 11–19.

Sweitzer, H. F., & King, M. A. (2004). *The successful internship: Transformation and empowerment in experiential learning* (2nd ed.). Belmont, CA: Brooks/Cole.

Szalacha, L. A. (2004). Educating teachers on LGBTQ issues: A review of research and program evaluations. *Journal of Gay & Lesbian Issues in Education, 1*(4), 67–79.

Talburt, S. (2004). Intelligibility and narrating queer youth. In M. L. Rasmussen, E. Rofes, & S. Talburt (Eds.), *Youth and sexualities: Pleasure, subversion, and insubordination* (pp. 18–39). New York: Palgrave Macmillan.

Taylor, C. (2002). Beyond empathy: Confronting homophobia in critical education courses. In E. P. Cramer (Ed.), *Addressing homophobia and heterosexism on college campuses* (pp. 219–234). New York: Harrington Park Press.

Taylor-Greene, S., Brown, D., Nelson, L., Longton J., Gassman, T., Cohen, J., Swartz, J., Horner, R., Sugai, G., & Hall, S. (1997). School-wide behavioral support: Starting the year off right. *Journal of Behavioral Education, 7*(1), 99–112.

Telljohann, S. K., & Price, J. H. (1993). A qualitative examination of adolescent homosexuals' life experiences: Ramifications for secondary school personnel. *Journal of Homosexuality, 26*(1), 41–56.

Thayer-Bacon, B. J., & Brown, S. (1995). *What "collaboration" means: Ethnocultural diversity's impact* (ERIC Document Reproduction Service No. ED 291 735). Washington, DC: Office of Educational Research and Improvement.

Thompson, A. (2002). The practices in and "out" of policy. *Journal of the Association for Persons with Severe Handicaps (JASH), 27*(1), 82–86.

Thompson, A. S., Bryson, M., & De Castell, S. (2001). Prospects for identity formation for lesbian, gay, or bisexual persons with developmental disabilities. *International Journal of Disability, Development and Education, 48,* 53–65.

Tolman, D. L. (2002). *Dilemmas of desire: Teenage girls talk about sexuality.* Cambridge, MA: Harvard University Press.

Trask, H. (1999). *From a native daughter: Colonialism and sovereignty in Hawai'i*

(rev. ed.). Honolulu: University of Hawai'i Press.
Tremble, B., Schneider, M., & Appathurai, C. (1989). Growing up gay or lesbian in a multicultural context. *Journal of Homosexuality, 17,* 253–267.
Troiden, R. R. (1979). Becoming homosexual: A model of gay identity acquisition. *Psychiatry, 42*(4), 362–373.
—— (1989a). The formation of homosexual identities. In G. Herdt (Ed.), *Gay and lesbian youth* (pp. 43–73). New York: Harrington Park Press.
—— (1989b). The formation of homosexual identities. *Journal of Homosexuality, 17*(1/2), 43–74.
Tucker, D. (Director/Writer). (2005). *TransAmerica* [Motion picture]. United States: Weinstein Company.
Turkle, S. (1997). *Life on the screen: Identity in the age of the internet.* New York: Simon and Schuster.
Turner, V. W. (1967). *The forest of symbols.* Ithaca, NY: Cornell University Press.
Unks, G. (1995). Thinking about the gay teen. In G. Unks (Ed.), *The gay teen* (pp. 3–12). New York: Routledge.
Uribe, V. (1994). Project 10: A school-based outreach to gay and lesbian youth. *The High School Journal, 77*(1/2), 108–112.
van Heeringen, C., & Vincke, J. (2000). Suicidal acts and ideation in homosexual and bisexual young people: A study of prevalence and risk factors. *Social Psychiatry Psychiatric Epidemiology, 35,* 494–499.
Vare, J. W., & Norton, T. L. (1998). Understanding gay and lesbian youth: Sticks, stones, and silence. *The Clearing House, 76*(6), 327–331.
Wallace, M., Peters, W., & Morgan, H. (Writers), & Morgan, H. (Producer). (1967, March 7). *CBS reports: The homosexuals.* [Television broadcast]. New York: CBS News.
Wells, A. (Director/Writer), & Mayes, F. (Writer). (2003). *Under the Tuscan sun.* [Motion picture]. United States: Touchstone Pictures. (2004). [DVD]. United States: Touchstone Home Entertainment and Buena Vista Home Entertainment Inc.
Wichstrom, L., & Hegna, K. (2003). Sexual orientation and suicide attempt: A longitudinal study of the general Norwegian adolescent population. *Journal of Abnormal Psychology, 112*(1), 144–151.
Wickens, E. (1993). Penny's question: "I will have a child in my class with two moms. What do you know about this?" *Young Children, 48*(3), 25–28.
Wulff, H. (1995). Introducing youth culture in its own right: The state of the art and new possibilities. In V. Amit-Talai & H. Wulff (Eds.), *Youth cultures: A cross-cultural perspective* (pp. 1–18). London: Routledge.
Wyss, S. E. (2004). "This was my hell": The violence experienced by gender non-conforming youth in US high schools. *International Journal of Qualitative Studies in Education, 17*(5), 709–730.
Zavalkoff, A. (2002). Teaching the teachers: Confronting homophobia and heterosexism in teacher education programs. In E. P. Cramer (Ed.), *Addressing homophobia and heterosexism on college campuses* (pp. 243–253). New York: Harrington Park Press.

Contributors

Corrine Bertram, Ph.D., is an Assistant Professor of Psychology and Women's Studies at Shippensburg University. Her research interests include an examination of moral communities and their scope of justice particularly feminist and women's organizations, feminist social psychology, qualitative methodologies, and youth participatory educational projects.

Lisa Bowleg, Ph.D., is an Associate Professor in the Department of Community Health and Prevention in the School of Public Health at Drexel University. Her research interests include (1) multiple minority stress, resilience, and coming out issues among Black/African American, lesbian, gay bisexual and transgender people (LGBT); and (2) the influence of social structural factors (e.g., racism, poverty, incarceration) and gender role and sexuality factors on sexual risk in Black/African American communities

David Lee Carlson is an assistant professor in secondary education. His research focuses on methods that prepare teachers to teach literature and multiple forms of writing in secondary urban schools. He completed a genealogy of portfolio assessment for his dissertation, pursuing an interest in how the post-modern methodologies of Michel Foucault can influence English education.

Dr. Kim Case joined the University of Houston-Clear Lake in 2005 as Assistant Professor of Psychology and Women's Studies. As a social psychologist, she applies queer theory, critical race theory, and feminist theory to her teaching, research, and service to the campus and surrounding community. Her research focuses on privilege awareness, prejudice reduction, and ally behavior with regard to sexual orientation, gender identity, race, and sex. Please send correspondence to caseki@uhcl.edu or Kim Case, University of Houston-Clear Lake, 2700 Bay Area Blvd., Box 35, Houston, TX 77058.

Marjorie Cooper-Nicols, Ph.D., is a school psychologist at the Children's Learning Center of the United Cerebral Palsy Association of Nassau County in New York. She earned a B.A. in Psychology from SUNY Geneseo, an M.A. in General Experimental Psychology from Bucknell University, and a Ph.D. in School Psychology at the University of Rhode Island in 2006. Her research interests include the school, familial, and social experiences of gay, lesbian, and bisexual (GLB) adolescents. She is hoping to parlay her research experience into her clinical practice as a school psychologist.

M. Sue Crowley is an Associate Professor in the School of Education at Binghamton University. Her research interests are focused on adolescent identity formation, impacts of child sexual abuse, and critical pedagogy. Her publications include a book, *The Search for Autonomous Intimacy: Sexual Abuse and Young Women's Identity Development*, and journal articles in *The Journal of Interpersonal Violence, Journal of Child Sexual Abuse, Journal of Family Issues, Women's Studies Quarterly*, and *Women and Therapy*, among others.

Thomas Scott Duke is an Associate Professor of Education at the University of Alaska Southeast, where he coordinates graduate programs in special education and teaches courses in special education, multicultural education, and qualitative research methods. He believes education can be a powerful vehicle for critical consciousness, individual liberation, and social transformation, and he is committed to the development of culturally responsive, socially just, and fully inclusive teaching and learning environments.

Stephen "Arch" Erich, Ph.D., LCSW, is an Associate Professor and Program Director of the BSW Program at the University of Houston-Clear Lake. His program of scholarship broadly centers on familial well-being and social justice concerns. Specifically, research topics include straight and gay/lesbian families who have adopted children and issues related to transgender well-being.

Gary W. Harper, Ph.D., M.P.H., is a Professor in the Department of Psychology and Director of the Master of Public Health Program at DePaul University. Dr. Harper's research and community intervention work focus on the HIV prevention and sexual health promotion needs of gay/bisexual male adolescents of color. His action research involves active collaboration with youth and community organizations. He is a former chair of the American Psychological Association's Committee on Lesbian, Gay, and Bisexual Concerns, and has published findings from his federally funded LGBT research in multiple peer-reviewed journals. Dr. Harper also has received several academic and community awards for his commitment to ethnic minority concerns in LGBT research, practice, and training.

Omar Jamil is a graduate student pursuing his doctorate degree in clinical psychology, with an emphasis on community psychology. His research interests and dissertation focuses on the sexual and ethnic identity development and integration processes among gay/bisexual/questioning male ethnic minority (Latino and African American) adolescents. Omar's research also examines the link between identity development and HIV risk behaviors, and he has been awarded the American Psychological Association's Minority Fellowship for his work in the field of HIV prevention and research.

Jeneka Joyce, B.A., is a Counseling Psychology doctoral student at the University of Oregon. Before pursuing doctoral studies, she served as an AmeriCorps member working collaboratively with teachers to close the achievement gap in high-poverty elementary schools. Her research interests include risk and protective factors for ethnic minority and sexual minority youth, adolescent psychosocial development, and the intersections between race/ethnicity, gender, religious/spiritual selves, and sexuality. She also teaches human sexuality class at a local church for high school adolescents. She has been an out member of LGBTQ communities for the past eight years.

Jes T. Kaminski, photographer, holds a BA in Art History and Women's Studies from Binghamton University. She works primarily in photography and art installation. Recently exhibited a series of photos emphasizing "women's work" through photo documentation and installation.

Dr. Heather Kanenberg, LMSW, is currently Director of Field Education and Assistant Professor with the University of Houston-Clear Lake Bachelor of Social Work Program. Her primary research interests include Public Policy Analysis and use of Feminist Policy Frameworks to review Public Health policies affecting women and children. In addition, Dr. Kanenberg engages in work that focuses on issues impacting the LGBTIQ and allied populations.

David Kilmnick, Ph.D., MSW, has over 20 years experience of working in and for the LGBT Community. Since founding Long Island Gay and Lesbian Youth (LIGALY) in 1993, David has led the organization from his master's project to a comprehensive network of three agencies that serve 60,000 LGBT youth, adults and seniors throughout the lifespan annually. He serves the Chief Executive Officer of The Long Island GLBT Services Network and it's three affiliate organizations - LIGALY, The Long Island GLBT Community Center and Services and Advocacy for GLBT Elders–Long Island. David is a professor at Stony Brook University, Nassau Community College, Walden University and the University of Maryland-University College.

Darla Linville is a Ph.D. Candidate in the Urban Education program at the City University of New York Graduate Center. She studies policies of sex education, sexual harassment and the hidden curriculum of gender and sexuality in schools. She is particularly interested in how student identities and affiliations within schools impact their academic standing, and inclusion in school culture.

Sean G. Massey, Ph.D., is Assistant Professor of Human Development in the College of Community and Public Affairs at Binghamton University, SUNY. His research interests include sexual prejudice and multidimensional attitudes, the experiences of LGBTQ parents, queer theory in social science, positive beliefs about gay men and lesbians, self and identity in the context of social stigma and sense of safety and community among LGBTQ people. His research has been published in *Journal of Homosexuality, Lesbian and Gay Psychology Review, Journal of GLBT Family Studies,* and *Journal of Social Issues.* He researched and co-authored a newspaper series "The Voices of Gay Austin" that was awarded Best News/Feature Story by the National Lesbian and Gay Journalist Association in 2001.

Ellen Hawley McWhirter is a professor and director of training of the counseling psychology program at the University of Oregon. Her scholarly interests include adolescent career development, adolescent risk behavior, and applications of the construct of empowerment to counseling, training, and consultation.

Maya O'Neil, M.S., is a doctoral candidate in the Counseling Psychology Program at the University of Oregon and is obtaining a concurrent degree in Mathematics. She is also a child and family therapist, a statistics and research design consultant, and a data analyst. Her research interests focus on the assessment of multicultural competence. She has been an out member of LGBTQ communities for the past nine years.

Christine M. Smith received her M.S.W. from Binghamton University. Her interests include postcolonial and feminist theories and critiques of transnational capitalism.

Maria Valenti is a doctoral candidate in the Ecological-Community Psychology program within the Department of Psychology at Michigan State University. She is interested in community based research and is currently working on a project with a non-profit organization serving runaway gay, lesbian, bisexual, and transgendered youth in the Detroit area.

Dr. Diane R. Wiener is an Assistant Professor of Social Work at Binghamton University. She has published widely in the areas of feminist and queer media criticism, mental health activism, and interdisciplinary cultural studies. Dr. Wiener has taught and worked in human services for over twenty years, including as a consultant on LGBTQ youth suicide prevention initiatives and as a teacher of LGBTIQ Studies.

AC	Adolescent Cultures,
SS	School & Society

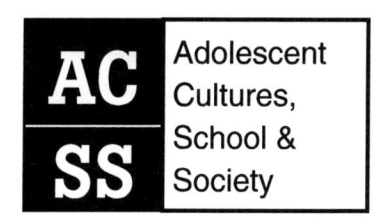

Joseph L. DeVitis & Linda Irwin-DeVitis
GENERAL EDITORS

As schools struggle to redefine and restructure themselves, they need to be cognizant of the new realities of adolescents. Thus, this series of monographs and textbooks is committed to depicting the variety of adolescent cultures that exist in today's post-industrial societies. It is intended to be a primarily qualitative research, practice, and policy series devoted to contextual interpretation and analysis that encompasses a broad range of interdisciplinary critique. In addition, this series will seek to provide a pragmatic, pro-active response to the current backlash of conservatism that continues to dominate political discourse, practice, and policy. This series seeks to address issues of curriculum theory and practice; multicultural education; aggression and violence; the media and arts; school dropouts; homeless and runaway youth; alienated youth; at-risk adolescent populations; family structures and parental involvement; and race, ethnicity, class, and gender studies.

Send proposals and manuscripts to the general editors at:
>Joseph L. DeVitis & Linda Irwin-DeVitis
>The John H. Lounsbury School of Education
>Georgia College & State University
>Campus Box 70
>Milledgeville, GA 31061-0490

To order other books in this series, please contact our Customer Service Department at:
>(800) 770-LANG (within the U.S.)
>(212) 647-7706 (outside the U.S.)
>(212) 647-7707 FAX

or browse online by series at:
>WWW.PETERLANG.COM